Falling Eagle—R

Andy\. -
Have enjoyed
knowing you so much.
Best of Luck Always.
Please keep in touch

FALLING EAGLE—
RISING TIGERS

Defusing the Next US Financial Time Bomb
with Solutions from Asia Pacific

Joe Hoft

Falling Eagle—Rising Tigers

ISBN 978-988-13527-0-5 (paperback)
ISBN 978-988-13527-1-2 (e-book)

Distributed by Inkstone Books
http://inkstone.chameleonpress.com

Typeset in Adobe Garamond by Alan Sargent
Front cover drawing by Becky Poen
Printed and bound in the United States

Preface

I have been interested in American history and politics since a very young age. I remember going to my hometown public library in my youth and checking out books on Washington, Lafayette, Lincoln, Lee, the Civil War and much more. I enjoyed history class in school and still to this day enjoy watching documentaries on television or reading books regarding almost any event in US or world history.

Along with my thirst for American history came an appreciation for the US founding fathers and the many other individuals who made the country great. Stories of courage and valor left me feeling proud of being an American. I admired men like Lincoln who gave so much for their country, indeed even their lives. The more I read, the more I was amazed with the many men and women who fought for not just their own freedom, but more so, for the freedom of others.

In more recent years, I have become more aware of the challenges facing America. In the process of creating this book, it became clear that the fundamentals underlying the world's number-one economy are frightening. Politicians in Washington are having difficulty finding a consensus on almost any matter and each day that passes, much more must be done to save America.

Two years ago, when riding on a commuter bus in Hong Kong, it hit me like a bolt of lightning—There are solutions that I have seen working in this region of the world that the US could adopt to mitigate its current malaise.

This book provides you with a clear understanding of the current social and economic condition of the US and more importantly, answers to save America. My hope is that you enjoy reading this book and see the solutions presented as the way forward.

Joe Hoft
Hong Kong, 2014

Contents

CHAPTER I

Introduction

The United States faces glaring challenges due to its spending and social programs. The generous welfare handouts in the US, which are in excess of revenues by more than $1 trillion annually, are unsustainable. On the other side of the globe there are prospering countries which are expected to continue their historical rise both economically and socially. These Asia Pacific countries provide real alternatives to the social and financial challenges of the US.

The United States is a great country and its contributions to mankind are immense. It was the first country to put a man on the moon. It has created numerous inventions in manufacturing and technology, and the United States is known as the "land of the free." For centuries people have given their lives trying to reach its shores. However, the US is now in a financial crisis. The economic turmoil in the world, which peaked in 2008, has left its mark and is a sign of things to come. This may not be clear to the average American because things appear the same today as they did yesterday, but a fiscal "time bomb" is ticking. The US is burdened with a massive debt load and social programs that are adding substantial sums to this amount annually. In each of the first four years of the Obama administration, the US has had more than $1 trillion deficits, and the future is set for more spending, not less.[1]

On the other side of the world, countries in Asia and the South Pacific, including Australia and New Zealand (collectively referred to as the "Asia Pacific"), are doing well and riding out the 2008 financial storm, if not thriving. There are a number of reasons for Asia Pacific's prosperity, but the major reason may be due to the governmental social programs throughout the region which are smart, efficient and effective.

In the United States, massive changes have occurred over the past century, moving the country more and more towards a socialist state. When the Great Depression came to the US in the 1930s, President

---

[1]   Christopher Chantrill, (2012, November 11). *Federal Budget FY 2012.* Retrieved 11 11, 2012, fromhttp://www.usfederalbudget.us/federal_budget_fy12

Franklin Roosevelt used it as a vehicle to push for social change. Social change in the US has not always gone so well and some changes have taken a long time to culminate in financial disaster. The 2008 financial crisis is an excellent example of this.

In his book *The Big Short,* Michael Lewis explains in great detail the factors that led to the financial collapse in 2008. Individuals with poor credit histories were provided "teaser" loans by financial institutions. These loans had low interest rates or required little or no proof of the borrower's ability to repay the loan. The loans were then bundled and sold to investors. Complex financial instruments were created to insure these investments, and the rating agencies classified these instruments as high quality without fully appreciating what they were rating. When the borrowers were not able to repay their loans, the whole system crashed.[2]

Politicians would have you believe that the 2008 financial meltdown was related to the more recent actions of one party or the other, but the roots of the 2008 housing market crisis really began in the 1930s with the creation of the Federal Housing Administration (FHA), which guaranteed banks' mortgage risks and the Federal National Mortgage Association (FNMA), which effectively insured mortgages by purchasing mortgages from lenders. Both shifted risks from the lenders to the US taxpayers. Then in 1977, the Community Reinvestment Act (CRA) was signed into law by President Jimmy Carter. This law was designed to promote home ownership for minorities by prohibiting banks from refusing mortgages in poor areas due to the loan's high risk. In addition, mortgage lenders were required under the 1975 Home Mortgage Disclosure Act (HMDA) to provide data about who they lent to. Then in 1991, HMDA rules were tightened and included specific demands for racial equality in the institution's lending.[3]

In 1992, the Federal Reserve Bank of Boston published a manual advising that a mortgage applicant's lack of credit history should not be viewed negatively in a loan assessment, that the borrowers should be allowed to deploy loans and gifts as deposits, and that unemployment benefits were valid income sources for lending decisions. The manual reminded banks that failure to meet CRA regulations violated equal

2   Michael Lewis, (2010). *The Big Short.* London: Penguin Books.
3   Charles K Rowley and Nathanael Smith, (2009). *Economic Contractions in the United States: A Failure of Government.* Fairfax: The Locke Institute, pp 88–89.

opportunity laws and exposed them to actual damages plus punitive damages of $500,000.[4]

"So the great housing bubble-party began. With credit-worthiness no longer relevant, the volume of subprime loans exploded."[5] This ultimately climaxed in 2008 with the subprime crisis that sent shock waves around the world and put financial markets in turmoil.

Another ticking time bomb is the colossal amount of debt which the US is amassing as a result of social programs. In October 2013, the federal debt load in the US surpassed $17 trillion for the first time in its history.[6] This amount may only be a part of the story. No government has ever accumulated the amount of debt that the US has in recent years. Some propose to solve the debt problem by cutting government programs, or cutting spending, or both, while others propose tax increases. Many Americans want neither option, but clearly, something has to be done. The current spending causing the annual deficits that lead to the ever increasing growth in the US debt is untenable.

The problem is not only with the federal government; state and local governments are overspending as well. What is the answer to the fiscal and social challenges facing the US?

What if there are programs or ideas in place elsewhere in the world that could be used in the US? *In fact, efficient and effective solutions are in place in Asia Pacific countries that provide real alternatives to the social and financial challenges of the US.*

The US

In addition to the policy changes the US government must make, there are cultural changes that must occur as well. Many Asia Pacific cultures have adapted to the multifaceted changes in the world today. Their adaptations have prevented them from accumulating deficits even close in size to that incurred by the US.

Greatness is part of America's birthright and lexicon. Its 18th-century founders had no doubt that they were embarking on a daring experi-

---

4   Ibid, p. 89.
5   Ibid. p. 89.
6   Stephen Dinan, (2013, October 18). "U.S. debt jumps a record $328 billion—tops $17 trillion for first time," *Washington Times.*

ment inspired by the highest ideals of the Enlightenment. In the 19th
century came Manifest Destiny, great migrations and the push to the
West, civil war and the end of slavery. The 20th brought titanic strug-
gles and famous victories against fascism and communism.

Even today, battered by recession, deep in debt, mired in war,
Americans remain proud of their country, and justly so. America still
towers over rivals in scientific virtuosity, military power, the vitality of
democracy and much else. Polls show that Americans are still among
the most patriotic people in the world. This summer 83% told Pew
that they were "extremely" or "very" proud to be American.[7]

The US is the third-largest country in the world by size with more
than 9.6 million square kilometers. Only Russia, with 17.1 million
square kilometers, and Canada, with nearly 10 million square kilometers, are larger.[8] With a US population of 310 million, only China,
with 1.3 billion, and India, with 1.2 billion, are larger in population.[9]

The American economy was again reported as the world's largest
national economy in 2012 with an estimated $15.7 trillion gross domestic
product (GDP). GDP is the annual market value of all officially
recognized final goods and services produced by a country. It is frequently used as a measurement of a country's economic health and size. The
US-reported GDP is larger than the entire European Union's GDP,
which was reported at $15.6 trillion in 2012. China had the second largest
GDP of any country in the world in 2012 at $12.4 trillion.[10] Not only
did the US have the world's largest economy in 2012 but it has had the
world's largest economy since at least the end of World War II.[11]

In 2011, the US remained the world's largest trader in merchandise
with imports and exports totaling $3.7 trillion. China and Germany
remained second and third, respectively. The United States remained the

7   *The Economist,* (2010, July 15). "Where has all the Greatness Gone?"
8   Nationsonline. (n.d.). "Countries of the World by Area." Retrieved May 4, 2013, from
    http://www.nationsonline.org/oneworld/countries_by_area.htm
9   Worldatlas.com. (2010). "Populations of All Countries in the World—Largest to Smallest."
    Retrieved December 17, 2012, from
    http://www.worldatlas.com/aatlas/populations/ctypopls.htm
10 CIA. (n.d.). *The World Fact Book.* Retrieved May 6, 2013, from
    https://www.cia.gov/library/publications/the-world-factbook/rankorder/2001rank.html
11 Kenneth Rapoza, (2013, March 23). "By The Time Obama Leaves Office, U.S. No Longer No.
    1," *Forbes.*

world's largest trader of commercial services in 2011 at $976 billion in trade. The US has recorded a surplus in services every year since the 1980s.[12]

In *Forbes* magazine's annual list of the 2,000 largest companies in the world, produced in early 2013, the US topped the rankings with 543 companies. Japan, with 251 companies, was second on the list with less than half the number of companies as the US, and China came in third with 136 member companies. The American company Apple was again the world's most valuable company, and the American company Wal-Mart Stores was the world's sales leader.[13]

The US has been the world's largest importer of oil since the 1970s but this may change because of the recent shale boom in the US and the offsetting reduction in imports.[14] The United States is the third largest producer of oil in the world, as well as its largest consumer.[15] It is the world's largest producer of nuclear power, accounting for more than 30% of worldwide nuclear generation of electricity, with 104 nuclear power plants producing 19% of the total electrical output for the country.[16]

The US has some of the most beautiful parks and historic views in the world, including the Statue of Liberty, the St. Louis Gateway Arch, the Lincoln Memorial, Mount Rushmore, the Grand Canyon, the Hawaiian Islands, Mount McKinley and the Golden Gate Bridge in San Francisco. The Midwest is full of farms that look like a giant quilt when viewed from a jet flying overhead. The Rocky Mountains are as majestic as the Gulf States are beautiful.

The US is the homeland of "the King"—Elvis, actress Marilyn Monroe and Mickey Mouse. Its music, movies and literature are sold around the world, and its retail goods are craved around the globe. It has an international population whose ancestors came from all parts of the globe. It is truly a unique nation in its multicultural and diverse

12   WTO. (n.d.). *World Trade Organization: World Trade Statistics 2012.* Retrieved May 7, 2013, from http://www.wto.org/english/res_e/statis_e/its2012_e/its12_highlights1_e.pdf, pp 15–17.
13   Scott DeCarlo, (2013, April 17). "The World's Biggest Companies," *Forbes.*
14   Benoit Faucon, (2013, April 3). "China to Overtake U.S. as World's Largest Oil Importer, OPEC Says," *Wall Street Journal.*
15   U.S. Energy Information Administration, (n.d.). "Countries." Retrieved May 7, 2013, from http://www.eia.gov/countries
16   World Nuclear Association, (2013, May 3). "Nuclear Power in the USA." Retrieved May 7, 2013, from http://www.world-nuclear.org/info/Country-Profiles/Countries-T-Z/USA—Nuclear-Power/

religions and people. Never before has the world seen such a marvelous and prosperous multicultural country as the Unite States.

The US has been the birthplace of many great men, but perhaps none as impressive as President Abraham Lincoln. Lincoln was President in the 1860s during the US Civil War. During his life he made many observations which are still applicable today. His most compelling for this day and age is perhaps the following: "If destruction be our lot, we must ourselves be its author and finisher."[17]

When looking at the fiscal challenges of this great nation, Lincoln's statement may be more relevant today than ever before. The federal debt load stands at over $17 trillion. Its social programs and government policies are cumbersome and at times ineffective. The politicians are at odds with each other and the people appear apathetic and unwilling to address the reality that government social programs are the root cause of the massive deficit spending.

The US is in a perilous situation. It must change from within. The last time the US faced such a perilous dilemma was over a century ago, when the country struggled with the institution of slavery. This problem was eventually resolved through civil war. Americans are in denial if they think today's dilemma: *how to take care of its poor, old and sick,* is any less challenging. The United States is in dire need of solutions! The good news is that there are solutions. The countries of Asia Pacific have policies and programs that are viable alternatives for the current budget-busting programs of the world's remaining super power.

Asia Pacific

In October 2012, a white paper was published by the Australian government titled *Australia in the Asian Century,*[18] which analyzed the explosive economic growth of Asian countries over the past few decades. Some relevant excerpts from this paper are noted and summarized below.

One of the most amazing statistics noted is that over the past 20 years, one-third of the world's population, located in Asia, has become part of the global economy and more are set to do so. "Living standards for billions of people in Asia have improved at a rate not previously experienced in human history."[19]

17   Abraham Lincoln, (1838, January 27). Address Before the Young Men's Lyceum of Springfield, Illinois.
18   Australian Government, (2012). *Australia in the Asian Century.* Canberra.

Asia's economic rise has been staggering but does not have a single "recipe," with each country adopting a different approach. Japan's rise to prosperity began shortly after World War II. Hong Kong's prosperity took hold as it set itself up as a regional and global financial center. Singapore's path was much more state-led with its leaders taking advantage of its favorable geographic location. South Korea's and Taiwan's strategies fostered entrepreneurship and innovation which established these two countries as technological powerhouses. In China, reforms began in 1978, when farmers were able to take responsibility for the profitability of their enterprises and were provided incentives to sell their own crops. In the 1980s, enterprises were able to take advantage of new market opportunities and "special economic zones" were created which provided concessions for private enterprise and foreign investment.[20]

Asia has become the factory for the world with integrated parts of the production process spreading across several different countries. Japan's economic rise led to cross-border value chains first developed for cars and electronics. As Japan developed, production costs rose and its companies began specializing in higher-skilled goods and services, and moved the labor-intensive assembly operation to South Korea, Hong Kong, Taiwan and Singapore. As production costs rose in these countries, businesses next relocated assembly processes to ASEAN (Association of Southeast Asian Countries) countries and finally to China. Now China has become the main assembly plant for Asia and the world.[21]

East Asia now accounts for one-third of the world's trade in manufacturing. China has become the main trading nation for all regional nations and is now the world's largest exporter. China is also now the world's largest energy consumer, having gone from consuming slightly half as much energy as the US in 2000, to slightly more today. As a result, China is now the world's largest producer and consumer of coal and accounts for almost half of the world's coal consumption. China has also become the world's largest consumer of steel, aluminum and copper, accounting for around 40% of global consumption of each. China and Japan rely on imports for their energy needs with China now the world's largest importer of coal and Japan the second-largest importer of coal and third-largest net importer of crude oil.[22]

---

19   Ibid, p. 30.
20   Ibid, p. 37–38.
21   Ibid, p. 41.

Asia is emerging as a global hub for innovation and technological development. In 2010, Japan overtook the United States as the leading producer of triadic patent families (a set of patents taken at the European Patent Office, the Japanese Patent Office and the US Patent and Trademark Office). South Korea was fifth. China overtook Japan in a number of innovation-related issues, including research and development expenditure and output of scientific publications. India's large and young population has influenced its research and development expenditure as its publications of scientific papers went from 2.1% of the world total in 2000 to 3.5% in 2010.[23]

The middle class in Asia is growing in wealth and mobility. With less income going towards life's necessities, demand has increased for a range of goods and services. "Between 2000 and 2011 the number of automobiles per 100 urban households in China is estimated to have risen from less than one to more than 18; the number of computers from eight to 80; the number of mobile phones from 16 to over 200; and microwave ovens from 16 to 60. While rates of growth in different consumer durables vary, similar patterns are evident across a whole range of goods."[24]

The Asian region is expected to be home to the world's fastest-growing middle class, whose emerging economies will become dominant consumer markets. "While recent studies differ on how to define and measure the global middle class, all point to the sheer magnitude of the shifts in Asia. One prominent study estimates that middle-class consumers in the Asia-Pacific region will increase by more than 2.5 billion people and account for around 60% of global middle-class consumption by 2030."[25]

Technology is changing the way people in Asia interact. "India now broadcasts more than 800 television channels, compared with only two in 1990. More than three in four people in Asia and the Pacific now use a mobile phone, compared with less than one in four in 2005; and 2.3 million more people in Asia and the Pacific are connecting to the Internet every week."[26]

Tourism throughout Asia has boomed. Popular culture is now shared across Asia as the region and world have discovered Japan's pop music

22   Ibid, p. 42–44.
23   Ibid, p. 45.
24   Ibid, p. 46.
25   Ibid, p. 62–63.
26   Ibid, p. 46.

and manga comics, Hong Kong cinema, South Korean television soaps and India's Bollywood films.[27]

The future for Asia is bright. The combined output of China and India will likely exceed that of the whole Group of Seven (G7) by early next decade and Asia alone is set to overtake the combined economic output of Europe and North America around the year 2025. India is now the world's third-largest economy and China could overtake the United States as the world's largest economy in 2014 in real purchasing power parity terms.[28]

Summary and Purpose

This book has two aims. The first is to provide an assessment of the current "state of the Union" in the US. No punches are held back. The US is in a dire situation economically and socially, and it must make some drastic fundamental changes now. Specifically, the US is broke and getting broker and the social programs that are the cause need a massive overhaul.

Something must be done in the US to address its social and economic problems, and US politicians must lead in this effort. However, in today's political climate the two political parties, the Democrats and the Republicans, can't even agree on what the current status is.

When root causes are identified and not just symptoms, then real solutions can be implemented. For example, when a man enters a hospital with a broken leg, the symptom of the issue may be the broken leg. The real issue may be that the man is an alcoholic and fell from a ladder drunk when cutting down a tree in his backyard. The "fix" in this situation is not just setting the man's leg and putting plaster on it to keep it stable while it heals. The "fix" is to do this while addressing the man's alcoholism so he does not injure himself or others in the future. This analogy is applied to the issues in the US presented in this book. The symptom may be that the US government is accumulating annual massive deficits. *The real issue in the US is that its social programs are broken and require a major overhaul.*

Some pundits may argue that the entire US political structure requires changing, which it may. But the premise in this book is to assume that the current capitalist/mixed economic system is a given and

---

27 Ibid, p. 46.
28 Ibid, p. 53.

the issues needing correcting are within the current social and political boundaries.

The second aim of this book is to provide hope through solutions and alternatives. As will be discussed throughout this book, real answers to the problems facing the US can be found in the Asia Pacific region today.

In the following chapters, the issues are defined and then a possible solution from Asia Pacific is presented. Applying these ideas in the US may not end up materially the same or come easily. However, it is encouraging to note that these solutions are working in Asia Pacific.

A final hope in developing this book is that this great country, the United States, has the humility to see its true challenges and the courage to change before it is too late.

CHAPTER 2

The Costs of Social Programs

In the US, in spite of nearly $16 trillion in welfare spending since 1964, the poverty rate at 15% is almost as high as the 19% rate when the programs to combat poverty were initially put in place. On the other side of the world, China still has poor people, but the Chinese have endured without much direct government assistance and as a result China is without the massive debt burden of the US.

US Annual Deficits, Debt and Unfunded Liabilities

A government deficit or surplus is measured by calculating the difference between receipts and spending.

The difference between deficits and debts is that deficits occur when government expenditures exceed revenues or receipts, usually measured on an annual basis. Debt is the amount a country borrows to support its continued existence. A country's debt is basically its accumulated deficits.[29]

Often the annual federal surplus or deficit is reported as a percent of gross domestic product. In a study by Luca Ventura and Tina Aridas that included most of the democratic countries in the world, the percent of expenditures in 2011 for each government ranged from a surplus of 12.5% of GDP for Norway and 0.8% for Korea and Switzerland; to severe deficits, including a 10.3% deficit for Ireland, 10% for the United States, 9.4% for the UK, 9% for Greece and 8.9% for Japan. For fiscal year 2012, the US was projected to have the largest annual deficit of all of these countries at 9.3%.[30]

The United States' "war on poverty" has greatly impacted the federal debt load. When President Obama took office in early 2009, the federal

29   Treasurydirect.gov. (2004, August 5). *Debt versus Deficit: What's the Difference?* Retrieved October 14, 2013, from http://www.treasurydirect.gov/news/pressroom/pressroom_bpd08052004.htm
30   Luca Ventura and Tina Aridas, (2012). "Public Deficit by Country," *Global Finance* magazine, Retrieved 11 11, 2012, from http://www.gfmag.com/tools/ /global-database/economic-data/10395-public-deficit-by-country.html#axzz2Ae3MwSuX

debt load was somewhere near $9.6 trillion. By fiscal year 2012, this had risen to $16.7 trillion. In each of Obama's first four years in office the annual deficit remained over $1 trillion per year.[31]

The total US federal debt is not easy to determine. In August of 2013, for example, the legal limit for the debt of $16,699,421,000,000 ($16.7 trillion) was set in a law passed by Congress and signed by President Barack Obama. The Treasury Department's Financial Management Service (FMS) publishes a "Daily Treasury Statement" and a "Monthly Treasury Statement." On May 17, 2013, the FMS reported that the official US debt was exactly $16,699,396,000,000. Then, even though the US government ran a deficit for the month of July 2013 in the amount of $98 billion, the debt reported was this same amount for the entire month. This debt amount remained $16.7 billion for 87 straight days through mid-August 2013, at just $25 million less than the legal limit. "If Treasury's daily statements were to declare that the government had borrowed an additional net $98 billion to cover the $98 billion deficit the Treasury declared in its monthly statement for July, the Treasury would be conceding that the government had already surpassed the legal limit on the debt—and has been violating the law by continuing to borrow additional money."[32] This unique accounting treatment continued for more than 150 days through October 16th 2013, while the federal government's debt still showed at the $16.7 billion amount.[33]

On Thursday October 17th, the first day the government was able to borrow money under a new deal put together between President Obama and Congress, the US debt jumped $328 billion, setting a new one-day record, raising the debt burden to over $17 trillion.[34] By the end of the first week after the new deal was set, the US government had accumulated an additional $375 billion in debt. At the rate of $375 billion per week, the public debt was on track to reach $22.7 trillion by the next debt ceiling deadline on February 7, 2014.[35]

31 Op cit, Chantrill.
32 Terence P. Jeffrey, (2013, August 14). "Treasury Ran $98 Billion Deficit in July—But Debt Stayed Exactly $16,699,396,000,000." Retrieved August 17, 2013, from http://cnsnews.com/news/article/ /treasury-ran-98-billion-deficit-july-debt-stayed-exactly-16699396000000
33 Terence P. Jeffrey, (2013, October 16). "150 Straight Days: Treasury Says Debt Stood Still at $16,699,396,000,000." Retrieved October 20, 2013, from http://cnsnews.com/news/ /article/terence-p-jeffrey/150-straight-days-treasury-says-debt-stood-still-16699396000000
34 Op cit, Dinon.
35 Ron DeLegge, (2013, October 22). "Will U.S. Public Debt Reach $22 Trillion by Feb. 2014?" Retrieved November 30, 2013, from http://www.etfguide.com/

When reviewing the numbers that add up to the federal debt load, it is clear that the increases are due to increases in federal government spending. The US federal budget in 2008 was $2.9 trillion a year. This included spending on military, welfare, healthcare, interest on debt and other costs. By year 2012, this had blossomed to $3.7 trillion. In almost every category, with the exception of defense, spending increased between 2008 and 2012 in both dollar amounts and percent of total federal government costs. With no observable decrease in spending, the debt load was expected to reach a staggering $17.5 trillion by the end of 2013.[36]

During budget deliberations in October 2013, it was pointed out that the US debt burden has grown more than twice the rate of the growth in GDP or economic output. In two years the US debt had grown $2.4 trillion but GDP had grown less than $1.2 trillion.[37]

Even more alarming than the US's annual deficits or federal debt burden is the amount of its unfunded liabilities. Unfunded liabilities are financial promises made with no money held in reserve to support these promises. For-profit organizations (e.g., companies or corporations) or not-for-profit organizations (e.g., charities) must report the amount of liabilities or promises they have made that are outstanding. For example, if you have promised your employees that they will receive a pension upon their retirement, then you must report this in your financial statements. In addition to reporting, a prudent company will set aside funds to pay for these promises when they become due. Companies may be legally prevented from taking money from the assets set aside for some of these obligations, and if a company or organization does not set aside adequate assets to support their liabilities, the organization could go bankrupt and face litigation as a result. Unfunded liabilities are a cause for concern in a company or corporation and a severe red light for anyone reviewing a company's balance sheet to determine its financial solvency and business practices.

The US government does not have to abide by these reporting and reserving measures. The government does not have to provide in its basic set of financial statements the amount of its total liabilities, the bulk of

/commentary/1138/Will-U.S.-Public-Debt-Reach-$22-Trillion-by-Feb.-2014

36   Op cit, Chantrill.
37   Daniel Halper, (2013, October 9). "U.S. Adds Two Times More Debt than Economic Output in Last 2 Years." Retrieved October 14, 2013, from http://www.weeklystandard.com/blogs/us-adds-two-times-more-debt-economic-output-last-2-years_762311.html

which are currently unfunded. Also, it does not have to set aside assets
to fund the obligations it has promised.

As of the end of 2012, the actual liabilities of the US federal government—including Social Security, Medicare, and federal employees'
future retirement benefits—were estimated to exceed $86.8 trillion, or
550% of annual GDP. In addition, for the year ending December 31,
2011, the annual accrued expense of Medicare and Social Security was
$7 trillion.[38] This means that these programs are adding $7 trillion
annually to the US debt load but this $7 trillion is not counted in the
amount of growing US debt or accounted for in its annual deficits. At
the current rate, the US will have almost $100 trillion in financial debt
and promises due at the end of 2014, but the public will only know
about the small portion of this amount, the already massive $17 trillion
in debt outstanding.

In late 2012, over 80 CEO's from some of America's largest corporations encouraged Congress to reduce the amount of US debt.[39] While
the US currently borrows at record low interest rates, the concern is that
this will change. This was the main concern of the individuals who
attended the "Tea Party" rallies beginning in 2009. Many Americans
were alarmed at the increases in federal government spending. How did
the US get to this point? The answer is in its war on poverty.

War on Poverty

The war on poverty started with admirable objectives. In his 1964 state
of the union address, President Lyndon Johnson declared "an uncondi-
tional war on poverty." The poverty rate at that time was 19% but it was
falling. The poverty rate has never since fallen below 10.5% and by 2012
was 15.1%, its highest level in nearly a decade. Clearly, something is
wrong with the US's war on poverty.[40]

In early 2014, it was noted that the poverty rate had stayed at 15% for
three years in a row. The poverty rate was 12.5% in 2007, before the
Great Recession.[41] In response, the federal government had plans to

---

38   Chris Cox and Bill Archer, (2012, November 26). "Cox and Archer: Why $16 Trillion Only
     Hints at the True U.S. Debt," *Wall Street Journal.*
39   Reuters. (2012, October 25). "US CEOs call action to reduce federal deficit." Retrieved 11 11,
     2012, from
     http://www.reuters.com/article/2012/10/25/congress-deficit-idUSL5E8LPJXY20121025
40   Michael Tanner, (2012, April 11) "The American Welfare State—How we spend nearly $1
     Trillion a year fighting poverty—and fail." *Policy Analysis,,* p. 2.
41   Dave Boyer, (2014, January 7). "That's rich: Poverty level under Obama breaks 50-year

spend more than $680 billion on 126 different programs to fight poverty. This did not include the nearly $284 billion in planned spending by state and local governments, nor did it include the costs related to middle-class entitlements Medicare and Social Security.[42]

"Welfare spending increased significantly under President George W. Bush and has exploded under President Barack Obama."[43] In 2012 it was noted that since President Obama took office, federal welfare spending had increased by 41% to more than $193 billion per year. "Despite this government largess, more than 46 million Americans continue to live in poverty. Despite nearly $15 trillion in total welfare spending since Lyndon Johnson declared war on poverty in 1964, the poverty rate is perilously close to where we began more than 40 years ago."[44]

According to the Heritage Center, since 1964, the US federal government has spent $16 trillion on welfare aid. Whether the amount is $12 trillion or $16 trillion, the amount spent on welfare aid is massive and welfare is the fastest growing part of the government, with the nation spending more on welfare than on national defense.[45]

Most welfare programs provide either cash, food, shelter, healthcare or some other form of assistance to those who qualify. Most programs are based on income but others target the homeless or locations where poverty is high.

In 2011 the federal government spent roughly $668.2 billion on those 126 [welfare] programs. That represents an increase of more than $193 billion since Barack Obama became president. This is roughly two and a half times greater than any increase over a similar time frame in US history, and it means an increase in means-tested welfare spending of about 2.4% of GDP. If one includes state and local welfare spending, government at all levels will spend more than $952 billion this year to fight poverty. To put this in perspective, the defense budget in this year (in 2011), including spending for the wars in Iraq and Afghanistan, totals $685 billion.[46]

record," *Washington Times.*
42   Op cit, Tanner, pp. 2–4.
43   William W. Beach and Patrick D. Tyrrell, (2012, February 8). "The 2012 Index of Dependence on Government," Washington DC: The Heritage Foundation, p. 14.
44   Op cit, Tanner, p. 1.
45   Op cit, Tyrrell, p. 16.
46   Op cit, Tanner, p. 12.

The poverty level for an US family of three in 2011 was an annual income of less than $18,530. Ironically, the US federal government spends more than $44,500 on a family this size through various government programs (e.g., food stamps, healthcare, education). Combined with state and local spending, the government spends $61,830 on a family of three.[47] Although this is what is spent, this is not the amount of money getting to the poor due to government waste and the bureaucracy built to oversee the government handouts. With the amount of spending on welfare, the war on poverty should have been won, but clearly it has not.

"We should focus less on making poverty more comfortable and more on creating the prosperity that will get people out of poverty."[48] By trying to reduce or eliminate poverty in the US, the federal government has itself become broke, and its policies encourage its citizens to remain broke.

Medicaid

In 2011, the single largest welfare program in the US was Medicaid. This spending includes healthcare costs for the poor but excludes long-term care and nursing home costs for the elderly.[49] News came out right after the November 2012 elections that one in five Americans are on Medicaid. More than 70 million were enrolled in 2011 as noted in a study by the Centers for Medicare and Medicaid Services, the agency that oversees the two healthcare entitlements, reporting that the number of participants enrolled in the program at any time of the year in 2011 was higher than ever before.[50]

Medicaid is a joint federal-state program that was put in place to combat poverty in the US. One study reported that the number of enrollees grew from 60 million in 2005 to 62.8 million in 2008, and in 2011 to 70 million. Medicaid grew by 5 million in the two years after 2009, after the end of the 2008 recession.[51] This estimate may be low. In 2013, the US Census Bureau reported that in the fourth quarter of

---

47   Ibid, Tanner, p. 2.
48   Ibid, p. 1.
49   Ibid, p. 3.
50   Matt Cover, (2012, November 9). "Record 70.4 million enrolled in Medicaid in 2011: 1 out of every 5 Americans." Retrieved November 10, 2012, from http://cnsnews.com/news/ /article/record-704-million-enrolled-medicaid-2011-1-out-every-5-americans
51   Ibid.

2011 the number of individuals in who lived in households in which one or more people received Medicaid benefits had risen to 82 million, a quarter of the entire US population.[52]

Medicaid is a massive federal program that is growing. A study of federal health data by researchers from the George Washington University School of Public Health determined that Medicaid program covered 48% of the 3.8 million births in 2010, jumping from 40% in 2008. Between 2008 and 2010, Medicaid covered 90,000 more women giving birth, an increase of 8%, as states expanded the federal-state health coverage plan.[53]

In 2010, Medicaid accounted for $246 billion in US federal government spending. Significant increases have occurred since 2008, well before the upcoming impact from the Patient Protection and Affordable Care Act (PPACA or Obamacare).[54]

The increase in spending in Medicaid is not only related to the increase in enrollees but also its wasteful processes. For example, in a report released by federal auditors in 2014, the Medicaid program overpaid for diapers by about $62 million in 2012. According to the auditors, only five state Medicaid agencies had implemented competitive bidding programs for disposable diapers.[55]

Medicaid, with all its waste, is expected to grow dramatically in the near future. Under the PPACA, the requirements for those on Medicaid will soften and more individuals will become eligible for the benefit. This comes into effect in 2014, when the maximum annual income for a family of four to be eligible for Medicaid will be $30,950.[56] The Supreme Court in a recent decision ruled that the federal government could not compel states to do this, making the expansion optional for state governments.[57] If the states choose to do this, the number of eligible

52 Terence P. Jeffrey, (2013, October 23)."Census: 49% of Americans Get Gov't Benefits; 82M in Households on Medicaid," Retrieved November 17, 2013, from http://cnsnews.com/news/ /article/terence-p-jeffrey/census-49-americans-get-gov-t-benefits-82m-households-medicaid
53 William Bigelow, "Almost Half of US Births Covered by Medicaid," (2013, September 8). Retrieved October 1, 2013, from http://www.breitbart.com/Big-Government/ /2013/09/08/Almost-Half-of-U-S-Births-Covered-by-Medicaid
54 Op cit, Tyrrell et al, p. 11.
55 Lachian Markay, (2014, January 27). "Medicaid Overpays Millions for Diapers." Retrieved February 16, 2014, from http://freebeacon.com/medicaid-overpays-millions-for-diapers/
56 Op cit, Cover.
57 Terence P. Jeffrey, (2014, April 7). "Americans on Medicaid Exceed Population of UK." Retrieved April 12, 2014, from http://www.cnsnews.com/news/article/ /terence-p-jeffrey/americans-medicaid-exceed-population-uk

individuals for Medicaid in the years ahead will significantly mushroom to even more unsustainable levels.

Food Stamps and Other Welfare Programs

The second largest welfare program in 2011 was related to food stamps. The Supplemental Nutrition Assistance Program (SNAP) cost tax-payers $72 billion in 2011.[58] Food stamps are basically cash equivalents provided to the poor which can be redeemed at stores throughout the US for food.

Although not released to the public until after the November 2012 elections, the number of US individuals receiving food stamp assistance reached an all-time high in October 2012. More than 47 million Americans were tallied as receiving food stamps in that month alone. These numbers are usually released at the end of the month, or the first day or two of the next month, but for October 2012 the numbers were withheld for nine days until after the election.[59] Since this was not a positive event for the Obama administration, it is no wonder the news was delayed.

Not only is the cost of the food stamp program exploding, but "food stamp trafficking" is way up as well. In 2013, the Food and Drug Administration released a report that showed that the rate of trafficking rose from 1% of total benefits in the previous study period of 2006–08 to 1.3% in the most recent study period of 2009–11, an increase of 30%. Food stamp trafficking is illegal, and while the percentage remains relatively low, the sharp increase in the SNAP program means the total annualized dollar amount of fraud reached a record level of $858 million in 2011, exceeding the previous high of $811 million in 1993.[60]

Other federal welfare programs in place include 33 housing programs under four different cabinet departments. The federal government has an additional 21 programs providing food and the ability to buy food for individuals who qualify. These are administered under three different departments and a separate agency. There are eight health programs

---

58   Op cit, Tanner, pp. 3–4.
59   Jim Hoft, (2012, November 11). "Figures—Obama Administration hid record food stamps till after election." Retrieved 11 11, 2012, from http://www.thegatewaypundit.com/ /2012/11/figures-obama-administration-hid-record-food-stamp-numbers-until-after-election/
60   Jeryl Bier, (2013, August 16). "Food Stamp Trafficking Up 30% From 2008 to 2011." Retrieved August 17, 2013, from http://www.weeklystandard.com/blogs/food-stamp-trafficking-30-2008-2011_748511.html

under the Department of Health and Human Services. In addition, there are 27 cash or general assistance programs run under six departments and five agencies. The exact number and list of agencies changes slightly from year to year as programs are eliminated and new ones created, but the number of federal government programs engaged in the war on poverty has remained at over 100 for nearly a decade.[61]

State and local governments provide additional funding for these programs and have programs of their own. In total, the federal government pays for about two-thirds of the cost of these programs, with different states and localities covering the remainder. The top ten list of government programs fighting poverty includes Medicaid and food stamps, as noted above. They are followed by the Earned Income Tax Credit, the Child Tax Credit, Pell Grants, Supplemental Security Income, the State Children's Health Insurance Program, housing vouchers, and TANF (Temporary Assistance for Needy Families). More than 4.5 million Americans receive benefits from these bottom eight programs.[62]

The welfare program numbers do not include the arrival of the PPACA. This program, enacted in 2010, is a massive increase to Medicaid by means of the setup of government controlled insurance exchanges. The PPACA is expected to add somewhere in the range of 19 to 25 million participants and an additional cost of $1 trillion or more to the national budget.[63]

Some pundits argue that the increase in the costs of the war on poverty is due to the recession that the US has experienced starting in 2007. However, after reviewing the current programs, it is also clear that the eligibility requirements for these programs have been loosened by the Obama administration.[64]

It can also be argued that the anti-poverty programs have reduced the rate, or at least the burden, of poverty on individuals. However, evidence suggests that "anti-poverty programs" are usually more concerned with protecting the prerogatives of the bureaucracy than with actually fighting poverty. But more important, the concept behind how we fight poverty is wrong. The vast majority of current programs are focused on making poverty more comfortable—giving poor people more food, better shelter, healthcare, and so forth—rather than giving

61   Op cit, Tanner, pp. 2–3.
62   Ibid, pp. 3–4.
63   Op cit, Tyrrell et al, pp. 13.
64   Op cit, Tanner, pp. 7–8.

people the tools that will help them escape poverty. And we actually have a pretty solid idea of the keys to getting out of, and staying out of, poverty, which are: (1) finish school; (2) do not get pregnant outside marriage; and (3) get a job, any job, and stick with it."[65]

Medicare, State and Local Liabilities and Decrease in Taxpayers

Medicare is quickly becoming insolvent. "Congress established Medicare in 1965 through Title XVIII of the Social Security Act. Medicare pays for healthcare for individuals ages 65 and above, and for those with certain disabilities. Medicare enrollment has steadily increased since its enactment due to increases in both population and individual life expectancy. In 1970, 20.4 million individuals were enrolled in Medicare. By 2010, the number of enrollees had more than doubled to 47.5 million."[66]

The increase in costs of Medicare is staggering. The expenditure rose by 86% from 1999 to 2010, when it reached $408 billion.[67]

In addition, the government is building up large amounts of unfunded liabilities related to the program.

> The Medicare trustees' 2011 annual report shows that the program
> faces $24.6 trillion in unfunded obligations under current law; under
> an alternative, even more plausible, scenario the estimate reaches $36.8
> trillion. Medicare Part A is already running yearly deficits, and accord-
> ing to the trustees, the Hospital Insurance Trust Fund will become
> insolvent in 2024.[68]

US state and local governments are also burdened with other huge debts and liabilities. In mid-July 2013, the city of Detroit announced that it was filing for bankruptcy. At the heart of Detroit's problem was a growing unfunded obligation to current and future retirees in the amount of $3.5 billion. Other US cities like Chicago and Los Angeles have similar estimated unfunded liabilities in the amounts of $36 and $30 billion, respectively. Estimates in 2010 were that US state govern-

65   Ibid, p. 10.
66   Op cit, Tyrrell et al, p. 10.
67   Ibid, p. 11.
68   Ibid, p. 12.

ments had unfunded liabilities related to pensions in the amount of $1.4 trillion.[69]

While the US population's dependence upon the federal government has increased, the number of taxpayers has decreased. Federal government spending is on the rise, even when accounting for inflation. Government resources spent on individuals in 2012 was 15 times the amount spent in 1962. In addition, "the percentage of people who do not pay federal income taxes, and who are not claimed as dependents by someone who does pay them, jumped from 14.8% in 1984 to 49.5% in 2009. This means that in 1984, 34.8 million tax filers paid no taxes; in 2009, 151.7 million paid nothing."[70]

"Any way that you look at it, we are rapidly becoming a society where more and more people rely on the government for their support."[71] The United States' war on poverty is a failure.

The significant growth in government spending along with the decrease in tax revenues is not sustainable. No longer is the debt burden only on the shoulders of current US taxpayers. Today's deficits in the US have created a burden for the current taxpayer's children and their children's children.

The social model used in the US today attempts to address social issues through massive spending, resulting in budget-busting deficits, debts and unfunded liabilities. China, the world's second-largest economy, has an alternative approach.

China's Economic Transition

In 1978, Deng Xiaoping took over as China's "paramount leader." China was then a very poor country that had endured the Japanese invasion in World War II, the Cultural Revolution under Mao and mass starvation through oppressive communist policies. The country was in a terrible state that required immediate and drastic changes in policy.[72]

One of the first things that Deng did was to recognize the potential in allowing individuals to acquire and maintain property rights. This capitalistic approach started in motion the greatest transformation of a

69 Todd Spangler, (2013, July 22). "Detroit not alone under mountain of long-term debt," *Detroit Free Press.*
70 Op cit, Tyrrell et al, p. 1.
71 Op cit, Tanner, p. 4.
72 Jonathan Fenby, (2009). *The Penguin History of Modern China—The Fall and Rise of the Great Power 1850–2009.* London: Penguin Books, p. xxxi.

country in world history. Deng recognized that some individuals would prosper before others. "Due to Deng Xiaoping's design of 'allowing some people to prosper first,' there is no doubt that the excellence of economic development has generally improved the people's living standards."[73]

In 1984, inspired by the success of recent reforms, the Party leaders decided to promote changes in national enterprises. "It was clarified that state ownership of enterprises may not be necessarily equivalent to the direct operation of the state. Rather, enterprises could be independent in management and responsible for their own profits and losses. Meanwhile, the income of workers should be based on their performance and the success of enterprises."[74]

As a result, today China has a space program, nuclear weapons and the largest standing army in the world with 2.2 million troops. It is still behind the US in military technology but gaining fast.[75] China now houses the world's largest building. Located in Chengdu, the building has offices, plenty of retail space, a university, hotels, a 14-screen IMAX Cineplex, a "Mediterranean village," and an artificial beach with a fake sun. The building is four times as large as the Vatican and three times as large as the Pentagon and its 420 acres of floor space is nearly the size of the entire country of Monaco.[76]

China has a permanent seat on the United Nations Security Council. It offered triple the aid of Western countries to Africa in 2007 and exerts soft power through diplomacy and assistance. China also has no qualms about relations with rogue states like Iran or North Korea if they can serve China's interests.[77]

The 2008 Olympics in Beijing were an official introduction to China's power and influence on the world's stage. Who can forget the opening or closing ceremonies of those Olympics, with the multitudes of individuals involved in these productions? The 2008 Olympics was China's call to the world that they had arrived.

China's economy has grown tenfold in the past three decades. In 2008 the People's Republic of China (PRC) was the world's second largest

73   Lei Jie, (2012, March). "China's Welfare Regime 1949–2011: the Key Role of the Communist Party of China," The University of Sheffield, Sheffield, England. Retrieved December 2012, from http://etheses.whiterose.ac.uk/2201/1/Lei,_Jie.pdf, p. 1.

74   Ibid, p. 96.

75   Op cit, Fenby, p. xxxii.

76   Tyler Falk, (2013, July 5). World's Largest Building Opens in China. Retrieved July 6, 2013, from http://www.smartplanet.com/blog/bulletin/worlds-largest-building-opens-in-china/23555

77   Op cit, Fenby, p. xxxii–xxxiii.

manufacturer with 15% of the output, just behind the US's 17%. At the end of 2008, its economy was worth 27.4 trillion yuan, equal to US$4 trillion, with purchasing power second in the world only to the US. China has a middle class estimated at near 80 million and at the end of 2007, there was thought to be up to 100 USD billionaires in China.[78]

In China's quest for growth, it has built relationships with countries like Venezuela for oil and Congo for copper. It has acquired Western practices in marketing and managerial skills and Western technology in almost all of its industries. Its small-sized town and village undertakings employ as many people as the whole American workforce. It makes 80% of the world's bestselling toys and Zhejiang province in eastern China makes a third of the world's socks, 40% of the world's ties, and 70% of its cigarette lighters.[79]

At the start of economic reform, the city of Wuhan in central China had no taxis. Today, it is estimated that it has 30,000. "In 2008, the PRC had 3,000 television stations, 1.3 million websites, 200 million Internet users (the highest number of any country), 540 million mobile phone users, and 137 handsets for every 100 urban inhabitants. Fast food chains proliferate. The showpiece city of Shanghai is Manhattan on steroids; rich young men there complain that development is changing the street pattern so fast that the GPS systems are out of date before they take delivery of the new limousines."[80]

Around the world, prices on commodities are greatly influenced by Chinese demand for raw materials and the PRC has become the greatest assembly plant the world has ever known, contributing materially to the profitability of US, Japanese and European firms. China's GDP has doubled between 2002 and 2008 and it has become the world's biggest producer of steel and aluminum. In the early years of the 21st century, it was estimated that half of the world's cranes were in use in the Chinese mainland.[81]

However, China's population is not as wealthy as that of the US on a per capita basis. China's GDP in 2009 was only a quarter of the United States', and was far smaller on a per capita basis.[82] However, the country is today set firmly on the world's stage. Along with its growth, China has challenges with a communist-controlled government and is one of

78   Ibid, pp. xxxiii–xxxiv.
79   Ibid, pp. xxxv–xxxvi.
80   Ibid, pp. xxxvii.
81   Ibid, pp. xxxvi–xxxvii.
82   Ibid, pp. xxxi.

the world's greatest polluters. These issues cannot be ignored but the incredible economic growth in this country has impacted its people in positive ways, increasing their standard of living immensely.

China's Social Programs

While the US is moving more and more towards a welfare state, China is moving more and more towards prosperity. "Since the launch of economic reform in 1978 more people (in China) have been made materially better off in a shorter span of time than ever before in human history."[83]

China's rise out of poverty has been dramatic. For example, considering a consumption threshold of $1 a day using the 1993 Purchasing Power Parities (PPP), the World Bank tracked a reduction of poverty from 652 million Chinese people in 1981 to 135 million in 2004. China's anti-poverty performance is even remarkable with a standard of $1.25 a day at 2005 PPP. "The numbers in poverty by this measure dropped from 848 million in 1981 to 351 million in 2004. This denotes that there were 517 ($1 standard) or 497 million ($1.25 standard) people who had escaped from absolute poverty during 1981–2004."[84] A half a billion Chinese citizens have risen out of poverty due to China's changing policies!

China has been able to make its transitions with low welfare spending. "East Asia has the most dynamic economies in the world. They have managed to combine this dynamism with social cohesion, an apparent "health miracle" and very low crime rates, while keeping their welfare expenditures low."[85]

> As early as 1980, Deng (Xiaoping) rejected any possibility of importing the welfare state into China. He insisted that the enhancement of welfare should be coordinated with the development of production. [He stated,] "We are poor and weak in foundation (*dizi bo*) with underdeveloped education, science and culture. We [are] oppose[d] to the argument of actualizing the welfare state in China now because it is impossible. We can only improve our living standards gradually on the basis of developing production. It is wrong to develop production

83   Ibid, pp. xxxiii.
84   Op cit, Jei, pp. 1–2.
85   Ibid, p. 3.

without raising people's living standard, but is also wrong, in fact impossible, to improve people's living standard without developing production."[86]

Through his arguments, Deng set the tone for China's rise out of poverty. Later in 2000, China's Premier Zhu Rongji discussed the welfare state:

> Our country is currently at the primary stage of socialism, in which productive forces are less developed. Thus, the contributions and the levels of entitlements could not be too high. Otherwise, it would be unaffordable for each quarter, damage economic development of the state and the competitiveness of enterprises. A huge deficit has been caused in some European countries because of the high standards of social welfare. The public and enterprises were dissatisfied after these countries were forced to reduce welfare or increase taxes.[87]

Zhu was right in seeing that you cannot provide a social program and then take it away and not expect a severe backlash from the people receiving or expecting to receive the benefits.

China's welfare spending is low but it is increasing. According to the Ministry of Human Resources and Social Security of the People's Republic of China, there were 284 million participants in the country's social security pension program in 2011, an increase of 27 million over the prior year. Of the participants, 216 million are paying into the plan and 68 million are receiving benefits. Of the new individuals in the plan in 2011, 22 million were paying into the plan and 5 million were receiving benefits.[88]

China had 473 million people enrolled in their medical plan in 2011, 143 million received unemployment benefits, 177 million received work-related injury benefits, and 139 million received maternity benefits. The total amount of revenue to cover all five of these programs (social security pensions, medical, unemployment, work-related injury and maternity) in 2011 was US$382 billion. The total outflow for these

86   Ibid, p. 123–124.
87   Ibid, p. 125.
88   Ministry of Human Resources and Social Security of the People's Republic of China, (2012). *2011 Social Services Review.* Beijing: Ministry of Human Resources and Social Security.

programs was $287 billion.[89] These numbers are significantly less than the comparable amounts in the US.

According to Tyrrell, the US federal government spent $1.7 trillion on social programs in 2010. This includes $680 billion on welfare programs to fight poverty, including Medicaid, food stamps and housing programs. It also includes the $1.053 trillion spent on Social Security and Medicare. These programs cover 67 million benefit participants or one-fifth of the US population. This does not include the beneficiaries of the PPACA program that is soon to come into effect.[90] Other sources show the US federal government spending more than $2.1 trillion in 2011 on health, welfare and pension benefits.[91]

When comparing these numbers to China, the results are very clear. The US spent somewhere near $2 trillion on social benefits in 2011 and China spent somewhere near $287 billion. The US spent nearly seven times as much on social programs in 2011 as China. According to the World Atlas, as of 2010, China had a population of 1.3 billion and the US 310 million.[92] Therefore China had more than four times the number of people living within its borders than did the US in 2010.

This adds up to the fact that the US paid approximately 30 times more per capita to its citizens in the form of social benefits than did the "socialist" country China in 2011.

Social Programs in Socialist and Capitalist Countries

When we think of an example of a socialist country, we probably think of Communist Party-run China, and when we think of a capitalist country the US is probably the first country that comes to mind. However, if socialism is measured by the amount spent on social programs, then the US is clearly a more socialist country than China. Even if you do not agree with this, it is hard not to see that the line between what is a socialist country and what is a capitalistic country has become blurred.

Socialist countries were led by idealists who preached equality and leveling the playing field. However, today the socialist countries are

89   Ibid.
90   Op cit, Tyrrell et al, pp. 8–27.
91   Op cit, Chantrill.
92   ´Op cit, World Atlas.

behind capitalist countries in providing social programs to their people in total dollars spent on social policies as well as per capita.

When the PRC stopped and looked at its situation after Mao's death in the 1970s, the picture was not great. As a matter of fact, the picture was dismal, and the reality was that the PRC was a very poor country and its policies needed drastic changes in order to catch up to the US. The first policy implemented was providing individuals the legal right to own property. In doing this, the PRC leaders recognized that some people would benefit before others. The principle of property rights was the catalyst for massive change. China still has problems with pollution, corrupt officials and other concerns, but with a half a billion people elevated out of poverty, it is clear China is moving in the right direction.

Meanwhile, on the other side of the Pacific in the US, the number of individuals living in poverty (as defined by the number receiving welfare benefits) has never been higher. The amount of spending by the federal, state and local governments for welfare, retirement, housing and other benefits has also never been higher. Rather than backing off on government subsidies, the Obama administration has moved full speed ahead in spending on welfare and other benefits.

As a result, socialist China is becoming more prosperous and the US is sliding over a fiscal cliff. Poverty is being reduced in China and poverty is on the rise in the US.

People who receive benefits from governments always want more rather than less. As even noted by the PRC leadership, it is very difficult to take away a benefit once provided. Perhaps this is human nature. In countries where there is no or limited welfare benefits from the government, people appear to be more willing to work for their livelihoods because there is no alternative. Government benefits promote an entitlement mentality, which promotes indolence, and this is not good for individuals or society as a whole. The products of entitlements are a stagnant economy and GDP as in the US, while the results of limited entitlements are a growing economy and an increased GDP as in China.

China is a country that thrives without massive government spending on social programs through reliance upon the family. There seems to be a belief in the US that without government spending on welfare related programs, there would be no support for the citizens of the country. This is not true as it ignores the fact that the family is and has been the primary support for the welfare of its citizens since the beginning of time. Churches and other community organizations have also supported their local citizens throughout history. One thing that is certain is that if the US continues with its current pace of government spending on welfare, sooner rather than later, Americans will know first-hand that the family is the primary support for the individual because there will be no more money available from a bankrupt United States.

CHAPTER 3

Australia's "Super"

The US Social Security system has been referred to as the world's largest Ponzi scheme, where individuals' payments made today don't even pay for the current recipients' benefits, let alone future needs. Australia's superannuation system is an alternative which provides for individual accounts based on amounts paid into the program with the payer selecting the fund and return they desire.

US Social Security

The Social Security Act was signed into law by President Franklin D. Roosevelt (FDR) on August 14, 1935. The law included several provisions for the general welfare of American citizens and created a social insurance program designed to pay retired workers, aged 65 or older, a continuing income. One of two major provisions of the law related to the elderly was "Title II: Federal Old-Age Benefits," which covered the social insurance program which we now think of as Social Security. In the original act benefits were to be paid only to the primary worker when he/she retired at age 65 and were to be based on payroll tax contributions that the worker made during his/her working life. Taxes were first collected in 1937 and monthly benefits began in 1940.[93]

By dollars paid, the US Social Security program is the largest government program in the world, and it is the single greatest expenditure in the federal budget.[94] In 1937, more than 53,000 Americans received benefits totaling $1.2 million; by 2008, nearly 50.9 million Americans were being paid Social Security benefits totaling more than $615 billion.[95]

---

93 Social Security Administration, (n.d.). *The Social Security Act.* Retrieved May 11, 2013, from http://www.ssa.gov/history/briefhistory3.html
94 Emily Brandon, (2010, August 9). "10 Things You Didn't Know About Social Security," http://money.usnews.com/money/retirement/articles/2010/08/09/ /10-things-you-didnt-know-about-social-security
95 Social Security Administration, (n.d.). "Historical Background and Development of Social Security." Retrieved May 11, 2013, from http://www.ssa.gov/history/briefhistory3.html

Since 1935, Social Security has provided the primary income for most retirees. It also has a component that provides for benefits for disabled Americans as well. The retirement portion of the program pays a monthly check based upon the recipient's income over a 35-year period. Current retirees become eligible for income from Social Security as well as for healthcare benefits from Medicare or Medicaid.[96]

Under Social Security, lower-income earners receive a higher proportion of their income than higher-income earners. For example, lower-income earners receive a benefit of about 70% of their pre-retirement income in Social Security while higher earners receive closer to 23%. In this regard, the system is not fair to higher-income earners. The system is not based upon need; millionaires receive the same benefits as low-income earners at age 65.[97]

Over recent years, the demographics that made the program affordable have changed and the program is crashing. Estimates were that in order to break even, Social Security needed at least 2.9 workers to pay taxes for each retiree who receives benefits. The current ratio has been near this but dropping because the Baby Boomers produced fewer children than their parents did and now are nearing retirement.[98]

Because of the recession, the Social Security program has been creating deficits since 2010. This is expected to be permanent per the Congressional Budget Office (CBO) and Social Security Administration (SSA). Between 1983 and 2009 workers paid more into the program than was necessary to meet the needs of current recipients but the excess funds were not invested by the government; they were spent on other programs.[99] Now that Social Security has gone bust, the excess funds required to keep it solvent will come from the federal government and add to the already massive deficit.

One criticism of the Social Security program is that benefits for enrollees are paid for by payroll deductions from today's working Americans, and because of this, it is a "Ponzi scheme" and therefore fraudulent. In the private sector, annuities, pensions, trusts, and similar investment vehicles are originated on a voluntary basis. These contracts are enforced by the courts and as clients pay money into the vehicles, the fiduciary invests the funds and the investment grows. Over a period

96   Op cit, Tyrrell, pp. 4 & 18.
97   Ibid, pp. 4 & 18.
98   Ibid, p. 18.
99   Ibid, p. 18.

of time, the client is paid back funds and accrued gains. The results of the investment depend on the investment climate. If the fiduciary or trustee violates the terms of the agreement, they can be sued, fined or jailed.[100]

In a "Ponzi scheme" a vehicle pays alleged "investment returns" to clients from the clients' own paid-in funds and with payments by subsequent clients, rather than from investments in fruitful assets or securities. In order to keep afloat, the scheme solicits new entrants by making false promises of high returns. The scheme has to keep adding new members to prevent its collapse. Eventually, outflows exceed inflows and the scheme collapses in insolvency. "Such schemes are rare and tend not to last long or grow large in a free market, since they aren't mandatory they ensnare increasingly suspicious clients, they attract legitimate rivals eager to expose them, and they invite publicity-hungry district attorneys to prosecute them."[101]

Whether the perpetrator of the Ponzi scheme deliberately creates the scheme or only ends up with it after years of "cooking the books," either way it is still fraud. The same can be said of Social Security in the US, whether President Franklin Roosevelt knew he was creating the world's largest Ponzi scheme or whether it just ended up this way, the fact remains that it has long since become a fraud. "Today fools or frauds dare deny it. Private-sector Ponzi schemes have built-in sensors, enemies, and anti-fraud laws to prevent and terminate them, while Social Security has the opposite: built-in perpetuators, coercion, muzzled and shrinking rivals, a growing pool of serfs, millions of admiring heralds, and a superficial air of legality."[102]

The very first Social Security recipient, Ida Mae Fuller of Ludlow, Vermont, paid just $25 in Social Security taxes, but the long-lived Mrs. Fuller collected $22,889 in benefits. She started collecting benefits in January 1940 at the age of 65 and lived to be 100 years old, dying in 1975.[103] Many Americans were like Mrs. Fuller in the beginning, in that they paid very little into the program and yet received a large annuity in return. In 1940, there were 159 workers supporting each social security

---

100 Richard M. Salsman, (2011, September 27). "Social Security is Much Worse Than a Ponzi Scheme—and Here's How to End It," *Forbes.*
101 Ibid.
102 Ibid.
103 Social Security Administration, (n.d.). *Historical Background and Development of Social Security.* Retrieved May 10, 2013, from http://www.ssa.gov/history/briefhistory3.html

beneficiary; by 1960 the ratio had decreased to five workers per retiree.[104] As noted above, today there are about three workers for every retiree.

Another criticism of the program is that the maximum amount of taxes promised to be paid into the scheme has been exceeded. American workers and employers pay FICA (Federal Insurance Contributions Act) taxes through automatic paycheck deductions. FICA and Medicare contributions, paid by both employers and employees, increased steadily from just 2.25% of pay between 1935 and 1953 to 4.50% by 1960, 6.90% by 1970, 8.10% by 1980 and 15.3% by 1990.[105]

In a pamphlet from 1936 used to publicize the program, the Social Security Administration promised that the most an employer and employee combined would ever pay was 6% of the worker's annual income, up to $3,000 by the year 1949. This rate was breached under President John F. Kennedy in 1962, and today's rate of 15.3% is more than double the original promised rate. In addition, today's rate applies to as much as $106,800 of annual income, which is more than *triple* the inflation-adjusted equivalent of what $3,000 was worth in 1949 (i.e., $28,642). So instead of paying $1,718 per year (6% on the inflation adjusted income of $3,000 from 1949), Americans are now forced to pay up to $16,340 per year (15.3% on income as high as $106,800), which amounts to a ten-fold increase on what was originally promised.[106]

One might expect that the massive inflows of cash into the program would be set aside and invested productively and be available for the payer when he or she eventually retires, but this is not the case.

In the 1960s, the federal government began raiding the Social Security fund which set aside the money provided by working Americans for their eventual retirement. The money from the fund was used for general outlays, and the government issued IOUs to itself in the form of non-tradable Treasury bonds worth $2.6 trillion in 2011. The amount of internal government bonds resulting from robbing the Social Security fund continues to grow, while now most inflows are spent immediately on current beneficiaries. This is a Ponzi scheme in its largest and simplest form. Private pensions or annuities provide their beneficiaries returns based on their contributions, plus investment returns, and assets are held in a legally-segregated accounts. This is not the case with Social

---

104 Social Security Administration, (n.d.). "Ratio of Covered Workers to Beneficiaries." Retrieved May 10, 2013, from http://www.ssa.gov/history/ratios.html
105 Op cit, Salsman.
106 Ibid.

Security as the government keeps the assets and now spends the current contributions on payments to beneficiaries and on other government programs.[107]

In the private sector, a fiduciary is not allowed to unilaterally alter the terms of your annuity or pension, against your well-being. If this were to happen, the fiduciary would be prosecuted, and you could file a civil action for restitution to retrieve your assets. With Social Security, the US government owns your assets, can and has changed the terms of the original agreement with the American people, spends the inflows on things other than Social Security and essentially pays for current outflows with the funds being paid into the program.[108]

Since 1935, the retirement income for seniors has been compared to that of a three-legged stool. One leg was the Social Security program, another leg was to consist of income from the recipient's employer-based pension and the third leg was the savings made by the individual throughout his career. Today this is not the case, as almost half of Americans work for employers who do not offer pension schemes, and most Americans are not able to save enough for retirement without a payroll-deduction saving plan. If you take away one leg of a three legged stool, it falls over. If you take away two legs. . . . "For workers without a pension plan, the reality of their retirement is closer to a pogo stick consisting almost entirely of US Social Security."[109]

In addition to Social Security being in danger, personal savings have also suffered. "By soaking up money that should have been invested for the future, US Social Security's high [contribution] tax rate makes it much harder for lower-income and moderate-income workers to accumulate any substantial savings."[110] Companies have also had difficulties saving for their employees.

> Complex government regulations also discourage the expansion of occupational pensions to cover a higher proportion of the workforce. Over the past few decades, the costs of traditional pension plans have skyrocketed, and thousands of [pension plans] have shut down. Efforts to develop innovative hybrid pension plans stalled when confusing laws and regulations resulted in lawsuits. . . . While most large employers

107 Ibid.
108 Ibid.
109 Op cit, Tyrrell et al, pp. 17–18.
110 Ibid, p. 18.

now offer defined-contribution plans, such as 401(k), these plans are subject to the Employee Retirement Income Security Act (ERISA). ERISA regulations are especially onerous for smaller employers, who usually lack the necessary expertise to comply with the act's complex legal requirements. As a result, small businesses hesitate to offer retirement savings plans to their workers for fear of either accidentally violating a regulation or facing the cost of hiring an outside expert.[111]

Boomers' Bummer

Over the next 20 years, 10,000 individuals in the US will retire every day.[112] "Over the next 25 years, more than 77 million boomers will begin collecting Social Security checks, drawing Medicare benefits, and relying on long-term care under Medicaid. No event will financially challenge these important programs over the next two decades more than this shift into retirement of the largest generation in American history."[113]

"Paying for these middle-class and upper-class entitlements in the coming years will require unprecedented levels of deficit spending. Focusing on Social Security and Medicare alone, Americans face $45.9 trillion in unfunded obligations over the next 75 years. That is more than $200,000 per American citizen."[114] Medicare has $24.6 trillion in unfunded obligations under current law, thus making Social Security's unfunded obligations somewhere near $21.3 trillion. Other estimates report the unfunded liability for Medicare at somewhere near $42.8 trillion with Social Security's unfunded liabilities at $20.5 trillion.[115] What this means in non-accounting terms is that the US government has promised more than $20 trillion in benefits to Americans who have paid into the current program.

Some politicians have made efforts to address the looming challenges with Social Security and Medicare. President George W. Bush after his 2004 re-election attempted to tackle these issues, but he had spent all his political clout on the wars in Afghanistan and Iraq. The Democratic members of Congress cheered during his speech to the assembly when he noted that his efforts had been blocked. Since then, the problems have not been addressed.

111   Ibid, p. 18.
112   Ibid, p. 4.
113   Ibid, p. 2.
114   Ibid, p. 4.
115   Op cit, Archer et al.

The inaction is perhaps because members of the government do not know of any viable alternatives to the status quo. In fact, there is a solution and it comes from the "Land Down Under"—Australia's superannuation program is the answer.

Australia's Superannuation

Australia and the US both faced problems in the 1980s related to their government-run old-age pension system. Australia did something about it—the US did not. In 1986, in an effort to address their system, Australia implemented an innovative retirement plan based primarily on mandatory private savings in "superannuation funds." This system became known as the "Superannuation Guarantee" and has since been modified and expanded over time.[116]

Superannuation's benefits include, firstly, more income for retirees than the previous system provided. Secondly, the country's savings rate increases as more people enter the program and add personal contributions to their nest eggs. Thirdly, there are reduced funding pressures on the federal government under the new scheme when compared to the former plan.[117]

In 1983, when Australia faced challenges with the pension scheme, politician and then Treasurer Paul Keating summarized the problem as follows: "We must let Australians know truthfully, honestly, earnestly, just what sort of international hole Australia is in. . . . If this government cannot get . . . a sensible economic policy, then Australia is basically done for. We will end up being just a third-rate economy. . . . Then you are gone. You are a banana republic."[118] This sounds eerily applicable to the situation today in the US.

In Australia, there was a strong consensus that an individual should be responsible for his or her own retirement savings. However, the government continued with a safety net for all individuals that guaranteed a minimum level of benefits. In effect, every individual was entitled to 25% of the average worker's salary, which was what was available and in place before the superannuation program was instituted.[119]

---

116 Daniel J. Mitchell and Robert P. O'Quinn, (1997, December 8). "Australia's Privatized Retirement System: Lessons for the United States." Retrieved 11 25, 2012, from http://www.heritage.org/research/reports/1997/12/australias-privatized-retirement-system, p.1.
117 Ibid, p. 2.
118 Ibid, p. 3.
119 Ibid, p. 6.

How Superannuation Works

Superannuation is a retirement savings scheme for Australian employees. It mandates that employers contribute 9% of eligible employee earnings into a fund in a fashion similar to FICA taxes in the US Social Security program. Superannuation is mandatory for employees, but is not mandatory for the self-employed. It works in a very similar fashion to any other investment portfolio, with the main exception being that you cannot generally access the superannuation funds until retirement or disability.[120]

To qualify for the superannuation program, an individual must be between the ages of 18 and 69 years old and be paid a minimum of $450 (before tax) of income in a given month. If under the age of 18, an individual must make at least $450 (before tax) a month and work more than 30 hours a week in the month. Employers are not required to make superannuation contributions in certain cases, such as to foreign nationals living in Australia under certain visas and other reasonable exceptions.[121]

Individuals can enter an agreement with their employers to have some of their salary or wages paid into their superannuation fund. This action may have tax advantages because the standard 15% tax on superannuation funds is probably less than the tax the individual would have paid if he/she had taken the money instead as salary. If an individual pays more into their fund than is permitted under the Australian regulations, the tax rate is much higher than for contributions below the limit.[122]

An individual can receive a distribution/payout from their superannuation based upon various events: retirement; death, terminal medical condition, permanent incapacity, financial hardship and attaining age 65.[123] The amount of distribution would be equal to the individual's fund balance.

The superannuation fund managers act as trustees under regulations codified in the Superannuation Industry (Supervision) Act 1993. There

120 Primorisifinancial. (n.d.). "What is superannuation?" Retrieved May 12, 2013, from
     http://primorisfinancial.com.au/superannuation/faqs/what-is-superannuation/
121 Australian Taxation Office, (n.d.). "Guide to Superannuation for individuals: Eligibility."
     Retrieved May 12, 2013, from
     http://www.ato.gov.au/individuals/content.aspx?doc=/content/00250233.htm&page=4
122 Australian Taxation Office. (n.d.). "Guide to Superannuation for Individuals: Contributions."
     Retrieved May 12, 2013, from
     http://www.ato.gov.au/individuals/content.aspx?doc=/content/00250233.htm&page=12&H12
123 Australian Government ComLaw (2013). *Superannuation Industry (Supervision) Regulations 1994—Schedule 1.* Retrieved May 12, 2013, from
     http://www.comlaw.gov.au/Series/F1996B00580

are very few governmental restrictions on the funds as well as governmental investment asset requirements. Many superannuation fund trustees provide individual members with the choice of a wide range of investment options and superannuation products with different investment goals. At the end of 2012, there were more than 470,000 funds available for Australian superannuation participants to choose from and more than 31 million member accounts.[124]

The superannuation fund accounts operate in a similar fashion to any other investment account. Different superannuation funds offer different investments of almost any asset, and as a consequence, a person's superannuation fund can be tailored to suit their individual needs. A participant can invest in a range of savings accounts, term deposits, managed funds, direct shares and property. Participants have control over the investment strategy and given that superannuation is normally a family's second biggest asset after their family home, it is vital that the investment strategy is suited to their own situation.[125]

In addition to fund performance, the superannuation funds may add disability or life insurance to the plans they manage. The fund trustees have a fiduciary duty to act in the best interests of their members, and insurance is seen as one of these avenues. There may also be tax advantages in obtaining these benefits, and the fees are deducted from investment earnings. This has created a very large market for these types of insurance products, not just for insurance companies but reinsurers as well. The advantageous tax treatment comes from the fact that amounts paid into a superannuation fund (at least 9% of salary) are taxed at a 15% rate, which is significantly lower than the income tax rate. Thus, insurance premiums are taken from a less-taxed account before investment earnings. The incentive for individuals to obtain insurance coverage also benefits the country by having fewer individuals to care for under its welfare and disability programs. The Australia Superannuation Guarantee is an example of how a sensible and smart social program in a country can have a positive impact on other social programs in that country.

The Australian government allows a range of tax concessions to both funds and contributors in an effort to make the superannuation pro-

---

124 Australian Prudential Regulation Authority, (2013, January 9). *Statistics: Annual Superannuation Bulletin.* Retrieved May 19, 2013, from http://www.apra.gov.au/Super/Publications/Documents/ /June%202012%20Annual%20Superannuation%20Bulletin.pdf, p. 5.
125 Op cit, Primorisifinancial.

gram more accommodating to its citizens. "In fact superannuation is one of the lowest taxed environments in Australia with contributions being taxed at 15%, investment earnings within the fund at 15% and capital gains at 10–15%. Compare this to someone who earns $100,000 being taxed at 40.5% on income, 40.5% on investment earnings and 40.5–47.5% on capital gains (assuming no health cover and on financial year 2010/11 income tax rates), superannuation can be a very tax effective vehicle for building wealth quicker than what could be possible with a personal investment strategy."[126]

In a move that sounds similar to recent actions by the US government, the tax advantages embedded in the superannuation legislation that encourage individuals to contribute to their individual accounts will soon change. Starting in July 2014, earnings of more than $100,000 on superannuation pensions and annuities will be taxed at 15%, instead of being tax free. When the superannuation fund is in the distribution phase, the earnings on the fund distributions have to date been tax-free. Superannuation earnings below $100,000 a year will remain tax-free. The Australian government said that around 16,000 people will be affected by this reform. Critics complained that this move was "quite cheeky" because only four or five years ago the government encouraged individuals to put up to $1 million into their superannuation funds tax-free, and now the new government in charge is taxing that income.[127]

Impact of a Superannuation Implementation in the US

Overall the results of the superannuation program to the Australian economy are positively staggering. The markets are liquid and growing. Results from a global pension assets study produced by Towers Watson & Company in early 2013 noted that the Australia pension fund assets are the fourth largest in the world. "Australia's total superannuation fund, which comes to US$1.6 trillion, has grown by 18% in the past decade in US dollar terms. However, Australia's pension fund assets, despite being bigger than the Australian economy, still trail the United States (which has US$16.8 trillion), Japan (US$3.7 trillion) and the UK (US$2.7 trillion), according to Towers Watson. The nation's superan-

---

126   Ibid.
127   ABC.net.au. (2013, April 6). *Government Double Dipping on Super Tax*. Retrieved May 12, 2013, from
      http://www.abc.net.au/news/2013-04-05/government-double-dipping-on-super-tax/4612322

nuation assets relative to GDP rose from 96% in 2011, to 101% in 2012, joining the Netherlands, Switzerland, the UK and the USA as countries where the ratio is higher than 100%."[128] *Australia's Superannuation Guarantee fund has grown significantly in real terms while the US Social Security has become a Ponzi scheme.*

It is quite impressive that a country the size of Australia, with a population of a little over 20 million, has the fourth largest pension fund assets in the world. This is due in large part to the Australian superannuation schemes.

Although the US has the largest holdings of pension assets in the world, if a superannuation-type plan were implemented in the US, the holdings for all pension plans in the US would increase significantly. The US federal government's revenues related to Social Security in 2012 were at $560 billion.[129] If this, or a portion of this amount, were added to pension programs in the US on an annual basis, the impact would be to increase the financial markets at historic rates.

According to the US Census Bureau in 2012, in the US the current mix of pension assets is: 27% related to Individual Retirement Accounts (IRAs); 26% related to defined contribution accounts; 25% related to federal, state and local pensions; 13% related to private pensions; and 9% related to annuities. Two-thirds of the defined contribution plans are related to 401(k) plans.[130] 401(k)s are plans where the participant defines an amount of contribution on a pre-tax basis to an account which assets are then available upon retirement to the individual. All of the various US pension plans and all other investors in the US markets would benefit from the US switching to a social security program similar to Australia's superannuation.

The rate of return for an individual's superannuation accounts would also be higher than the returns of the current Social Security program.

> Under the current Social Security system, each generation now and in the future loses the difference between the return to real capital that would be obtained in a funded system and the much lower return in

128 Sophie Cousins, (2013, February 7). "Australia's pension fund assets are world's fourth largest."
     Retrieved February 11, 2013, from http://www.investordaily.com/cps/rde/xchg/id/style/
     /15983.htm?rdeCOQ=SID-0A3D9632-A44542EA
129 Op cit, Chantrill.
130 U.S. Census Bureau, S. A. (2012). "Banking, Finance, and Insurance: Retirement Assets by
     Type of Asset: 1990 to 2010." Retrieved February 11, 2013, from
     http://www.census.gov/compendia/statab/2012/tables/12s1216.pdf

the existing unfunded program. Shifting to a privatized system of individual mandatory accounts that can be invested in a mix of stocks and bonds would permit individuals to obtain the full real pre-tax rate of return on capital. This would mean a larger capital stock and a higher national income.[131]

The concept of implementing a superannuation scheme in the US is not new. In 1997, Harvard University professor of economics, Martin Feldstein, promoted a similar plan.

Conservative assumptions imply that Social Security privatization would raise the well-being of future generations by an amount equal to 5% of gross domestic product (GDP) each year as long as the system lasts. Although the transition to a funded system would involve economic as well as political costs, the net present value of the gain would be enormous—as much as $10–20 trillion.

Such a private savings program would solve Social Security's long-run financial problems without the necessity for either huge tax increases or draconian benefit cuts. At the same time, it would yield enormous benefits to the economy. In short, privatizing Social Security can increase real incomes for everyone while ensuring a dignified retirement for future retirees.[132]

If the US were to move to a program like that of Australia's superannuation, it would place at least part of the responsibility for retirement back on the individual. Higher long-term returns on individual accounts would be much better than the current government-run Ponzi scheme. The Social Security program would no longer be a liability to the federal budget. The number of jobs created as a result would be significant, and the markets would increase substantially.

Implementing Superannuation in the US
If Australia can implement a superannuation social security system then why can't the US? Both are developed English-speaking countries. Both

131   Martin Feldstein, (1997, January 31). "Privatizing Social Security: The $10 Trillion
       Opportunity." Retrieved February 11, 2013, from http://www.cato.org/pubs/ssps/ssp7.html
132   Ibid.

have democratic forms of government and both are high-income countries. But a change in policy in the US will require changes in attitude by both US politicians and citizens. Some recommendations by proponents of this plan regarding the implementation are as follows:

- The shortcomings of the current US Social Security system must be explained. The government programs will not be enough to live on comfortably in old age. An individual must take some responsibility himself.
- The privatization of Social Security will lead to larger nest eggs than the current system.
- The change to a superannuation-type scheme will not alone balance the US budget but it is one of many significant changes that will help the country in the long run.
- The new superannuation system should protect existing beneficiaries with the understanding that benefit reductions to existing retirees would be a major political liability for reform.[133]

The most important of these points is the fourth, which recommends not taking away anything already promised to current participants. If you bring this idea up in even casual conversations, the average American will belittle the idea because of fears of the government not making good on its current promises. Many people are dependent upon Social Security income or are counting on it being there in their old age. In order for the successful implementation of superannuation in the US, lawmakers must make good on their commitments. This will be difficult to do in the short run but immensely beneficial in the long run.

One way to do this when implementing a superannuation scheme would be to award all current enrollees with IOUs on the amounts currently promised. These would become due when the beneficiary's assets are distributed. By staggering payments of the government IOUs over time as the amounts come due, the US government could preclude a multi-trillion dollar one-time payout for amounts currently due to plan participants. These IOUs could be increased by a given rate promised by the government equal to the measly current rate of interest or one reflecting a more reasonable rate of return.

---

133 Op cit, O'Quinn et al, pp. 11–12.

Changes have to be implemented with the US Social Security program as it is now as bankrupt as the other social programs in the US. The superannuation model is a viable and smart alternative that is working in Australia. The US could take a giant step forward in implementing a similar solution for hard-working, soon-to-be-retired Americans. This solution would fix the old age retirement benefit solvency problem that Social Security has created while at the same time providing substantial nest eggs for future retirees. Additionally, the stock market would rise substantially while moving the solution for old age retirement from the US federal government back to the individual where it belongs.

The US Social Security program is running down the same track as other programs created during the 1930s that have already derailed the US economy. Just like the Fannie Mae and FHA programs led to the 2008 financial disaster, Social Security in its current state is a ticking financial time bomb. "Since the scheme began in 1935 the full force of the US government has compelled a growing portion of citizens to suffer by it, such that we all do so by now. A scheme of such widespread, compulsory fraud is unprecedented in US history, and one of the most shameful (and popular) of FDR's schemes."[134]

The Australian Prudential Regulation Authority noted in its recent publication regarding superannuation schemes:

> It is generally accepted that for markets to work effectively, there must be firms competing for consumers' business, and consumers making choices about various value propositions. . . . Markets have two sides and for a market to be working effectively, the demand side and the supply side need to be operating well: suppliers need to be competitive and consumers need to be able to exercise their market power.[135]

Indeed, it is clear that the Australian superannuation scheme works effectively, while the US Social Security system does not.

---

134 Op cit, Salsman.
135 Op cit, Australian Prudential Regulation Authority, p. 8

CHAPTER 4

Obamacare versus Hong Kong Healthcare

Hong Kong is known for its efficient and effective government services and healthcare program. However, as with the US, the costs for healthcare in Hong Kong are unsustainable. Hong Kong's proposed Health Protection Scheme is an alternative currently being vetted that reduces the burden on the government while improving the quality of public healthcare services in the long run. It differs from Obamacare in many ways.

The Emotional Aspects of Obamacare

When President Barack Obama took office in early 2009, there was much hope and excitement. Although the economies of the world had undergone a recent major downturn, the new administration had promised to make changes necessary to shore up the economy while maintaining fiscal responsibility.

President Obama was in an exceptional situation. Not only had he won the presidency, but the Democratic Party had also retained its majorities in both the House of Representatives and the Senate. The President was placed in the happy situation where his policies would easily fly through both houses of Congress and become law. The result was many new and controversial laws and acts; however, none were as controversial as the Patient Protection and Affordable Care Act (PPACA aka Obamacare).

Although the US was in the worst recession it had been in since the Great Depression of the 1930s, the new President and his Democratic colleagues in Congress began publicizing the advent of a new healthcare law shortly after passing the trillion-dollar stimulus package in the first month of Obama's presidency. The stimulus was put together without any Republican input, despite the Democrats' promise to be transparent during the election, and it would add nearly $1 trillion in spending to an already unbalanced federal budget. The administration's next project was to overhaul the entire healthcare system.

In September 2009, after less than a year in office, President Obama gave a speech to Congress about his healthcare proposal, making the following statements:

- Individuals will be required to carry basic health insurance.
- I will not sign a plan that adds one dime to our deficits—either now or in the future.
- [N]othing in this plan will require you or your employer to change the coverage or the doctor you have.
- If you strike out on your own and start a small business, you will be able to get coverage. We will do this by creating a new insurance exchange—a marketplace where individuals and small businesses will be able to shop for health insurance at competitive prices.
- This exchange will take effect in four years, which will give us time to do it right.
- [T]he reforms I'm proposing would not apply to those who are here illegally.
- [U]nder our plan, no federal dollars will be used to fund abortions, and federal conscience laws will remain in place.
- Reducing the waste and inefficiency in Medicare and Medicaid will pay for most of this plan.[136]

After much debate, the law was finally brought forward in the Democrat-controlled House of Representatives for a vote. The Democrat leader and Speaker of the House at the time, Nancy Pelosi, stated before the vote, "We have to pass the bill so that you can find out what is in it, away from the fog of controversy."[137] The House passed the "Affordable Health Care for America Act" in November 2009. One Republican voted for the legislation along with 219 Democrats and 215 members voted against the bill.[138] The result was hardly a bipartisan venture.

Next, the Senate took on Obamacare. The majority leader, Harry Reid, cut deals with Democratic Senators including Mary Landrieu of

136 Toby Harnden, (2009, September 10). "Transcript of Barack Obama's health-care speech." Retrieved December 15, 2013, from http://blogs.telegraph.co.uk/ /news/tobyharnden/100009074/transcript-of-barack-obamas-health-care-speech/
137 Debra J. Saunders, (2012, October 11). "Nancy Pelosi says she read Obamacare Bill." Retrieved January 13, 2013, from http://blog.sfgate.com/djsaunders/2012/10/11/nancy-pelosi-says-she-read-obamacare-bill/
138 US House.Gov, (2009, November 7). *FINAL VOTE RESULTS FOR ROLL CALL 768.* Retrieved December 15, 2013, from http://clerk.house.gov/evs/2009/roll768.xml

Louisiana, Ben Nelson of Nebraska and Bill Nelson from Florida, and eventually, on Christmas Eve of 2009, the Senate passed the legislation with the 60 votes needed without a single Republican vote.[139]

The Democrats in the Senate knew that they would have problems passing the law so they decided to pass it as a revenue bill, but because all revenue bills have to originate in the House, the Senate found HR3590, a military housing bill, took essentially all of the original wording out of it, and turned it into the Patient Protection and Affordable Care Act.[140]

The bills that were passed by the House and Senate were different bills, due to the additions and changes made in the Senate. The dilemma was that a bill needs to be passed by both bodies to become law. The Senate bill did not stand a chance in the House because it contained funding for abortion, which a group of Democratic representatives openly opposed, and it held the deals for Louisiana, Nebraska and Florida, previously mentioned. Conversely, the House bill could not pass the Senate because it did not have abortion coverage, or the riders demanded by Landrieu, Nelson and Nelson.[141]

More problems for the Democrats arose in January 2010. The Massachusetts Senate seat held by the late Democratic Senator Ted Kennedy was shockingly won by a Republican, Scott Brown. Brown had promised to kill Obamacare. Suddenly, the Democrats did not have the 60 votes needed in the Senate.[142] So the Democrats in the House and the Senate made an agreement. The members in the House agreed to pass the Senate bill if the Democratic Senators would agree to pass a supplementary bill in the House with their changes to the Senate's bill. So the House passed the Senate bill, without a single Republican vote, as well as the Reconciliation Act of 2010.[143]

The second bill passed by the House, the Reconciliation Act of 2010, next needed to be passed by the Senate to become law. But without the 60 votes needed, the Democrats used the "reconciliation" ruling. Under

---

139 Sundance. (2013, October 14). "Obamacare 'Settled Law'? NBC's David Gregory Used The Primary Talking Point Again Yesterday...." Retrieved December 15, 2013, from http://theconservativetreehouse.com/2013/10/14/ /obamacare-settled-law-nbcs-david-gregory-used-the-primary-talking-point-again-yesterday/
140 Crawfordbroadcasting.com. (2012, October 15). "How Obamacare Became the 'Law of the Land'." Retrieved December 15, 2013, from http://www.crawfordbroadcasting.com/Vecchio_Archives/ /How%20Obamacare%20Became%20Law.pdf
141 Op cit, Sundance.
142 Ibid.
143 Op cit, Crawfordbroadcasting.com.

this rule, which had only been used for budget item approval in the past, budget items could be passed with only 51 votes. Both laws were signed by Obama with neither earning a single Republican vote. Democrat Representative Alcee Hastings of the House Rules Committee said during the bill process: "We're making up the rules as we go along."[144] The PPACA became the only major legislation in US history ever enacted on a strict party-line vote.[145]

Obamacare Overview

Why was there so much concern about Obamacare? One reason is that the US healthcare industry is very large and growing. According to a presentation by Big 4 accounting firm Deloitte and Touche (D&T), the US healthcare industry in 2008 accounted for 17% of the US GDP. In 2009, $9,200 was spent per capita on healthcare. Multiplied by 310 million people, that is a nearly $3 trillion industry.[146]

The PPACA implementation comes in three material phases over 10 years. During the first stage in the years 2010 through 2013, 105 new agencies or programs were scheduled to be created. These required coordination between states and the federal government, and coordination at the federal government level between agencies themselves.[147]

During the second phase, occurring in the years 2014 through 2016, the individual mandate comes into play, exchanges are created and other programs are piloted. This is the period of the most dramatic changes. In the third phase, during 2017 and beyond, the "new normal" arrives, with legislation rulemaking and appropriations coming into play.[148]

The law itself is very complex and cumbersome. It creates 68 grant programs, 47 bureaucratic entities, 29 demonstration or pilot programs, six regulatory systems, six compliance standards and two entitlements. The law was 2,841 pages long and the Secretary of Health and Human Services has 2200 references in the law and 600 new authorities, none of which can be challenged. Obamacare includes 150 new bureaucracies

---

144 Ibid.
145 Ann Coulter, (2013, September 25). "Cruz Control should be standard on GOP models."
    Retrieved December 9, 2013, from
    http://www.humanevents.com/2013/09/25/cruz-control-should-be-standard-on-gop-models/
146 Jean Yves-Gueguen, Paul Keckley, Howard Mills and Andrew Freeman, (2010, December 21).
    "The Impact of Health Care Reform on the Financial Services Industry." Deloitte
    Development LLC, pp. 4 & 28.
147 Ibid, p. 6.
148 Ibid, p. 6.

and boards that are created between doctor and patient and 17 new mandates on insurance.[149]

Benefits Promised by Obamacare

The benefits of Obamacare, as noted by its proponents, include:[150][151]

- You can add your children up to age 26 to your health insurance plan.
- Your insurance company cannot limit the coverage you receive over your lifetime.
- If you have a child with a pre-existing condition, you no longer have to worry about losing coverage if you change your insurance.
- If you or another adult has a pre-existing condition, you will get the same protection as your child in 2014. Until then, if you get denied coverage by a new insurance company, you can get temporary health insurance coverage from the state.
- Insurance companies must spend at least 80% of premium payments on medical services, instead of advertising and executive salaries. If they can't, the money goes back to you.
- You may not have to pay a fee (co-pay) for wellness or pregnancy exams.
- Preventative care and screening such as mammograms and pap smears are free.
- Small business owners get a tax credit to help provide coverage for their employees.
- If your job does not provide insurance, you will be able to buy into an insurance exchange with costs based on your income.

Most Americans would not be opposed to legislation enforcing some if not all of the above benefits. However, it is the items in the other 2,840 pages of the PPACA that have received criticism.

149 Dailybail.com. (n.d.). "Obamacare Complicated? Check out the Flowchart." Retrieved January 15, 2013, from http://dailybail.com/home/obamacare-complicated-check-out-the-flow-chart.html

150 Kimberly Amadeo, (2012, October 11). "Obamacare Summary: How Obamacare affects you." Retrieved January 29, 2013, from http://useconomy.about.com/od/criticalssues/a/Obamacare-Summary.htm

151 Teresa Albano, (2012, July 12). "Top 10 Reasons to Love Obamacare." Retrieved January 29, 2013, from http://www.peoplesworld.org/top-10-reasons-to-love-obamacare/

Criticisms of Obamacare

At the time of its passing and since, the PPACA has not been very popular. In a national telephone survey poll by Rasmussen Reports taken as recently as July 2012, 52% of likely US voters favored repeal of the healthcare law, while 39% were opposed.[152]

Some states have taken the law directly to the voters. In August 2010, the state of Missouri addressed Obamacare in a proposition on their ballot. Missouri's measure prohibiting the enforcement of the individual mandate to buy health insurance was approved on a statewide ballot with an overwhelming 71% of the vote.[153]

Individuals and politicians have called for the repeal of the law. "Beyond the unprecedented mandates, new taxes, massive entitlement expansion, unworkable and costly insurance provisions, and its failure to control costs, the new law concentrates enormous power in the US Department of Health and Human Services (HHS). It creates a giant network for the federal micromanagement of health plans, benefits, insurance markets, and unprecedented intervention into the details of health care financing and the delivery of medical care."[154]

Individual Mandate

The "individual mandate" provision of the PPACA forces Americans to purchase health insurance or pay a penalty. Robert E. Moffit of the Heritage Foundation writes:

Under Section 1501, individuals will be assessed a monetary penalty if they do not purchase a health insurance plan that meets the federal definition of "minimum essential benefits." Congress finds, in Section 1501(a), that health care is inextricably connected with interstate commerce thus claiming a constitutional power to require that citizens purchase a specified level of coverage. The penalty for failure to make such a purchase is to be the *greater* of a flat dollar amount or a percent-

152 Ed Morrissey, (2012, July 2). "Rasmussen Post Scotus No Change in Obamacare Popularity." Retrieved January 19, 2013, from http://hotair.com/archives/2012/07/02/ /rasmussen-post-scotus-no-change-in-obamacare-popularity/
153 Rob Bluey, (2010, August 4). "Obamacare Loses Big in Missouri Voters Reject Individual Mandate." Retrieved January 19, 2013, from http://blog.heritage.org/2010/08/04/ /obamacare-loses-big-in-missouri-voters-reject-individual-mandate/
154 Nina Owcharenko, (2010, November 9). "The Case Against Obamacare: Repealing Obamacare and Getting Healthcare Right." Retrieved January 19, 2013, from http://thf_media.s3.amazonaws.com/2011/pdf/TheCaseAgainstObamacare.pdf

age of income, phased in from 1% to 2.5% of income by 2016. The penalty is to be phased in over a three-year period, with the flat dollar amount set at $95 in 2014, $325 in 2015, and $695 in 2016.[155]

This mandate applies to all citizens in the US with exemptions including incarcerated persons, illegal aliens, foreign nationals, and members of "recognized religious sects or divisions" with accepted tenets or teachings that would forbid the person from accepting public or private insurance.[156] When the law came out there was speculation that this religious exemption applied to Muslims, as Muslims consider insurance to be a form of gambling, risk taking and usury and therefore banned under Sharia law. This is yet to be determined in the courts.[157]

"Under section 1502, the Internal Revenue Service is authorized to enforce the health insurance mandate and to collect the penalties."[158] In order to do this, the PPACA provides for the IRS to hire up to 16,500 new IRS agents.[159]

The requirement for Americans to purchase health insurance or pay a fine has been perhaps the most controversial aspect of the new law, setting off a number of state lawsuits and state countermeasures. As of January 2011, over half of all the states, plus the 350,000-member National Federation of Independent Businesses (NFIB), had filed suits challenging the constitutionality of the mandate, while legislation opposing it had been introduced in 42 states. The NFIB claimed that the mandate deprived its members of their liberty and property interests without due process of law in direct violation of the Fifth Amendment of the US Constitution.[160] This is why 70% of Americans opposed the individual mandate per a tracking poll by the Henry J. Kaiser Family Foundation in August 2010.[161]

Adding to the problems with the individual mandate, the administration was inconsistent with its message, with "President Obama

155 Robert E. Moffit, (2011, January 18). "The Case Against Obamacare: Obamacare and the Individual Mandate: Violating Personal Liberty and Federalism." Retrieved January 19, 2013, from http://thf_media.s3.amazonaws.com/2011/pdf/TheCaseAgainstObamacare.pdf
156 Ibid.
157 Snopes. (n.d.). "Health Insurance Exemptions." Retrieved January 19, 2013, from http://www.snopes.com/politics/medical/exemptions.asp
158 Op cit, Moffit.
159 Kurt Nimmo, (2012, July 3). "Thousands of New IRS Agents to be Hired to Enforce Obamacare." Retrieved December 29, 2012, from infowars.com: http://www.infowars.com/thousands-of-new-irs-agents-to-be-hired-to-enforce-obamacare/
160 Op cit, Moffit.
161 Ibid.

originally opposing an individual mandate but then endorsing it. The President stated that the penalty was not a tax, but then administration lawyers insisted it was, stressing that Congress's sweeping taxing power was the linchpin of their argument for the mandate's constitutionality." However, according to the Congressional Budget Office in a memorandum in 1994, "The government has never required people to buy any good or service as a condition of lawful residence in the United States."[162]

In upholding the state of Virginia's challenge to the constitutionality of the individual mandate, US District Court Judge Henry Hudson in December 2010 wrote the following:

> A thorough survey of pertinent Constitutional case law has yielded no reported decisions from any appellate courts extending the Commerce Clause or the General Welfare Clause to encompass regulation of a person's decision not to purchase a product, notwithstanding its effect on interstate commerce or role in a global regulatory scheme. The unchecked expansion of Congressional power to the limits suggested by the Minimum Essential Coverage provision would invite unbridled exercise of federal police power. At its core, this dispute is not simply about regulating the business of insurance—or crafting a scheme of universal health insurance coverage. It's about an individual's right to choose to participate.[163]

The individual mandate, requiring Americans to purchase health insurance or be fined (i.e., taxed), opens the door for future government mandates coercing individuals to perform actions that they morally and rationally may not want to perform. Based on the individual mandate alone, how can anyone be "pro-choice" and yet support Obamacare?

George Washington University Law Professor Jonathan Turley wrote in 2011 that,

> There is a legitimate concern for many that this mandate constitutes the greatest (and perhaps the most lethal) challenge to states' rights in US history. With this legislation, Congress has effectively defined an uninsured 18-year-old-man in Richmond as an interstate problem like a polluting factory. It is an assertion of federal power that is inherently at odds with the original vision of the Framers.[164]

162 Ibid.
163 Ibid.

The purpose of the PPACA was to provide insurance to the uninsured in America. However, even with the mandate, the Congressional Budget Office estimated in 2010 that in 10 years, 23 million Americans would remain without insurance.[165] This projection was revised in 2012 when the CBO stated that they believed the number of uninsured non-elderly Americans in 2022 would instead be closer to 30 million.[166]

> Given the combination of the law's health insurance rules—the elimination of pre-existing condition restrictions and guaranteed issue and the compressed ratio of ratings between older and younger enrollees—and the relatively light mandate penalties, there will be incentives for millions of Americans, facing much higher insurance premiums than they are today, to go without coverage. Faced with paying a light penalty and a heavy premium, they would have every incentive to pay the light penalty and sign up for insurance if they get sick and drop out of coverage when they get well. This will induce a severe case of adverse selection, as the less stable pools are disproportionately populated with older and sicker enrollees, resulting in a deadly cost spiral.[167]

It was misleading to state that the need for the new program was because too many Americans were uninsured in the first place. According to the CBO, there are currently 53 million Americans who are uninsured.[168] However, what was not mentioned is that under current law in the US, "federally funded hospitals must treat ("stabilize") persons entering hospital emergency rooms."[169] Although these individuals do not have insurance, the hospitals have a legal obligation to pay for their care. Therefore, to state that they do not have healthcare insurance may be accurate but nevertheless they are covered for care under the status quo.

In addition, Obamacare encourages "free riders," persons who forgo health insurance coverage that they often cannot afford, to use hospital

---

164　Ibid.
165　Ibid.
166　Patrick Burke, (2012, August 8). "CBO: Obamacare will leave 30 million uninsured."
　　　Retrieved January 20, 2013, from
　　　http://cnsnews.com/news/article/cbo-obamacare-will-leave-30-million-uninsured
167　Op cit, Moffit.
168　Op cit, Burke.
169　Op cit, Moffit.

emergency rooms to secure care when they get sick or injured. These costs will result in higher taxes and private insurance premiums.[170]

To make matters worse, the PPACA includes a massive expansion of Medicaid, a major contributor to existing emergency room overcrowding, and this will result in rapidly aging, ailing, and unstable pools in the existing health insurance markets. As Harvard economist Martin Feldstein said, "The resulting rise in cost to insurance companies as the insured population becomes sicker would raise the average premium, strengthening that incentive."[171]

Kagan's Case

The legality of the individual mandate came to a head in the summer of 2012 when the Supreme Court presented its ruling. Of the nine judges, two were recent appointees of Barack Obama, including Justice Elena Kagan.

Kagan's previous role was that of Solicitor General. The dilemma for Kagan was that the federal statute "requires Justice Kagan to disqualify herself if she, as a federal employee (solicitor general) "participated as counsel" or as an "adviser," or she "expressed an opinion concerning the merits of the particular case in controversy."[172]

The government (after much prodding) released emails that raised serious questions whether Justice Kagan, had in fact, expressed any opinion regarding the constitutionality of the act. These emails showed that her deputy solicitor general emailed Kagan about the issue, and she replied that she wanted to talk over the phone (with no paper trail). Emails also showed that her deputy solicitor general at that time believed Kagan "definitely" wanted her office involved in the administration's defense against legal challenges to the PPACA. The deputy solicitor general was the public face involved in the Obamacare defense while Justice Kagan stayed in the background.

In spite of the evidence showing at least a perceived engagement with Obamacare, Justice Kagan did not recuse herself from the matter of the individual mandate.

---

170 Ibid.
171 Ibid.
172 Ronald D. Rotunda, (2011, December 15). "ROTUNDA: Kagan Must Recuse Herself from Obamacare Case," *Washington Times*.

In June of 2012 the Supreme Court upheld the PPACA's individual mandate as a tax. Chief Justice John Roberts joined the four liberal judges, including Justice Kagan, in their interpretation of the law. "Twenty-six states sued over the law, arguing that the individual mandate, which requires people to buy health insurance or face a fine starting in 2014, was unconstitutional. Opponents cast the individual mandate as the government forcing Americans to enter a market and buy a product against their will, while the government countered that the law was actually only regulating a market that everyone is already in, since almost everyone will seek health care at some point in his or her life."[173]

"The Supreme Court had to violate the Constitution's separation of powers to uphold Obamacare as a 'tax'—despite the fact that no elected body could ever have enacted such a massive tax hike even with the sleazy parliamentary tricks used to pass this bill."[174] The result of this decision was that the American citizen was now forced to purchase health insurance, or pay a "tax." This result was shocking to most Americans because the administration said over and over again that the PPACA would not raise taxes.

New Taxes

Obama's pledge of no tax increase for Americans making less than $250,000 a year "was thrown out the window" when he signed the healthcare law, says John Kartch, communications director with Americans For Tax Reform (founded by anti-tax crusader Grover Norquist). Seven of the Obamacare tax hikes affect the entire US population.[175] Overall, Obamacare includes 20 new or higher taxes on American families and small businesses, making the law one of the largest tax increases in US history.[176]

Eighteen separate tax increases will cost taxpayers $503 billion between 2010 and 2019, with three of the major tax hikes making up nearly half of the new taxes imposed by Obamacare.[177]

173 Liz Goodwin, (2012, June 28). "Supreme Court upholds Obamacare individual mandate as a tax." Retrieved January 20, 2013, from http://abcnews.go.com/Politics/OTUS/ /supreme-court-upholds-obamacare-individual-mandate-tax/story?id=16669186
174 Op cit, Coulter, September 2013.
175 Ashlea Ebeling, (2012, June 28) "ObamaCare's 7 Tax Hikes On Under $250,000-A-Year Earners," *Forbes.*
176 Ryan Ellis and John Kartch, (2012, June 28). *Full List of Obamacare Tax Hikes.* Retrieved January 20, 2013, from http://www.atr.org/full-list-ACA-tax-hikes-a6996
177 Curtis Dubay, (2011, January 20). "The Case Against Obamacare: Obamacare and New Taxes:

- Section 1401 of the PPACA imposes a 40% tax on healthcare plans that are deemed by the government as excessive. These "Cadillac" health insurance plans are those valued in excess of $10,200 for individuals and $27,500 for families. These amounts increase annually for inflation, and the tax takes effect in 2018. They are projected to raise $32 billion by 2019.
- Section 1411 increased the Medicare Hospital Insurance portion of the workers' payroll tax. This tax increases the employee's portion of that tax from 1.45% to 2.35% for families making more than $250,000 a year (and for individuals making more than $200,000). Along with the employer's portion, the total rate is increased to 3.8% on every dollar of income over $250,000 starting in 2013.
- Section 1411 also imposed a new payroll tax on investment income. This new tax applies the new higher 3.8% Medicare tax to investment income, including capital gains, dividends, rents, and royalties, and also became effective in 2013. The two Medicare tax hikes in Section 1411 are expected to raise $210 billion in new taxes between 2013 and 2019.[178]

The key point to raise here along with the raising of taxes is that taxes "transfer money from productive private hands to the less efficient public sector. A politicized allocation is less efficient than market-based allocation because political decisions do not consider the highest-value use of resources, while the private sector considers such issues and therefore does a better job of assigning resources where they will contribute the most to economic growth."[179]

Other arguments against increased taxes are that higher tax rates decrease the incentives for individuals to work and save more. The ultimate implication is that increasing taxes do not reduce deficits.[180] This has been seen time and again as noted in this book's chapter regarding taxes. When President Obama said individuals will be required to have insurance, he neglected to note that the penalty for not having insurance will be a large penalty . . . er . . . tax.

Destroying Jobs and the Economy." Retrieved January 12, 2013, from http://thf_media.s3.amazonaws.com/2011/pdf/TheCaseAgainstObamacare.pdf
178   Ibid.
179   Ibid.
180   Ibid.

Impact on the Federal Budget

Despite the taxes, the PPACA will cause a massive increase in the deficit. The federal government's finances were a wreck before the law was passed. This was why Democratic lawmakers who pushed for its passage "felt compelled to try to calm worried Americans by claiming that the law would cut projected federal budget deficits in addition to covering the uninsured."[181]

The Congressional Budget Office's official estimate showed that the PPACA's healthcare provisions would cut projected deficits by $124 billion over the period from 2010 to 2019. However, the CBO's cost estimate was not the whole story. "A close examination of what the CBO said, as well as other evidence, makes it clear that the deficit reduction associated with PPACA (Obamacare) is based on budget gimmicks, sleights of hand, accounting tricks, and completely implausible assumptions. A more honest accounting reveals the new law as a trillion-dollar budget buster."[182]

When a bill is provided to the CBO for projections, the CBO must assume that the bill will be enacted as written, even in cases where this is improbable. For example, the PPACA has $575 billion in projected cuts to Medicare. Regarding this and the planned cuts in payments to physicians under what is known as the "sustainable growth rate" formula, CBO Director Douglas Elmendorf wrote:

> [C]urrent law now includes a number of policies that might be difficult to sustain over a long period of time. For example, PPACA and the Reconciliation Act reduced payments to many Medicare providers relative to what the government would have paid under prior law. On the basis of those cuts in payment rates and the existing "sustainable growth rate" mechanism that governs Medicare's payments to physicians, CBO projects that Medicare spending (per beneficiary, adjusted for overall inflation) will increase significantly more slowly during the next two decades than it has increased during the past two decades. If those provisions would have subsequently been modified or implemented incompletely, then the budgetary effects of repealing PPACA and the relevant provisions of the Reconciliation Act could be

---

181 James C. Capretta and Kathryn Nix, (2011, January 21). "The Case Against Obamacare: Obamacare and the Budget: Playing Games with Numbers." Retrieved January 20, 2013, from http://thf_media.s3.amazonaws.com/2011/pdf/TheCaseAgainstObamacare.pdf

182 Ibid.

quite different—but CBO cannot forecast future changes in law or assume such changes in its estimates.[183]

The CBO could not address in their projections the future changes in the law that will be necessary in order to keep Medicare afloat. Medicare's Chief Actuary echoed these concerns. "If Medicare savings do not materialize, new spending under PPACA will be added to the deficit."[184]

In addition to the unrealistic assumptions that Medicare spending will increase at a rate significantly less than the current rate, which is highly implausible with the current population mix, the new law also assumes that Medicare's payments to physicians also decrease over time. The current law supposes that physicians will face a 25% decrease in payments for Medicare patients, which will restrict patient's care as more doctors are unable to assist patients due to not being reimbursed fully for their costs.[185]

While pushing his bill through the Democratic Congress, President Obama did not want to include the costs of increasing Medicare in the Obamacare bill because it would explode the myth of it being a deficit reducer. Instead, the solution was to pass separate legislation to address this. "But it does not matter to taxpayers if the President's ideas are passed in one bill or many. All that matters is the total cost. And the President's total bill for health care—with an unfinanced 'doc fix'— shows massive deficits, not deficit reduction."[186]

The CBO's projections assumed that all cuts to existing programs and new revenues created by PPACA were to be used to pay for new spending. However, this is not the case, as Obamacare increases Medicare taxes and imposes cuts in Medicare that are double-counted as offsets for new programs, but are also pledged to extend Medicare's solvency. "They cannot do both."[187]

The CLASS Act is another source of double-counted savings in the initial projections presented by the CBO. The CLASS Act creates a new, federally-run long-term care insurance program. Beneficiaries began paying premiums to this program in 2011 but do not receive benefits for five years. This frontloading of revenues created the illusion of $70

183   Ibid.
184   Ibid.
185   Ibid.
186   Ibid.
187   Ibid.

billion to pay for new spending under the PPACA; however, these revenues will actually be used to pay out benefits in later years. Democratic Senator Kent Conrad from North Dakota called this "a Ponzi scheme of the first order, the kind of thing that Bernie Madoff would have been proud of."[188]

Obamacare also created a new subsidy program for low- and middle-income Americans to purchase insurance in healthcare exchanges. The CBO predicted that 19 million Americans would benefit from the exchanges at a cost of $460 billion by 2019.[189]

> But the new law includes substantial incentives for employers to drop existing coverage and allow employees to instead purchase taxpayer-subsidized coverage. Former CBO director Douglas Holtz-Eakin points out that many businesses could drop their employee health plan, raise wages to make up for the lost benefit, pay the employer penalty for not offering insurance, and still come out ahead. These incentives, exacerbated by the various new insurance rules that will cause a faster rate of growth in employer plan premiums, will cause the cost of the subsidy program to greatly exceed initial projections.[190]

The final and possibly the most obvious flaw in the budget projections is that when putting together the budget for the PPACA, the CBO was provided a law where in the first ten years there is only six years of full-fledged spending but includes ten years of revenues as the costliest provisions do not come into effect until 2014.[191]

The reality is that Obamacare will result in trillions in unaffordable deficit spending, which will impact taxes, the economy and the financial burden put on future generations for years to come.[192] President Obama stated that Obamacare will not add to the deficit. He was not even close.

Employers and the Employer Mandate

In addition to the individual mandate, the PPACA also includes what is called the "employer mandate." The rationale behind this was to increase the number of individuals with health insurance. This new law

188 Ibid.
189 Ibid.
190 Ibid.
191 Ibid.
192 Ibid.

creates a "tax penalty on firms with more than 50 workers that fail to provide 'adequate' coverage for their employees. The result is government intrusion into voluntary arrangements made between employer and employee. The cost of the tax penalty will ultimately be borne by workers (lower wages and fewer jobs), shareholders (lower profits), and consumers (higher prices)."[193]

> Section 1513 of PPACA amends the Internal Revenue Code of 1986 by adding "Section 4980H.Shared Responsibility for Employers Regarding Health Coverage." This section imposes tax penalties on certain firms that fail to offer adequate healthcare coverage to their employees. Beginning in 2014, all companies with 50 or more full-time employees (or their equivalent) that do not offer "qualified" health insurance or pay at least 60% of premiums to their workers will face financial penalties if at least one employee receives subsidized coverage in an exchange. The annual tax penalty will be equal to $2,000 for every fulltime employee (or their equivalent) beyond the first 30 workers.[194]

Even though businesses may offer health insurance to their employees, they can still face tax penalties. In cases where companies offer insurance to employees who qualify for tax credits in a health insurance exchange and one employee enrolls in a plan through an exchange, and qualifies for a subsidy, the company will face a tax penalty. The penalty will be either $3,000 per employee receiving a subsidy or $2,000 for each of their total full-time employees, whichever is less, when exempting the first 30 employees.[195]

The employer mandate will be enforced by requiring businesses to provide additional information to the IRS about the health insurance offered to each employee by the company.

> The employer mandate will change the nature of the employer-employee relationship, as employers will want detailed household information, such as family size and income for each family member, from each of their employees. The economic effects of the employer mandate will likely be lower profits for many businesses, lower wages

---

193 Brian Blase, (2011, January 19). "The Case Against Obamacare: Obamacare and the Employer
     Mandate: Cutting Jobs and Wages." Retrieved January 20, 2013, from
     http://thf_media.s3.amazonaws.com/2011/pdf/TheCaseAgainstObamacare.pdf
194 Ibid.
195 Ibid.

for millions of workers, increased unemployment, and higher prices for many goods and services.[196]

Not only do IRS personnel have increased workloads, but employers have more forms to complete while Obamacare tramples all over employee confidentiality.

Shortly after Obama's win in the 2012 election, the ramifications of this new legislation began to take place as numerous companies began laying people off in an effort to deal with the new costs.[197] The owner of Papa John's pizza company, John Schnatter, announced that he would reduce employee hours from 40 to 28 beginning January 1, 2013. Jimmy John Liataud, the founder and CEO of Jimmy John's Sandwich Company, made similar comments to Fox News: "If you have 40 or 50 employees at a restaurant, and the penalty is $2,000, and you're going to pay $80,000 or $100,000 penalty, there goes the profit in your restaurant."[198]

In addition to companies, school districts and other public entities have begun cutting the hours of staff to less than 30 hours a week. It was reported that the school district in Lafayette, Indiana, cut the hours of 200 support staff to no more than 29 hours per week. The school system in Bangor, Maine, began preparations for tracking and capping the number of hours worked by substitute teachers to ensure that they would not work more than 29 hours a week.[199]

School districts across the nation reported similar stories. This all happened because the PPACA defines a "full-time employee" as anyone working an average of 30 hours a week, rather than the traditionally accepted 40-hour work week. This rule caused a growing number of employers to cut the hours of their workers, and according to one study by the University of California Berkeley Labor Center, at least 2.3 million workers were at risk. "This provision of the health law is not in the best interests of the country, and it needs to change."[200]

---

196 Ibid.
197 J.D. Rucker, (2012, November 10). "The Two Stages of Obamacare Layoffs." Retrieved January 20, 2013, from
    http://www.redstate.com/jdrucker/2012/11/10/the-two-stages-of-obamacare-layoffs/
198 Laura Alexander, (2012, November 15). "2013 Small businesses Cut Employee Hours to Avoid Healthcare Insurance." Retrieved January 20, 2013, from http://www.examiner.com/article/2013-small-businesses-cut-employee-hours-to-avoid-healthcare-insurance
199 Susan Collins and Joe Donnelly, (2013, July 18). "ObamaCare's Definition of a Full-Time Job Needs Revising," *Wall Street Journal.*
200 Ibid.

In mid-2013 it became apparent not only to the *Wall Street Journal* editors but also to the Obama administration that the employer mandate was a "train wreck." In early July 2013, before the 4th of July holiday weekend, Mark Mazur, the deputy assistant Treasury secretary for tax policy, published a blog post postponing the insurance reporting rules and tax enforcement of the employer mandate until 2015. *Journal* editorial staff stated:

> These columns fought the Affordable Care Act from start to passage, and we'd now like to apologize to our readers. It turns out we weren't nearly critical enough. The law's implementation is turning into a fiasco for the ages, and this week's version is the lawless White House decision to delay the law's insurance mandate for businesses, though not for individuals. . . . The provision was supposed to start in January, and delaying it is like Ford saying its electric car is ready to go, except the electric battery doesn't work.[201]

Speaking for the administration, Mazur blamed the complexity of the requirements as the reason for the delay, which was probably an admission that Treasury's information technology was not ready to process and cross-check paperwork across the 5.7 million businesses in America in order to implement the employer mandate. The Obama administration has issued "over eight interim final rules, three final rules, 20 requests for comment, 21 proposed rules, one information collection request, two amendments to the interim final rules, six requests for information and one frequently-asked-questions document"[202], to clarify the implementation of the employer mandate. The *Wall Street Journal* editors commented:

> This selective enforcement of laws has become an Administration habit. From immigration (the Dream Act by fiat) to easing welfare reform's work requirements to selective waivers for No Child Left Behind, the Obama administration routinely suspends enforcement of or unilaterally rewrites via regulation the laws it dislikes. Now it is doing it again on health care, without any consultation from, much less the approval of, Congress.[203]

201 Joe Rago, (2013, July 3). "Employer Mandate? Never Mind." *Wall Street Journal.*
202 Ibid.
203 Ibid.

In spite of the Obama administration postponing the implementation of the employer mandate, the impact was clear. Of the 953,000 jobs created in the US through the first seven months of 2013, 77% or 731,000 were part-time.[204] Employers simply are not hiring individuals for more than the 30-hour work week.

Benefit Mandates

The US Department of Health and Human Services has a set of provisions that impose various benefit requirements on employer-sponsored health plans and major medical policies sold by health insurers. The impact of these is that health insurance benefits will eventually become very uniform, reducing the number of choices for individuals in selecting their coverage, and as a result, the costs of insurance will go up for millions of Americans as these plans will be forced to limit the amount of services patients can consume.[205]

"Benefit mandates" are requirements in the PPACA that force insurance companies to write insurance policies within certain specified guidelines. A report by Edmund Haislmaier noted numerous provisions. "Section 1001(5) of PPACA requires that, effective for plan years starting in the fall of 2010, health insurers and employer plans must cover numerous preventive services with no enrollee cost-sharing."[206] The key words here are "no enrollee cost-sharing." As is plain to see, if the enrollee is not paying for the new benefits, then someone else is, which will either be the entire pool participating in the policy, or the government, and that ultimately means the US taxpayer.

"Section 1001(5) prohibits health insurers and employer plans from setting lifetime coverage limits 'on the dollar value of benefits' effective for plan years starting in the fall of 2010 and prohibits plans from setting annual coverage limits starting in 2014."[207] That plans must not set limits to coverage is perhaps good in that it prevents companies from walking

---

204 Tyler Durden, (2013, August 2). "Obamacare Full Frontal: Of 953,000 Jobs Created In 2013, 77%, Or 731,000 Are Part-Time. Retrieved August 4, 2013, from http://www.zerohedge.com/news/ /2013-08-02/obamacare-full-frontal-953000-jobs-created-2013-77-or-731000-are-part-time
205 Edmund F. Haislmaier, (2011, January 20). "A Case Against Obamacare: Obamacare and Insurance Benefit Mandates: Raising Premiums and Reducing Patient Choice." Retrieved January 27, 2013, from http://thf_media.s3.amazonaws.com/2011/pdf/TheCaseAgainstObamacare.pdf
206 Ibid.
207 Ibid.

away from the very sick and needy. This can even be priced into insurance policies; however, it will ultimately lead to higher premiums to cover these new plan adjustments. Americans will be paying higher premiums for cover they may not want.

"Section 1302(c) limits deductibles for employer plans in the small-group market to $2,000 for self-only coverage and $4,000 for family coverage, indexed after 2014 to the growth in average per capita premiums."[208] Deductibles are costs that must be paid by insureds before the insurance coverage kicks in. The higher the deductible, the lower the premiums. Setting a limit on the deductibles will increase premiums, and those inclined to limit medical insurance costs in lieu of other priorities will be forced to pay higher insurance premiums.

Haislmaier also notes that Obamacare grants more discretionary authority to unelected federal officials to micromanage health insurance coverage than state legislatures have ever granted to state insurance regulators. He believes that more regulations are the likely outcome, and that the HHS will be more intrusive rather than less, based on the recent appointees at the HHS.[209]

With greater regulation comes increased costs from administrative processing activities. Also, the benefit mandates will mean the loss of insurance for many. Estimates in 2013 were that nearly 16 million Americans will lose their coverage due to their old policies not complying with the new benefit mandates.[210]

The US individual health insurance market consists of around 19 million people. About 85% of these plans were not grandfathered under Obamacare, which amounts to about 16 million insureds. These policies must comply with the law at their next renewal period. In late 2013, these 16 million people received letters from their carriers saying that they would have to re-enroll in order to avoid a break in coverage and comply with the benefit mandates. As a result, many of these insureds were expecting to see some pretty big rate increases.[211]

The rate increases have caused millions to lose their insurance because they simply cannot afford the new policies. A study in late 2013 by the Manhattan Institute reported that underlying premiums will increase

208 Ibid.
209 Ibid.
210 John McCormack, (2013, October 23). "Millions of Americans are losing their health plans because of Obamacare." Retrieved January 4, 2014, from http://www.weeklystandard.com/
     /blogs/millions-americans-are-losing-their-health-plans-because-obamacare_764602.html#
211 Ibid.

by 41% on average for those seeking insurance on their own.[212] When President Obama guaranteed Congress and the American people in his September 2009 speech that Americans would not lose their insurance coverage because of Obamacare or that they would be able to shop for insurance at competitive costs, he was incorrect.

Exchanges and Subsidies

The PPACA creates a new program for low- and middle-income Americans, enabling them to purchase insurance in new health exchanges while offering subsidies to most individuals who purchase insurance in the newly created health insurance exchanges. The CBO predicted in 2011 that 19 million Americans would benefit from this generous new entitlement program at a cost of $460 billion by 2019.[213] These subsidies are the most expensive component of Obamacare.[214]

According to Brian Blasé and Paul L. Winfrey, the subsidies discourage work by eligible individuals, and other taxpayers are forced to pay higher taxes in order to finance the subsidies.[215]

Blasé and Winfrey noted that in the PPACA, there is an enormous "cliff effect," where earning additional income results in the loss of the subsidy. The subsidies are based not only on income, but also on age. A family of four headed by a 60-year-old would lose more than $15,000 worth of tax credits as household income passes a certain threshold. The subsidy also encourages individuals to retire early and to change the way they report income. "This subsidy structure also penalizes upward income mobility and marriage."[216] It sounds good to retire early, but ultimately, someone has to pay for it, and it will be the taxpayer.

Obamacare is set up such that "many businesses could drop their employee health plan, raise wages to make up for the lost benefit, pay the employer penalty for not offering insurance, and still come out ahead. These incentives, exacerbated by the various new insurance rules that

---

212 Avik Roy, (2013, November 4). "49-State Analysis: Obamacare To Increase Individual-Market Premiums By Average Of 41%," *Forbes*.
213 Op cit, Nix et al.
214 Brian Blase and Paul L. Winfree, (2011, January 20). "The Case Against Obamacare: Obamacare and Health Subsidies: Expanding Perverse Incentives for Employers and Employees." Retrieved January 27, 2013, from http://thf_media.s3.amazonaws.com/2011/pdf/TheCaseAgainstObamacare.pdf
215 Ibid.
216 Ibid.

will cause a faster rate of growth in employer plan premiums, will cause the cost of the subsidy program to greatly exceed initial projections."[217]

The exchanges set up under the PPACA have also been the cause for criticism. "If a state chooses not to establish an exchange, the federal government will step in and establish an exchange for that state."[218] A new government bureaucracy will be required to administer the exchanges.

Under Section 1311 of the PPACA, the Secretary of Health and Human Services is to make grants to state officials so that they can establish a healthcare exchange in each state. The Secretary is sanctioned to determine the amounts of the grants and is able to renew these for each state that is meeting "such benchmarks as the Secretary may establish."[219] States are also to establish a Small Business Health Options Programs for employees of small businesses. States may also to establish multi-state exchanges. Under Section 1321(c)(1), the HHS Secretary is required to establish and run exchanges in states that do not set up exchanges by January 1, 2014.[220]

The exchanges detailed above are designed to facilitate the purchase of a "qualified" health plan for both individuals and employers and are to be set up as either a state government agency or a "nonprofit" entity. The HHS Secretary under this section of the law has broad authority to issue rules and set standards governing the creation and operation of the exchanges.[221]

One of the first problems noted about the exchanges was that they are a direct assault on the states' authority to regulate health insurance. "Under the US Constitution, as the US Supreme Court has strongly affirmed, Congress can exercise no such authority over state officials."[222]

The exchanges also possess inherent new costs which will ultimately be pushed to the taxpayers in the states. In addition, Obamacare imposes a "one-size-fits all" approach that ignores state differences. "Before enactment of PPACA, only two states had enacted health insurance exchanges: Massachusetts and Utah. In their design and function and how they have been implemented, each is very different and serves very different policy objectives."[223]

217   Op cit, Nix et al.
218   Robert E. Moffit, (2011, January 18). "The Case Against Obamacare: Obamacare and Federal Health Exchanges: Undermining State Flexibility." Retrieved January 27, 2013, from http://thf_media.s3.amazonaws.com/2011/pdf/TheCaseAgainstObamacare.pdf
219   Ibid.
220   Ibid.
221   Ibid.
222   Ibid.

The exchanges were to be in place in late 2013. The result was described as "fundamentally flawed" and "not ready for primetime." The main vehicle for the introduction of the PPACA was the website which applicants were hoping to log on to and obtain an array of options for affordable health insurance. However, constant glitches kept people from logging into the exchanges. Reporters normally favorable to Obamacare simply gave up in frustration because they could not sign up. Consumers who were lucky enough to get through the system were stunned to learn that their premiums had skyrocketed by thousands of dollars. One Pennsylvania mother said that she could either pay her increased premiums or pay for her kids to eat, but she could not do both.[224]

During the 2013 rollout, extremely personal information was leaked from the system in Minnesota, and software security experts from McAfee predicted millions of identity theft victims.[225] The data hub created to exchange personal health and financial information on users is a ripe target for computer hackers and identity thieves. Critics claimed that it was not tested for security flaws before being put into use.[226] In spite of the President stating in his September 2009 speech to Congress that plenty of time would be given to roll out the law properly, the initial introduction was a mess.

Overall, the exchanges and subsidies in Obamacare serve to inhibit competition and infringe upon state rights and the individual's choice of the insurance programs they desire. By increasing the administrative burden to individuals, companies and the government, the subsidies and exchanges also increase the overall costs to the taxpayers for health insurance.

Health Insurance Premium Restrictions

The PPACA set new mandates on insurance companies and on employer sponsored health plans. These entities are barred from imposing pre-existing condition exclusions in any circumstances, are limited

223 Ibid.
224 Ben Sasse, (2013, October 15). "BEYOND 'GLITCHES': Obamacare Nightmare Just Beginning." Retrieved January 4, 2014, from http://www.breitbart.com/Big-Government/2013/10/15/obamacare-rollout-disasster
225 Ibid.
226 Paul Bedard, (2013, July 22). "Obamacare data hub a 'honey pot' for ID thieves, warn critics." Retrieved July 27, 2013, *Washington Examiner,* http://washingtonexaminer.com/ /obamacare-data-hub-a-honey-pot-for-id-thieves-warn-critics/article/2533323

in the amount of insurance premiums the entity can charge based upon age of the insured and require insurers to provide individual insurance on a guaranteed issue basis.[227]

> Effective in 2014, Section 1201(4) of PPACA imposes new federal rules on how health insurers may "rate," or price, their products. Under the new rules, insurers will be allowed to vary premiums for coverage in the individual and small group markets using only four factors: (1) by self only versus family coverage, (2) by geographic "rating area," (3) by age, and (4) by tobacco use.[228]

For tobacco users, the maximum rate allowed in the new law is not to be more that 150% of a non-smoker's rating. The largest deviation between ages allowed will be a "3 to 1 ratio." This means that a plan cannot charge a 64-year-old more than three times what the same plan charges a 21-year-old for the same coverage starting in 2014.[229]

The impact of the premiums changes noted above is huge. Lower premiums for older Americans will be covered through increases for younger Americans. The older group's premiums may not be minimized in this new approach, but the premiums for the younger generation sure will be increased.

Young non-smokers are the individuals who lose most with this new law. The natural variation of age in medical costs is elders consume about five times as much in medical costs as the younger generation. The incentive for young people is not to insure and take the risk of getting sick when their premiums rise substantially in 2014. This is why the individual mandate was put in place, to "tax" youngsters who do not opt for health insurance.[230] This is an example of government trying to adjust a market characteristic of a group—the consequence is a different class is ultimately discriminated against.

> Economists commonly lament public policies that transfer resources to a particular group because such policies ignore the "law of unintended

---

227 Edmund F. Haislmaier, (2011, January 20). "The Case Against Obamacare: Obamacare and Insurance Rating Rules: Increasing Costs and Destabilizing Markets." Retrieved January 27, 2013, from Heritage.org:
       http://thf_media.s3.amazonaws.com/2011/pdf/TheCaseAgainstObamacare.pdf
228 Ibid.
229 Ibid.
230 Ibid.

consequences." Economists point out, for example, that the law of unintended consequences is at work when workers' wages fall in response to a mandated increase in benefits or when employment falls in response to an increase in the minimum wage. As Henry Hazlitt said in *Economics in One Lesson,* "Depth in economics consists in looking for all the consequences of a policy instead of merely resting one's gaze on those immediately visible."[231]

In addition to the restrictions on premiums, health insurance companies now have to report where their money is spent, with limitations on the costs outside of direct premium costs. This has a major impact on health carriers. "Many commercial insurance agencies depend heavily on group health for major shares of their revenue and profitability; so many carriers (not just health insurers) are potentially affected."[232]

The Protection of the Right to Life

The PPACA contains several provisions that undermine the US government's longstanding policy denying public subsidies for elective abortions and healthcare plans that provide coverage for elective abortions. In addition, Obamacare fails to protect insurers, providers and personnel who decline to provide, pay for, provide coverage of, or refer for abortions.[233]

Section 1303 of the PPACA provides substantial federal subsidies for private healthcare plans that are offered through health insurance exchanges and will cover elective abortions. "Under separate law (specifically, the Hyde Amendment to the annual Labor–Health and Human Services spending bill) federal funds appropriated to HHS by Congress cannot be spent for health benefits coverage that includes elective abortion. Section 1303 bypasses this limitation."[234]

In the summer of 2012, a group of plaintiffs including the Catholic Archdiocese of New York, the Catholic Archdiocese of Washington, D.C., the University of Notre Dame—43 Catholic dioceses and

---

231 Thomas DeLeire, (n.d.). "The Unintended Consequences of the Americans with Disabilities Act." Retrieved March 19, 2013, from
http://www.cato.org/sites/cato.org/files/serials/files/regulation/2000/4/deleire.pdf
232 Op cit, Freeman et al, pp. 21–23.
233 Chuck Donovan, (2011, January 19). "The Case Against Obamacare: Obamacare and the Ethics of Life: Weakening Medical Conscience and the Protection of Life." Retrieved January 28, 2013, from http://thf_media.s3.amazonaws.com/2011/pdf/TheCaseAgainstObamacare.pdf
234 Ibid.

organizations total—filed a dozen federal lawsuits against the Obama administration for violating their constitutionally guaranteed freedom of religion, citing new regulations that force healthcare plans to cover sterilizations and abortion drugs.[235]

In February 2013, the Obama administration released new HHS mandate rules to expand the number of religious groups that can opt out of subsidizing abortion. This reaction was due to a number of decisions in court related to lawsuits filed by dozens of religious businesses and organizations where the Obama administration was put under court order to make changes to the law. However, some Americans still argued that the new changes did not go far enough and still forced religiously-run companies to comply with the law.[236]

Companies were next to file suit against the government in regards to the mandate requiring these companies to include abortion in their healthcare plans. In the summer of 2013, Hobby Lobby, represented by the Becket Fund for Religious Liberty, received a preliminary injunction against the abortion pill mandate. The Becket Fund released the following in regards to the ruling: "Every American, including family business owners, should be free to live and do business according to their faith. We commend the court's ruling which is a victory for religious freedom and freedom of conscience. The Obama administration claims 'unwavering' support for religious freedom, but the only thing unwavering is the administration's tenacious opposition to that freedom."[237]

In late 2013, the Little Sisters of the Poor filed a class-action lawsuit on behalf of multiple religious organizations that provide health benefits. Their lawsuit was filed to protect them against fines for refusing to provide access to abortion-inducing drugs.[238]

The Charlotte Lozier Institute, a pro-life group, noted that federal dollars will be given to those states that are expanding Medicaid—

235 Jennifer LeClaire, (2012, May 22). "43 Catholic Groups File Suit Against Obamacare." Retrieved January 28, 2013, from http://www.charismanews.com/us/33460-43-catholic-groups-file-suit-against-obamacare
236 Steven Ertelt, (2013, February 1). "New HHS Mandate Rules Force Hobby Lobby and Any Religious Biz to Comply." Retrieved February 2, 2013, from http://www.lifenews.com/2013/02/01/new-hhs-mandate-rules-force-hobby-lobby-any-religious-biz-to-comply/
237 Alliancedefendingfreedom.org. (2013, July 19). "Hobby Lobby wins injunction against HHS abortion pill mandate." Retrieved July 21, 2013, from http://www.alliancedefendingfreedom.org/News/PRDetail/8338
238 Joel Gehrke, (2013, September 24). "Little Sisters of the Poor sue over Obamacare fines, contraception requirement." Retrieved December 8, 2013, from *Washington Examiner,* http://washingtonexaminer.com/ /little-sisters-of-the-poor-sue-over-obamacare-fines-contraception-requirement/article/2536338

which, in many states, includes abortion coverage. They noted that federal dollars will be given to individuals to help them purchase health insurance plans which may include abortion coverage. According to the Institute, "Obamacare's annual net increase in insured abortions that are either fully publicly funded through Medicaid or heavily subsidized through the exchanges could be as high as 71,000 to 111,500."[239] In President Obama's speech to Congress and the nation in 2009, he promised that taxpayers would not fund abortions through the Affordable Care Act. This also was not true.

Impact on Medicare and Medicaid

Medicare Advantage is a program put in place in 2003 which provides for elderly assistance with healthcare. James Capretta, who was a member of President G.W. Bush's team that worked with Congress in passing the Medicare legislation, notes that "Medicare Advantage (MA) plans are private insurance options available to Medicare beneficiaries. The Patient Protection and Affordable Care Act (PPACA) cuts deeply into the projected payments to MA plans. Millions of Medicare beneficiaries enrolled in MA plans, or who would have been enrolled if not for the cuts, will experience very substantial reductions in the value of health care services provided to them by the Medicare program."[240]

According to Capretta, these cuts will force participating MAs to raise their premiums, increase their deductibles and co-payments (i.e., amounts per prescription or hospital visit paid by the participant), and eliminate some coverage for things like preventive services. The change in the MAs will then force beneficiaries back into the traditional Medicare system which has the problems that MAs were put in place to correct. "Moreover, downsizing the role of MA plans will make it more difficult to pursue the kinds of structural changes that are needed to ensure that Medicare can be financially sustained over the long term."[241]

The PPACA includes many "impressively complex" formulas for payment reductions to Medicare. The payment reductions may lead to

239 Molly Henneberg, (2013, November 22). "Does ObamaCare subsidize abortions?" Retrieved January 4, 2014, from
   http://www.foxnews.com/politics/2013/11/22/does-obamacare-subsidize-abortions/
240 James C. Capretta, (2011, January 20). *A Case Against Obamacare: Obamacare and Medicare Advantage Cuts: Undermining Seniors' Coverage Options*. Retrieved January 27, 2013, from http://thf_media.s3.amazonaws.com/2011/pdf/TheCaseAgainstObamacare.pdf
241 Ibid.

reductions in seniors' access to care, will not enhance Medicare's solvency and are unlikely to survive.[242]

Another section of the PPACA provides for the Congress to establish an Independent Advisory Board, composed of 15 members appointed by the President and confirmed by the Senate. The purpose of the Board is to reduce the growth of Medicare spending. However, the problem with the Board is that it is prohibited from offering any important reforms.[243]

It was estimated in 2011 that roughly half of the gains in Obamacare's insurance coverage will be as a result of a massive expansion of Medicaid. "The Medicaid program, with its soaring price tag and dubious level of care for recipients, is in serious need of reform, not expansion. Increasing enrollment in this program by a third is a major flaw of the new health care law."[244]

Back in 2011, it was noted that the Congressional Budget Office and the Centers for Medicare and Medicaid Services projected that the PPACA will increase federal spending on Medicaid by between $75 and $100 billion *annually*. In addition, it was estimated that as the number of insureds in Medicaid rises, the number in private plans decreases by about 60%. This is because several million individuals below the new income threshold who currently have private coverage will be swept into Medicaid when Obamacare takes effect.[245]

When the PPACA exchanges opened up in late 2013, the impact on Medicaid was even more alarming than first projected. By early December 2013, 1.6 million Americans had enrolled in Obamacare. The not-so-good news was that 1.46 million of these actually signed up for Medicaid. Before 2013, Medicaid was America's third-largest government program, trailing only Social Security and Medicare as a proportion of the federal budget. It was feared that if the trend for more people to sign up for Medicaid than private insurance continues, it could bankrupt both federal and state governments.[246]

242 Robert E. Moffit, (2011, January 19). "The Case Against Obamacare: Obamacare and Medicare Provider Cuts: Jeopardizing Seniors' Access." Retrieved January 27, 2013, from http://thf_media.s3.amazonaws.com/2011/pdf/TheCaseAgainstObamacare.pdf
243 Robert E. Moffit, (2011, January 19). "The Case Against Obamacare: Obamacare and the Independent Payment Advisory Board: Falling Short of Real Medicare Reform." Retrieved January 27, 2013, from http://thf_media.s3.amazonaws.com/2011/pdf/TheCaseAgainstObamacare.pdf
244 Brian Blase, (2011, January 19). "A Case Against Obamacare: Obamacare and Medicaid: Expanding a Broken Entitlement and Busting State Budgets." Retrieved January 27, 2013, fromhttp://thf_media.s3.amazonaws.com/2011/pdf/TheCaseAgainstObamacare.pdf
245 Ibid.

The cost increases to Medicaid and Medicare as a result of Obamacare are a ticking time bomb. Ultimately, the US taxpayer will pay for these additional costs. President Obama stated to Congress in September 2009 that reducing waste and inefficiency in Medicare and Medicaid would pay for the PPACA. In fact, Obamacare causes increased government spending on both programs by billions.

Administrative Costs and the Intrusion of Privacy

The burden placed on individuals, companies and corporations to comply with Obamacare is significant. The drastic increases in costs to comply with the new law provide no value to the sick and those needing healthcare services. The costs for insurers to comply with new regulations have forced insurance companies to raise the premiums they charge on healthcare policies. The nation's biggest health insurers said they expected premiums to rise by between 20% and 100% for millions of people when key provisions of Obamacare roll out in January 2014.[247]

The complexity of the law itself multiplies the adminsitrative costs. The original law includes both the Patient Protection and Affordable Care Act and the Health Care and Education Reconciliation Act. By October of 2013, government bureaucracies had published approximately 11,588,500 words of Obamacare regulations, while there are only 381,517 words in the original law itself. The ratio is 30 words of regulations for each word from the original law due to the various agencies having published 109 regulations spelling out how the law is to be implemented.[248] All of these regulations create compliance costs for the private sector.

The Obama administration has a poor record of job creation, but one small segment will do well. Community organizers or "navigators" will be hired by the federal government to assist individuals in signing up for Obamacare subsidies. These individuals will have access to an incredible amount of private data related to individuals and companies.

246 Michael D. Tanner, (2013, December 7). "ObamaCare created a Medicaid time bomb." *New York Post.*

247 Tom Murphy, (2013, March 14). "Insurers warn of overhaul-induced sticker shock." Retrieved March 14, 2013, from Yahoo.com:
    http://news.yahoo.com/insurers-warn-overhaul-induced-sticker-shock-152538504—finance.html

248 Penny Starr, (2013, October 13). "11,588,500 Words: Obamacare Regs 30x as Long as Law." Retrieved January 5, 2014, from http://www.cnsnews.com/news/article/penny-starr/ /11588500-words-obamacare-regs-30x-long-law

These organizers will be guided by the new Federal Data Hub, which will give them access to reams of personal information compiled by federal agencies ranging from the IRS to the Department of Defense and the Veterans Administration. "The federal government is planning to quietly enact what could be the largest consolidation of personal data in the history of the republic," Paul Howard of the Manhattan Institute and Stephen T. Parente, a University of Minnesota finance professor, wrote in *USA Today*.[249]

In early 2013, lawyers representing the US House Oversight and Government Reform Committee were told that the newly hired navigators will have access to sensitive data such as Social Security numbers and tax returns and there will be no criminal background checks required for them. These navigators do not even have to hold high-school diplomas. In the age of Wikileaks and IRS abuses, many Americans are concerned that their personal data cannot be safe with the US government. The navigators will have to take a 20–30 hour online course about how the 1,200-page law works. This "is like giving someone a first-aid course and then making him a med-school professor."[250]

The complexity of the PPACA, along with the highly sensitive nature of the information needed to administer the law, is staggering.

Summarizing the Problems With Obamacare

To summarize Obamacare is difficult; however, one individual did just that in one sentence. Republican Dr. Barbara Bellar, a licensed attorney and an adjunct faculty member at DePaul University and Benedictine University, a former Major in the US Army Reserves and the Republican candidate for the Illinois State Senate seat in 2012, gave a speech including this (long) senence:

> We're going to be gifted with a healthcare plan we are forced to pur-
> chase, and fined if we don't, which purportedly covers at least 10
> million more people, without adding a single new doctor, but provides
> for 16,000 new IRS agents, written by a Committee whose Chairman
> says he doesn't understand it, passed by a Congress that didn't read it
> but exempted themselves from it, and signed by a President who

249 Stephen T. Parente and Paul Howard, (2012, December 6). "Potential ObamaCare privacy
      nightmare." *USA Today*.
250 John Fund, (2013, July 22). "Obamacare's Branch of the NSA." *National Review*.

smokes, with funding administered by a Treasury Chief who didn't pay his taxes, for which we will be taxed for four years before any benefits take effect, by a government which has already bankrupted Social Security and Medicare, all to be overseen by a Surgeon General who is obese and financed by a country that's broke. So, what the blank could possibly go wrong?[251]

Although her comments were sound and the video of her statement hit the blogosphere and went viral, it did not help her with her constituents as she went on to lose her bid for the Illinois State Senate seat.[252]

The PPACA is a massive bill that will significantly change healthcare in the US. The costs are astronomical and the intent is for government control of a major facet of Americans' lives. The program was passed in the Democratic Congress without a single Republican vote and with part of it never being passed in the US Senate by the 60-member vote normally necessary for such legislation. As a result, the Democrats lost control of the House of Representatives in the bi-annual election cycle in 2010 and have not taken back control since. Obamacare is still today very unpopular in the US.

Of the numerous statements about healthcare made by President Obama in September 2009 to Congress, the only one that was true was that individuals would be required to maintain healthcare. He did not mention, however, that premiums would be more expensive or that those not buying health insurance would incur tax penalties. All the other statements noted above that were made by the President during his 2009 speech were false. Even the statement about illegal aliens not qualifying for Obamacare was false. This was the statement that caused Representative Joe Wilson to call out, "You lie." It turns out that illegal aliens will qualify for Obamacare.

Representative Wilson was vindicated in August 2011, when the Department of Health and Human Services announced that it was funneling cash to 67 community health centers where the money would be used for migrant farm workers. HHS also noted that the immigration status of these farm workers would not be ascertained before free care was given, meaning that illegal aliens could be given Obamacare fund-

251   Ballotpedia.org. (2012). "Barbara Ruth Bellar." Retrieved January 13, 2013, from
       ballotpedia.org:http://ballotpedia.org/wiki/index.php/Barbara_Ruth_Bellar
252   Ibid.

ing. Approximately $8.5 million would target services for migrant and seasonal farm workers, who would not be asked about their citizenship or other matters not related to the treatment needs.[253]

For all the reasons noted above, Obamacare should be repealed. The American people want and need a "do-over." What could be used as a model?

A significantly different healthcare program is in operation in the Asia Pacific region, one which demonstrates a viable alternative to Obamacare: the Hong Kong healthcare program.

Hong Kong Healthcare

Hong Kong has a population of 7 million people and is one of the most densely populated areas on earth, peaking in its Kwun Tong district with 54,530 persons per square kilometer. In spite of its dense population, Hong Kong is among is one of the healthiest populations on earth. Its people enjoy a life expectancy of 85.9 years for females and 80 years for men, which are among the highest in the world.[254]

The Hong Kong Department of Health (under the Food and Health Bureau) is the government's health adviser and agency to execute healthcare policies and statutory functions.[255] The Hong Kong Hospital Authority "manages 41 public hospitals and institutions, 47 Specialist Out-patient Clinics and 74 General Out-patient Clinics throughout Hong Kong. The general clinics offer general healthcare and medical services to patients in need, while the specialist clinics strive to keep pace with the latest medical and scientific advances."[256]

Hong Kong has a relatively low healthcare expenditure when compared to other developed countries. "Spending on healthcare (which tends to be resistant to economic downturns) ticked up to an estimated 6.2% of GDP in 2009, based on WHO definitions. This is still low

253 Warner Todd Huston, (2011, August 14). "Obama DID Lie: Obamacare Now Paying for Illegal Immigrants." Retrieved January 7, 2014, from http://www.conservativecrusader.com/articles/ /obama-did-lie-obamacare-now-paying-for-illegal-immigrants

254 Hong Kong Government, (2012, January). "Hong Kong: The Facts." Retrieved May 19, 2013, fromhttp://www.gov.hk/en/about/abouthk/factsheets/docs/population.pdf

255 Hong Kong Department of Health, (n.d.). "About Us." Retrieved May 19, 2013, from http://www.dh.gov.hk/english/aboutus/aboutus_mv/aboutus_mv.html

256 Hong Kong Department of Health, (n.d.). "Introduction." Retrieved May 19, 2013, from http://www.ha.org.hk/visitor/ha_visitor_index.asp?Content_ID=10008

compared with healthcare spending of 16.3% of GDP in the US, 10.6% in Germany and 7% in Japan."[257]

The structure of healthcare expenditure in Hong Kong has been changing. In the early 1990s, expenditure was predominantly in the private sector. In recent years, public-sector expenditure has become more significant, now accounting for well over one-half of all health spending. "Healthcare spending in Hong Kong is being pushed up by the same factors that are affecting most developed economies: an aging population, the emergence of innovative and expensive medical technologies, new sources of demand and rising consumer expectations."[258]

Estimates in 2009 were that total healthcare spending in Hong Kong would increase from an estimated US$13.2 billion in 2009 to US$16.6 billion in 2014. It was estimated in 2009 that the increase in expenditures would be driven in part by expanding public health investment. But consumer health spending was also expected to increase from around US$5.6 billion in 2009 to US$7.8 billion in 2014, driven by rising disposable incomes.[259]

"In fiscal year 2008/09 (April–March) total public spending on healthcare stood at an estimated HK$36.8 billion (US$4.7bn)."[260] In May 2012, the 2013 Hong Kong budget was presented to the public, and the government had already set aside HK$45 billion for healthcare in the budget (US$5.8 billion).[261]

Today, healthcare in government hospitals in Hong Kong is not free but is heavily subsidized. Fees can be waived for individuals receiving social security assistance. The disadvantage of the government hospitals is that waiting lists can be long. Public subsidies cover around 95% of care costs and including virtually all in-patient care costs. Most of Hong Kong's in-patient admissions are in public hospitals, but the vast majority of outpatient consultations are provided by private doctors. The level of coverage of private medical insurance is remarkably low in Hong Kong.[262]

257 Asiahealthspace.com (2010, July 20). "Healthcare Country Profile: Hong Kong." Retrieved February 2, 2013, from http://www.asiahealthspace.com/?p=3283
258 Ibid.
259 Ibid.
260 Ibid.
261 Educationinnovation.net (2012, May 2). "Education—Healthcare Get Priority in Hong Kong's New Budget." Retrieved February 2, 2013, from http://enterpriseinnovation.net/ /article/education-healthcare-get-priority-hong-kongs-new-budget
262 Op cit, Asiahealthspace.com.

Hong Kong's ratio of an estimated 1.5 doctors per 1,000 people in 2009 was below that in Germany (3.8 per 1,000), the US (3.3) and Japan (2.2). "Hong Kong had an estimated five hospital beds per 1,000 people in 2009, a level that has been broadly stable in recent years. The Hospital Authority runs 48 specialist outpatient clinics and 74 general outpatient clinics. Around 4,760 doctors—roughly 40% of the 11,961 doctors registered in Hong Kong—are employed by the Hospital Authority. Most other doctors are general practitioners in the private sector."[263]

Healthcare in Hong Kong has not been without some controversy. Private hospitals in Hong Kong were reported in late 2012 to have violated terms of their rent-free leases by omitting mandatory facilities, distributing profit surpluses and skimping on free beds required by the terms of their grants—without proper consultation with the Health Department. "The majority of the city's 11 private hospitals are run by non-profit churches. Land grants of many of the hospitals frequently stipulate a ban on distribution of profits and there is a mandatory requirement for provision of low-cost beds."[264]

Despite these shortcomings, for the most part, the system has run smoothly for many decades. The more pressing issues facing Hong Kong are the same ones facing other countries related to costs and the sustainability of quality care. In July 2005, the Hong Kong government began a process to address its healthcare challenges.

Hong Kong Healthcare Reform

When reviewing the Hong Kong Healthcare Reform proposal, it is striking to see the care and respect for its citizens that the Hong Kong government has taken during the reform process. This is apparent when reading the current version of the proposal online. The reform process has not been pushed upon the Hong Kong citizens and hastily voted into law, as was the case with Obamacare.

The Hong Kong Health and Medical Development Advisory Committee (HMDAC) issued the discussion paper *Building a Healthy Tomorrow* in July 2005.

---

263 Ibid.
264 Kahon Chan, (2012, November 15). "Slam on Private Hospitals." Retrieved February 13, 2013, fromhttp://www.cdeclips.com/en/hongkong/Slam_on_private_hospitals/fullstory_76783.html

The discussion paper surveyed the healthcare system and made a number of recommendations on how the service delivery model should be changed. The recommendations covered various aspects of the healthcare system including primary medical care, hospital services, tertiary and specialized services, elderly, long-term and rehabilitation care services, integration between the public and private sectors, and infrastructural support. They received broad support from the community and stakeholders. Based on the recommendations by the HMDAC, the government published the Healthcare Reform Consultation Document *Your Health, Your Life* on March 13, 2008 and put forward a comprehensive package of reform proposals to meet the challenges brought about by the changing demographic profile and rising medical costs. These include[d] four proposals on healthcare service reform and a proposal for healthcare financing reform by considering the introduction of supplementary healthcare financing through six possible supplementary financing options. The government conducted the first stage public consultation on the healthcare reform from March to June 2008 with a view to engaging the community and stakeholders and building a consensus to reform the healthcare system and enhance its sustainable development.[265]

The first stage of consultation reflected the widely shared concern over the long-term sustainability of the Hong Kong healthcare system. There was a consensus from Hong Kong citizens to move forward with the reform proposals. At the same time, the people of Hong Kong expressed their divergent views on the supplementary financing options presented, and the citizens expressed reservations against mandatory supplementary financing options in general. "A greater proportion of the public preferred voluntary choice for individualized healthcare and favored voluntary private health insurance."[266]

The Hong Kong government expressed its commitment to healthcare reform based upon the community's views and agreed to uphold the public healthcare system as the safety net for the whole population. The government also made a commitment to healthcare by increasing its annual recurrent expenditure on healthcare from HK$30.5 billion (US$3.9 billion) in 2007–08 to HK$36.9 billion (US$4.7 billion) in

---

265 Food and Health Bureau, H. (2010, October). "My Health My Choice." Retrieved February 2, 2013, from http://www.myhealthmychoice.gov.hk/en/fullConsolDoc.html, p. 1.
266 Ibid, p. iv.

2010–11. The Hong Kong government stated that it aimed to increase its healthcare budget to 17% of the government's recurrent expenditure in 2012.[267]

In Hong Kong's second stage public consultation, announced in the 2009–10 Policy Address, the government put forward a supplementary healthcare financing scheme. The voluntary Health Protection Scheme (HPS) aimed to ease pressure on public healthcare by encouraging individuals who are able and willing to subscribe to private health insurance as an alternative to public healthcare, which will still be available to all eligible Hong Kong residents. In addition, the government pledged to draw HK$50 billion (US$6.4 billion) from the government's fiscal reserve to support healthcare reform.[268] Thus Hong Kong's healthcare is a mix of private and public healthcare, with everyone covered by the public system at a minimum.

Hong Kong's voluntary HPS was created to provide more choices to better enable people with health insurance to stay insured, and make premium payments at older ages and meet their healthcare needs through private services. It was designed to enhance transparency, competition, value-for-money and consumer protection in private health insurance and private healthcare services.[269]

The HPS plans are voluntary for both individuals and insurance companies. HPS plans are required to provide features that offer advantages over existing private health insurance products currently available in the market. Some of these enhanced HPS plan features are:

- Insurers are prohibited from turning away subscribers who are to be guaranteed renewable for life.
- Insurers must have published age-banded premiums subject to adjustment guidelines.
- Insurers must cover pre-existing medical conditions subject to waiting period and time-limited reimbursement limits.
- Insurers must cap on premiums plus high-risk loading at three times the published premium rates.
- Insurers must ensure portability for insureds upon leaving employment.
- Insurers must have standardized health insurance policy terms and definitions.

---

267 Ibid, p. iv.
268 Ibid, p. v.
269 Ibid, p. vi.

- Insurers must include the government regulated health insurance claims arbitration mechanism.
- HPS makes higher risk groups insurable with the creation of a high-risk reinsurance pool.
- HPS promotes transparent medical fees by packaged charging for common procedures."[270]

To enable the higher-risk groups to have access to health insurance, the HPS introduced a High Risk Pool (HRP). "All high-risk policies, defined as those policies with risk premium assessed to exceed the cap for premium with high-risk loading (i.e., three times the published premium of Standard Plans) will be put into the HRP. The HRP is proposed to be a reinsurance mechanism operated by the industry and regulated by the government, funded by the premium of high-risk policies (corresponding to Standard Plans) and reinsurance premium from participating insurers. Where necessary, injection by the government would be considered in case the viability of the HRP is in jeopardy due to a large proportion of higher risk people joining health insurance plans under the HPS, when the HRP premium cannot meet the claims pay-out."[271]

A key objective of the HPS is to encourage people with health insurance to stay insured as they reach older ages. However, age-banded premiums for voluntary health insurance are bound to increase sharply with the age of the insured as their healthcare utilization increases. Three proposals are in the second stage of public consultation of the HPS to address saving for future premiums. One is for HPS plans to be required to incorporate a savings component, where an insured would pay a higher premium at a younger age to offset the premium increases at an older age. The second alternative is for individuals subscribing to HPS plans to have an option to save to a savings account, and the accrued savings can then be freely used on or after age 65. Incentives via government contributions to the savings account are being considered, subject to the savings being used to pay HPS premium from age 65. The third alternative is to encourage HPS subscribers to choose to save by their own means. Incentives via premium rebates in proportion to their length of staying insured under the HPS would be considered, provided

270 Ibid, p. viii–ix.
271 Ibid, p. xi.

that they continue to pay premiums from age 65 using their own savings.[272]

The second stage public consultation proposed that financial incentives make use of the HK$50 billion fiscal reserve. Healthcare reform was to be considered in three different areas. The first area was to use earmarked funds to address the issue of insurance for high-risk individuals. The government should allow high-risk individuals to join HPS without requiring other insured persons to pay excessive premiums to compensate for the high-risk group. To buffer the excess risk, the government could inject into the HRP where necessary. Secondly, the earmarked funds could be used for premium discounts for new subscribers which would attract individuals, especially the young, to join HPS plans. The government is considering incentives for all new joiners plans to enjoy up to a 30% no-claim discount on the Standard Plan premium immediately upon joining. Thirdly, funds could be used for savings on future premiums to enable the insured to continue to afford health protection under the HPS at an older age. The government incentives could be proportional to the length of time an insured continuously stayed in the HPS.[273]

The second stage public consultation concluded that the HPS is dependent upon the participation of insurance companies in shifting the healthcare risks from the government to the private sector. They stated:

> Implementation of the HPS requires participation of private health insurers and private healthcare providers. To this end, the proposals for the HPS are designed with a view to safeguarding consumer interests in private health insurance and private healthcare services, while ensuring that it should be practically feasible and financially viable to offer health insurance plans and provide private healthcare services under the HPS. To ensure competition and choice under the HPS, there is a need for more interested private health insurers to participate and offer sufficient and attractive choices of health insurance plans under the HPS. The HPS is formulated taking into account the views of the insurance industry, and we expect that private insurers in the insurance industry would be interested in participating in the HPS.[274]

272 Ibid, p. xii.
273 Ibid, p. xiv–xv.
274 Ibid, p. xiii–xiv.

In 2010, the Hong Kong Food and Health Bureau (FHB) commissioned the actuarial firm Milliman Limited to design actuarially sound insurance product templates and to develop policy options for the provision of incentives to enable the HPS to operate effectively. Milliman noted several key risks and methods to mitigate these risks, and noted that, ultimately, some form of government incentive will be required to encourage members to stay on the scheme through the older ages to reduce lapse rates from their current high levels.[275]

The Hong Kong government proposed an action plan to be carried out by the first half of 2013. The plan was intended to establish a platform to engage with stakeholders; formulate a supervisory framework for health insurance and healthcare service markets under the scheme; and facilitate the development of healthcare services.[276]

It is expected that the HPS will encourage demand for private healthcare in Hong Kong. The development of private hospital facilities will be encouraged, including four new private hospital developments at already designated sites. Also, a dedicated office will be established within the Food and Health Bureau to support the action plan. It will also coordinate and take forward initiatives and the purchase of private healthcare services.[277] Hong Kong's plan is well under way with some experts suggesting the HPS will be fully functioning by 2016.

The differences between the well-thought-out "plan of attack" with dialogue open to the private and public sectors and practical implementation of a revised healthcare system like that of Hong Kong; and Obamacare are significant. The programs and implementation are light years apart. The already apparent results of both programs are a prudent, functioning, transparent and financially sound program in Hong Kong and an expensive, excessively bureaucratic and very unpopular government cluster-clutter with Obamacare.

Healthcare Summary

When President George W. Bush was in office an effort was made at Medicare reform. Medicare, the government program put in place in

275 Chye Pang-Hsiang, (2010). *Milliman Limited: Feasibility Study on the Key Features of the Health Protection Scheme*. Hong Kong: Milliman Limited.
276 Kevin Bowers, (2011, October 25). "Assessing the impact of healthcare reform on insurance." Retrieved February 15, 2013, from http://www.internationallawoffice.com/ /newsletters/detail.aspx?g=1f4a5c60-ed19-40aa-a60e-cbfc7c2c7e3d
277 Ibid.

1965 to help seniors with their healthcare costs, didn't cover prescription drugs and was going broke. President Bush put together a group who worked with a bipartisan Senate team of two Democrats and two Republicans in drafting a bill to address the issues with Medicare. A bill was eventually passed in 2003 that provided prescription drug coverage to seniors through private insurance options. President Bush wrote:

> Thanks to competition between private-sector plans, the average monthly premium for prescription drug coverage dropped from an initial estimate of $35 to $23 [per individual] the first year. By 2008, the initial estimate of $634 billion had dropped below $400 billion. The Medicare prescription drug benefit became one of the few government programs ever to come in well under budget. Market forces had worked. And we had moved America's healthcare system in the right direction: away from government control and toward the choices and competition of a private market system, which is the best way to control costs in the long run.[278]

Two things become clear when comparing the Medicare Advantage Program and the PPACA. The first is that the Medicare Advantage program had bipartisan support. Members of both the Democratic and Republican parties were involved in drafting the law and were part of its passage. The PPACA, in contrast, was created by Democrats who refused to consider or incorporate Republican ideas regarding healthcare. The second major difference is that Medicare Advantage introduced market forces to the health insurance arena while Obamacare does the opposite.

Current US public healthcare programs are even more deficient when compared to Hong Kong's programs. First and foremost, Hong Kong citizens' opinions were considered as well as those of insurance companies and healthcare providers.

When the PPACA was hastily pushed into law, the opinions of the Republican lawmakers were not considered or invited. Insurance companies were condemned as being unethical entities which deny people coverage while their CEOs enjoy lavish salaries and perks. Individuals who spoke out against the law were condemned as being racist, and the

---

278 Bush, G. W. (2010). *Decision Points*. New York: Crown Publishers, pp. 281–287.

opinions of the majority of individuals who provide healthcare, the doctors, were for the most part ignored.

The costs of Obamacare have been understated and misleading and the complexity is not necessary. The Hong Kong HPS is a model for healthcare reform around the world. Obamacare is not.

It is difficult for the average citizen to even get their mind around the costs that are currently being incurred. According to William W. Beach, Director of the Center for Data Analysis at the Heritage Foundation and Patrick D. Tyrrell, Research Coordinator in the Center for Data Analysis, in 2010, the US spent $408 billion on Medicare and $246 billion on Medicaid.[279] These costs do not include the various additional federal, state and local government healthcare costs.

In total, with a total population of around 310 million,[280] the US spends $2,100 per capita for just Medicare and Medicaid alone. Hong Kong has a population of around 7 million[281] and has set aside a budget for public healthcare spending of $5.8 billion in 2013.[282] Thus Hong Kong spends only $800 per capita on public healthcare. The US therefore spends 2.5 times more on public healthcare per capita than does Hong Kong, not including Obamacare and other US federal, state and local government healthcare programs.

Another contrast between Obamacare and the proposed Hong Kong HPS is the thought put into making health insurance products more marketable and desirable to the consumer. The US law requires insurance companies to create rate scales where the premiums on older members cannot exceed three times the lowest premium rates. This encourages insurance companies to charge more to younger members in order to pay for the reduction in premiums on the elderly, also mandating that younger individuals obtain healthcare coverage or pay a fine. The Hong Kong HPS instead requires that insurers put caps on premiums plus high-risk loading at three times the published premium rates and provides for insurance on high-risk members by creating a pool shared amongst insurance companies and funded by the premium of high-risk policies and reinsurance premiums from insurers. The HPS is voluntary for insurance companies and individuals alike, no mandates

279 Op cit, Tyrell et al, p. 11.
280 Op cit, Worldatlas.com.
281 Hong Kong Government, (2013, July). "Hong Kong: The Facts." Retrieved March 22, 2014, fromhttp://www.gov.hk/en/about/abouthk/factsheets/docs/population.pdf
282 Op cit, Educationinnovation.net.

are necessary and fines are not assessed on individuals who decide they don't want to pay for health insurance at the current time.

A final point regards the most influential factor driving the increase in healthcare costs in the US—malpractice insurance costs for doctors and healthcare professionals and firms. In the US, the cost to medical doctors for malpractice insurance is excessive and growing. This is because any doctor can be sued at any time for almost any act taken, or not taken, which may be even remotely related to their performance in providing healthcare. Tort liability is a major issue which the PPACA does not address.

The Hong Kong healthcare regime is one that works. America would be prudent to mirror the Hong Kong HPS as a solution for both future solvency and quality of care. In addition, the US could save billions in healthcare costs by creating public hospitals rather than public healthcare regimes, bureaucracies and policies. The costs to administer the healthcare programs in the US are excessive. As American economist Thomas Sowell commented, "It is amazing that people who think we cannot afford to pay for doctors, hospitals, and medication somehow think that we can afford to pay for doctors, hospitals, medication *and* a government bureaucracy to administer it."[283]

283   Thomas Sowell, (1980). *Knowledge and Decisions*, chapter: "What society expends?"

CHAPTER 5

All Blacks, All Care

The enchanting islands of New Zealand have the only system in the world that provides 24-hour coverage for all accidental physical injuries as well as other mental injuries, workplace injuries and occupational diseases. The amazing fact to non-Kiwis is that this program replaces tort liability—no individual or company can be sued for accidental injuries. The care is better and more comprehensive than that of other developed countries, and the cost savings to society are significant.

Disability Overview

Current estimates are that around 10% of the world's population, or roughly 650 million people, live with a disability. In most of the Organization for Economic Co-operation and Development (OECD) countries, females have a higher disability rate than males. Disability rates in the world population are also higher among groups with lower educational levels, and on average, 19% of less-educated people have disabilities compared to 11% among the better-educated.[284]

There is a correlation between disability and poverty: poor people are at more risk of acquiring a disability. This is because they lack access to good nutrition, healthcare, sanitation, and safe living and working conditions. Once disabled, people around the world face barriers to education, employment, and public services that can help them escape poverty.[285]

In recent years, disability benefit claims have increased in industrialized countries, with some reporting increases as high as 600%. These increases encourage governments and other entities to search for ways to get people back to work.[286] It is much more beneficial for a govern-

284 Disabled-world. (n.d.). "World Facts and Statistics on Disabilities and Disability Issues." Retrieved March 9, 2013, from http://www.disabled-world.com/disability/statistics/
285 Ibid.
286 Ibid.

ment or company to pay an individual to work, rather than to pay someone *not* to work. It also is more rewarding for an individual to earn an income as a result of working, rather than staying at home collecting disability payments. These rewards are both monetary and emotional.

In the United States, the chance that an individual will become disabled at some point in his/her career is very high. "Despite dramatic reductions in the physical demands of the workplace in recent decades and significant improvements in medical care, workers in industrialized economies face a substantial lifetime risk of developing a work-limiting disability. The US Social Security Administration estimates that a 20-year-old US worker has a three in ten chance of becoming disabled before reaching full retirement age."[287]

Estimates of current disabilities vary depending on source of data. According to estimates derived from a 2006 Census report, 18.6% of the US population had a disability lasting any length of time, and 6% of the population has had disabilities lasting six months or longer. Not surprisingly, persons with disabilities have higher healthcare costs because of their poorer health status. These costs fall predominantly on private insurance and public insurers Medicare and Medicaid.[288]

Online medical resource site WebMD lists the following as most likely causes of disability:

- Arthritis and other musculoskeletal problems are the most common causes of long-term disability and make up as much as a third of all disability cases.
- Heart disease and stroke, although thought of as sudden medical events, are often related to chronic conditions. People can live with heart disease for decades. Studies show that heart disease accounts for 17% of all health costs in the US.
- Cancer is the fastest growing cause for disability despite more effective treatments.
- Mental health problems like depression, bipolar disorder, and other conditions are the most common reason that people file for Social Security disability in the US.

287 David H. Autor, (2011, November 23). "The Unsustainable Rise of Disability Rolls in the United States: Causes, Consequences, and Policy Options." Retrieved March 8, 2013, from http://economics.mit.edu/files/7388, p. 2.
288 Wayne Anderson, (n.d.). "The Impact of Disability on Health Care Costs." Retrieved March 10, 2013, from http://www.rti.org/files/fellowseminar/fellowseminar_longtermcare_anderson.pdf

- Diabetes is a fast-rising cause of disability. Along with obesity, diabetes is related to other health problems like heart disease, but also is very expensive to treat.
- Nervous system disorders like multiple sclerosis (MS), Parkinson's disease, amyotrophic lateral sclerosis, epilepsy and Alzheimer's disease, account for numerous disability cases with MS being the leading cause of disability among young adults.
- Finally, pregnancy is effectively a disability, but in the US, most women don't get paid maternity leave. Most pregnant women in the US have to use sick days and vacation days to support their income until the baby arrives and they return to work.[289]

According to a 2011 Long-Term Disability Claims Review, the following were the leading causes of new disability claims in 2010:

- Musculoskeletal/connective tissue disorders caused 27.5% of new claims.
- Cancer was the second-leading cause of new disability claims at 14.6%.
- Injuries and poisoning caused 10.3% of new claims.
- Cardiovascular/circulatory disorders caused 9.1% of new claims.
- Mental disorders caused 9.1% of new claims.[290]

Approximately 90% of disabilities are caused by illness rather than accidents.[291]

US Disability System

Since 1956, the US Social Security Disability Insurance Program (SSDI) has served to insure workers and their families against impoverishment and loss of medical care in the event of disability. At present, the program provides disability insurance to 153 million non-elderly Americans and pays monthly benefits to 8.4 million disabled workers and 2 million dependent spouses and children. Although the

289 R. Morgan Griffin, (n.d.). "Leading Causes of Disability." Retrieved March 9, 2013, from http://www.m.webmd.com/a-to-z-guides/features/top-causes-disability
290 Council for Disability Awareness, (n.d.). "Chances of Disability: Disability Statistics." Retrieved March 15, 2013, from http://www.disabilitycanhappen.org/chances_disability/disability_stats.asp
291 Ibid.

majority of insured workers will never suffer from a work-limiting disability, it is arguable that most benefit from the SSDI program nevertheless because it provides economic security and, potentially, peace of mind that would be difficult to obtain from any other source.[292]

Approximately one-third of US workers are covered by employer-provided, long-term disability insurance policies (PDI). These policies work with SSDI by providing the insured additional wage replacement benefits upon contracting long-term disability. "Unlike SSDI, wage benefits in PDI policies are generally time-limited, are typically not indexed for inflation, and do not include medical coverage. PDI benefit payments are offset by SSDI benefits one-for-one."[293]

In addition to SSDI and PDI protection, a third layer of protection against disabilities in the US is the Supplemental Security Income (SSI) program. SSI is the second major federal disability entitlement program that applies the same medical criteria as SSDI but, unlike SSDI, does not require that an individual have prior work history for eligibility. "Cash transfers under SSI are substantially smaller than under SSDI and are contingent on the beneficiary having very low income and assets. Medical coverage under SSI is provided through Medicaid rather than Medicare (which accompanies SSDI)."[294]

To qualify for SSDI benefits, a non-blind worker must have recent work activity as calculated by the Social Security Administration. The calculation takes into account an individual's recent work history, ending with the quarter in which the disability began. In general, workers disabled in their 20s must have worked in one-half of the calendar quarters "beginning with the quarter after the quarter in which age 21 is attained and ending with the calendar quarter in which the disability began."[295] SSDI provides a formula for qualifying for benefits under the program. To do all these qualification calculations require a huge population of administrators.

SSDI's expenditures are extremely high and growing rapidly. In 1957 the total annual benefit paid for disability by the Social Security

292   Op cit, Autor, p. 2.
293   Ibid, p. 2.
294   Ibid, p. 11.
295   Social Security Administration, (2013, February). *Annual Statistical Supplement to the Social Security Bulletin, 2012.* Retrieved March 10, 2013, from http://www.ssa.gov/policy/docs/statcomps/supplement/2012/supplement12.pdf, p.12.

Administration was $130 million. Disability benefits in 1957 were 2.7% of the cost of Social Security retirement benefits. By 1980, this had increased to over $12 billion annually, almost 16% of the cost of Social Security retirement benefits. By 2011, the total annual benefit paid by Social Security Administration on disability was $114 billion, or 22% of the cost of Social Security retirement benefits.[296]

According to David Autor, Professor of Economics at the Massachusetts Institute of Technology: in 2010, SSDI cash transfer payments actually totaled $124 billion. He also reported that the cost of Medicare for SSDI beneficiaries in 2010 was $59 billion. "These outlays, exceeding $1,500 for every US household, comprised 7.3% of federal non-defense spending the previous year—a sum that is larger than interest payments on the federal debt. In the last two decades, outlays for SSDI grew at 5.6% in real terms, compared to just 2.2% for all other Social Security spending."[297]

Autor also noted that "most ominously, SSDI expenditures now exceed by 30% the payroll tax revenue dedicated to funding the program. The Trustees of the Social Security Administration project that the SSDI Trust Fund will be exhausted between 2015 and 2018, at least two decades ahead of the trust fund for Social Security retirement benefits."[298] Clearly, the SSDI portion of Social Security is seriously underfunded.

The cost increase of SSDI is due to the increase in the number of adults receiving SSDI. Between 1989 and 2009, the share of adults receiving SSDI benefits doubled, rising from 2.3% to 4.6% of Americans aged 25 to 64. "The rapid expansion of SSDI contributes significantly to the deteriorating financial health of the overall Social Security system since both depend on the Social Security payroll tax."[299]

The total number of people in the US receiving federal disability benefits reached a record 10,982,920 in November 2013, up from the previous record of 10,978,040 set in May 2013 according to data from the Social Security Administration. This number is greater than the total population of the countries of Greece, Portugal, Tunisia and Burundi.

---

296 Ibid, p. 5.14.
297 Op cit, Autor, p. 3.
298 Ibid, p. 3.
299 David H. Autor and Mark Duggan, (2010, December). "Supporting Work: A Proposal for Moderninzng the US Disability System." Retrieved March 10, 2013, from http://www.americanprogress.org/wp-content/uploads/issues/ /2010/12/pdf/autordugganpaper.pdf, p. 2.

The month of November 2013 was also the 202nd straight month that the number of disabled workers in the United States increased, with the last decrease occurring in January 1997.[300]

The fraction of middle-age adults reporting a disability has been roughly stable over the last two decades, averaging approximately 10% among both men and women. However, what has changed greatly is the fraction of individuals who receive disability benefits. Between 1988 and 2008, the fraction of middle-aged men and women aged 40 to 59 receiving SSDI benefits rose by 45% among males (from 3.9% to 5.6%) and 159% among females (1.9% to 5.0%).[301]

> The expanding size and cost of the SSDI program would not be inherently problematic if this expansion reflected a rising rate of disability among working-age adults and if the program's mounting expenditures enabled these individuals to maintain employment and self-sufficiency. Unfortunately, neither is the case.[302]

The steep increase in SSDI costs has corresponded with a significant decline in the employment rates of working-age individuals with disabilities. The employment rate of males in their 40s and 50s with a self-reported disability fell from 28% in 1988 to 16% in 2008 (approximately a 40% decline). The employment rate of comparably aged males without a disability held roughly constant at 87% to 88%. For females in this same age range with disabilities, the employment rate declined slightly (from 18% to 15%), while the employment rate of their counterparts without a disability rose from 66% to 76%.[303]

> The simultaneous occurrence of these two trends—declining employment among working-age people with disabilities and rising SSDI receipt—underscores that the two key policy challenges of the SSDI program are two sides of the same coin. The SSDI program is growing in size and cost because it is supporting a rising rate of dependency and a declining rate of labor force participation among adults with disabilities.[304]

---

300 Terence P. Jeffrey, (2013, December 3). "10,982,920: More Americans on Disability Than People in Greece." Retrieved December 8, 2013, from http://cnsnews.com/news/ /article/terence-p-jeffrey/10982920-more-americans-disability-people-greece
301 Op cit, Duggan et al, pp. 2–3.
302 Ibid, p. 2.
303 Op cit, Duggan et al, pp. 2.

Causes for the Expansion in US SSDI Costs

To be insured by the SSDI program, an individual must have worked in at least five of the ten most recent years prior to the onset of disability. Once insured, a worker is qualified to receive SSDI benefits if SSA determines that, due to a medical condition that has lasted or is expected to last for at least one year or result in death, the worker is unable to either engage in her previous work or to adjust to a different type of work. If benefits are awarded, SSA begins making monthly cash payments to the beneficiary five months from the onset of disability. Monthly benefits currently average $1,150 for new awardees and are indexed to the Consumer Price Index. Two years following the onset of disability, beneficiaries also become entitled to Medicare benefits. Both cash and Medicare benefits continue until the beneficiary experiences a medical recovery, passes away, or reaches the full retirement age. In the latter case, he transitions to Social Security retirement. Autor and Duggan (2010) estimate that in 2009, the present value of cash and medical benefits for a new SSDI awardee at the average age of enrollment of 48.8 years was $270,000.[305]

In 1956, when Congress created SSDI, the ability to work was considered mutually exclusive with disability. "Reflecting this understanding, the 1956 law defines disability as the 'inability to engage in a substantial gainful activity in the US economy'—in other words, the inability to work. The SSDI program still uses this definition. It provides income support and medical benefits exclusively to workers who are out of the labor force and, based on SSA's criteria, not expected to return."[306]

Over the half century since SSDI was created, the line between the ability and the inability to work hase blurred due to changes in jobs as well as enhancements in medical technology that enable disabled individuals to work and maintain economic self-sufficiency. "The Americans with Disabilities Act of 1990 (ADA) forcefully articulates this contemporary understanding of disability, stating that 'The Nation's proper goals regarding individuals with disabilities are to assure equality of opportunity, full participation, independent living, and economic self-sufficiency. . . .' The SSDI program has not been altered to reflect this

304 Ibid, p. 2.
305 Op cit, Autor, p. 4.
306 Ibid, p. 4.

changed understanding, however. Two decades after the ADA's passage, SSDI remains unable to provide assistance to workers with disabilities until their condition has made it infeasible for them to work."[307]

The employment provisions of the ADA exemplify the law of unintended consequences. Provisions of the ADA have *harmed* the intended beneficiaries of the Act, not helped them. "ADA was enacted to remove barriers to employment of people with disabilities by banning discrimination and requiring employers to accommodate disabilities (e.g., by providing a magnified computer screen for a vision-impaired person). However, studies of the consequences of the employment provisions of ADA show that the Act has led to less employment of disabled workers."[308]

> Why has ADA harmed its intended beneficiaries? The added cost of employing disabled workers to comply with the accommodation mandate of ADA has made those workers relatively unattractive to firms. Moreover, the threats of prosecution by the Equal Employment Opportunity Commission (EEOC) and litigation by disabled workers, both of which were to have deterred firms from shedding their disabled workforce, have in fact led firms to avoid hiring some disabled workers in the first place.[309]

A recent case involves a California nonprofit, Placer ARC, dedicated to helping people with special needs. This entity is being sued for allegedly discriminating against a former deaf employee. According to the federal lawsuit, the employee was given an interpreter during mandatory staff meetings, but when she transferred to a different location three years later, her attorneys claim that she had to begin taking notes instead and that her supervisors failed to provide an interpreter for her during daily staff meetings and forced her to speak only in English, failing to provide reasonable accommodations.[310]

The fact that ADA has made disabled individuals unattractive to firms is not a surprise. "After all, if you raise the price of a good or service, you must expect that less of it will be bought. Likewise, theories of labor

---

307 Ibid, p. 5.
308 Op cit, DeLeire.
309 Ibid.
310 Hemphill, A. (2013, March 26). "Deaf Woman Suing Former Employer For Not Providing Sign Language Interpreter." Retrieved March 31, 2013, from http://sacramento.cbslocal.com/ /2013/03/26/deaf-woman-suing-former-employer-for-not-providing-sign-language-interpreter/

demand predict that when a group of workers becomes more expensive, firms will hire other workers or substitute capital for labor."[311]

Before the ADA was put into effect, SSDI costs were increasing, until in the mid-1980s, President Ronald Reagan's administration clamped down on excessive costs with an aggressive program of "continuing disability reviews," which led to the summary termination of benefits for close to 400,000 SSDI recipients. "Taking place against the backdrop of the severe and early 1980s recession, these steps provoked a national backlash. Congress responded by halting the reviews and, in 1984, liberalizing the program's screening criteria along several dimensions. Most important, [the Democratic] Congress directed the Social Security Administration to give additional weight to pain and related subjective factors in making its disability determination decisions, and to relax its strict screening of mental illness by placing less weight on diagnostic and medical factors and relatively more weight on the ability to function in a work setting. A key consequence was that applicants with difficult-to-verify disorders such as muscle pain and mental disorders could more easily qualify for benefits."[312]

The impact of the 1980s' changes on SSDI program enrollment was not immediately evident because the US economy climbed out of the deep recession in the years following the SSDI reforms. But when economic conditions deteriorated in the early 1990s (and with the advent of the ADA legislation), SSDI costs resumed their rapid growth. Between 1989 and 2009, the proportion of adults receiving SSDI benefits doubled, from 2.3% to 4.6% of Americans aged 25 to 64, while cash payments to SSDI recipients (adjusted for inflation) tripled to $121 billion. Along with this, Medicare expenditures for SSDI recipients rose from $18 billion to $69 billion. "This growth coincided with a dramatic change in the characteristics of SSDI recipients, with a steadily increasing share of awards made to individuals with musculoskeletal conditions and mental disorders, and a corresponding decline in the share of awards for cardiovascular disease and cancer, the two most common diagnoses prior to the 1984 liberalization."[313]

The growth of the SSDI roles is not only due to changes in the program's eligibility criteria. The labor market has played a key role with research showing that workers are most likely to apply for SSDI benefits

311 Op cit, DeLeire.
312 Op cit, Autor, p. 5.
313 Ibid, p. 6.

following job loss. This is also evident when noting the positive correlation between the national unemployment rate and the SSDI application rate. The decline in earnings and employment opportunities for US workers with high school or lower education over the last three decades has also made SSDI an increasingly attractive option for the unemployed.[314] The SSDI award is like an annuity that pays inflation-adjusted monthly income plus full medical benefits until the time of retirement. Not many individuals with marginal employment prospects would give that up in favor of finding a job in a difficult market.[315]

The increase in SSDI participants is not due to the US population becoming less healthy. Evidence shows that the percentage of middle-aged adults reporting a disability has been roughly the same over the past few decades. In addition, there is little evidence that the health of the working-age population is deteriorating.[316]

The simultaneous occurrence of two trends—decreasing employment among working-age people with disabilities and rising SSDI receipts—underlines the two key policy challenges of the SSDI program. "The SSDI program is growing in size and cost in substantial part because it is supporting a rising rate of dependency and a declining rate of labor force participation among adults with disabilities."[317]

The trend of a significant portion of the US population away from the "family as the provider" and towards the "government as the provider" ideal is the underlying cause of this increase in disability payments. In contrast, in underdeveloped nations, an individual works until they die with no support from the government. Neither of these extremes is workable in developed countries, but what is clear is that the current disability system in the US is in need of major repair.

Prescriptions for SSDI Solvency

Various efforts have been made to reform SSDI. However, these efforts have not worked due to not addressing the root causes of increasing costs. According to MIT's Autor, the previous efforts have been fruitless because "they make one or more fundamental mistakes: limiting SSDI awards by denying applicants rather than reducing applications; revok-

---

314   Ibid, p. 5.
315   Ibid, p. 13.
316   Ibid, pp. 6–7.
317   Ibid, p. 8.

ing benefits of individuals who have no other means of financial support and thus strong incentives to get back on the system; and reducing the penalties for gainful employment when these are, by and large, too late to matter."[318]

Recent efforts to terminate benefits to beneficiaries have not worked. "Following passage of a 1996 law outlawing the provision of disability benefits for drug and alcohol addiction, the SSA removed from the rolls approximately 210,000 beneficiaries whose primary impairment was drug and alcohol addiction. Between 50 and 60% of these terminated claimants re-qualified for SSDI benefits under other impairments, primarily mental illness."[319] Revoking the benefits of the needy is also not politically viable, and highly motivated applicants find a way to make it back on the SSDI rolls.[320]

Autor believes that the goal of SSDI reform should be to increase the participation of individuals with work-limiting disabilities in the labor force and thus reduce the number applying for long-term SSDI benefits. To accomplish this goal, the government needs to change the incentives faced by firms and workers.[321]

SSDI is currently funded as part of the Old-Age, Survivors, and Disability Insurance) payroll tax charged at a rate of 12.4% split between employer and employee for all US workers on the first $107,000 of wage and salary income. The SSDI component of this tax is a flat rate of 1.8% of the 12.4% payroll tax on covered earnings, which is insufficient to cover the program's current costs as evidenced by the fact that the SSDI Trust Fund is nearing exhaustion.[322]

US employers who pay into the SSDI system have no incentive to minimize SSDI claims since their payroll taxes are independent of the claims their workers make. One suggestion is to "experience-rate" the SSDI payroll tax so that employers will feel the cost of SSDI claims. "Under this scheme, employers whose workers make more frequent claims on the SSDI system would pay higher SSDI payroll taxes."[323]

"Experience-rating" SSDI is a simple proposal that has been used for decades in state unemployment insurance and workers' compensation systems. Adding an experience-rating scheme to the SSDI payroll tax

318 Ibid, p. 11.
319 Ibid, p. 11.
320 Ibid, p. 12.
321 Ibid, p. 13.
322 Ibid, p. 14.
323 Ibid, p. 14.

system would probably not necessitate new data collection since employers currently report payroll tax data to the federal government for each employee. It also may not be challenging for the Social Security Administration to link payroll data to SSDI awards. It is therefore plausible that SSA could implement an experience-rated SSDI payroll tax without imposing substantial new reporting requirements or administrative burdens on employers.[324]

"Any SSDI reform that makes firms partly liable for workers' SSDI claims faces the delicate task of creating incentives for firms to accommodate workers with disabilities when appropriate without penalizing firms for either bad luck (e.g., a worker developing heart disease) or worker moral hazard."[325] Experience-rating firms on SSDI claims does create incentives for firms to limit the number of claims from their institutions.

Another alternative for reducing SSDI inflows, as presented by Autor, is for SSDI to leverage existing private disability insurance (PDI). "Under the PDI proposal, employers would be required to carry disability insurance policies, the cost of which could be partly charged back to employees. Policies would be competitively sold, and employers would have the option to self-insure. Premiums would be experience-rated for firms with fifty or more full-time equivalent employees. Premiums for smaller firms would be industry-rated. Insurers would be allowed to vary the premium with the average age of employees at a firm as well as with the firm's industry. The proposed policy would support workers from 90 days to 2.25 years following onset of disability, providing partial income replacement, vocational rehabilitation, and workplace accommodations geared toward helping individuals maximize work-readiness and self-sufficiency. After receiving PDI benefits for 24 months, individuals who are unable to engage in substantial gainful employment would transition into the SSDI system. The screening criteria for SSDI would be unchanged."[326] This alternative is promising because it brings third parties into the disability equation who have a profit motive which would inhibit fraudulent or weak disability cases from receiving awards.

The PDI proposal has additional strengths and weaknesses. The plan's strength is that it encourages firms to minimize disability costs— since private sector policies depend in part on an employer's claims

324 Ibid, pp. 14–15.
325 Ibid, p. 16.
326 Ibid, p. 18.

history—while providing individuals with work limitations with access to an infrastructure for supporting ongoing employment and managing the financial toll of work limitations that are provided with PDI coverage.[327]

The PDI policy noted by Autor has the goal of accommodating and remedying the disability before it leads to job loss and labor force withdrawal. "It is a widely held view among vocational rehabilitation practitioners that maintaining the worker's link to the current employer is critical to successful labor force reintegration; once the current employment tie is severed, the hurdle to reentering becomes substantially higher."[328]

The challenge with the PDI proposal as a solution for reducing SSDI costs is that Americans are ideologically opposed to mandates from the government. Another challenge with the PDI proposal is its complexity. While the SSDI experience-rating proposal requires only modest modifications to the existing payroll tax scheme, the PDI proposal would require developing policy standards, verification systems to ensure that these policies were in place and the resources at the SSA to manage the system.[329]

Other remedies have been proposed to reduce the costs of SSDI. However, none of these address the rising costs to society as a whole of outrageous legal settlements as a result of accident and malpractice suits. Currently if you become disabled in the US, you either receive government assistance for life or you "win the lottery" with the proceeds from a settlement of a legal dispute.

Accidents and the US Legal System

Indeed, few features of the American legal system are as distinctive as American accident law institutions. The United States relies much more heavily than most other developed legal systems on private law and tort litigation to compensate accident victims and deter potential causers of harm. It is well known, for example, that tort litigation rates are considerably higher in the United States than in Western Europe. Where the US system is characterized by juries, contingency fees, and

327 Ibid, p. 18.
328 Ibid, p. 19.
329 Ibid, p. 20.

relatively high damage awards (including punitive damages), other developed systems of accident law tend to be characterized by more systematic social insurance systems, comparatively low damage awards (including damages caps on non-pecuniary damages), loser-pays attorneys' fee rules, limitations on group litigation, and professional judges rather than juries. In world-comparative terms, ours [the US's] is (as Judge Jack Weinstein has described it) an "exotic" system of accident law.[330]

American accident law has its roots in the Anglo-American tradition of individual private dispute resolution. However, as US accident law has developed, it has become more and more peculiar, as recent developments make abundantly clear. A $28 billion damages verdict against the corporate giant Philip Morris for one person's death is a reminder of the extraordinary and exceptional power—virtually unique to the United States—of tort juries. In addition, lawyers have begun to aggregate tort claims into class actions in areas ranging from pharmaceuticals and asbestos to tobacco and handguns.[331]

Over 15 million lawsuits will be filed this year in state courts in the US. This is the equivalent of one new lawsuit every two seconds, or one lawsuit for every 12 adults in America.[332] Many of these cases will be legitimate but some will be bordering the absurd. Below is a list of some of the more ludicrous accident-related court cases litigated in the US:

- In February 1992, Stella Liebeck ordered "a cup of coffee to go" from McDonalds. Liebeck was sitting in the passenger seat of her nephew's car, which was pulled over so she could add sugar to her coffee. While removing the cup's lid, Liebeck spilled her hot coffee, burning her legs. It was determined that Liebeck suffered third-degree burns on over six percent of her body. Originally, Liebeck sought $20,000 in damages. McDonalds refused to settle out of court. However, they should have. Liebeck was ultimately awarded $200,000 in compensatory damages, which was reduced to $160,000 because she

330 John Fabian Witt, (n.d.). "Thinking Historically about American Accident Law." Retrieved March 16, 2013, from
     http://www.law.columbia.edu/law_school/communications/reports/winter2003/accidentlaw
331 Ibid.
332 Legalreform-now.org, (n.d.). "Legal Process Reform: Reduce the large number of lawsuits." Retrieved March 16, 2013, from http://www.legalreform-now.org/menu3_3.htm

was found to be 20% at fault. She was also awarded $2.7 million in punitive damages.

- In September 1988, two Akron, Ohio-based carpet-layers named Gordon Falker and Gregory Roach were severely burned when a three-and-a-half-gallon container of carpet adhesive was ignited by the hot-water heater it was sitting next to. Both men felt the warning label on the back of the can was insufficient. Words like "flammable" and "keep away from heat" didn't prepare them for the explosion. They filed suit against the adhesive manufacturers, Para-Chem. A jury obviously agreed since the men were awarded $8 million for their troubles.

- In 1992, 23-year-old Karen Norman accidentally backed her car into Galveston Bay after a night of drinking. Norman could not operate her seat belt and drowned. Her passenger managed to disengage herself and make it to shore. Norman's parents sued Honda for making a seat belt their drunken daughter (her blood alcohol level was 0.17%—nearly twice the legal limit) could not open underwater. A jury found Honda 75% responsible for Karen's death and awarded the Norman family $65 million. An appeals court threw out the case.[333]

People in the US never used to sue for hot coffee spills or for obvious neglectful behavior. In the 1970s, a million-dollar verdict for an accident was headline news, but today, people sue for billions. The obvious villains are greedy lawyers and a culture that has lost its sense of personal responsibility. "But there's a chicken that laid those eggs—the American judiciary abdicated its role as gatekeeper in the 1960s, and started letting anyone sue for almost anything. Embarrassed by their complacency on racial and gender discrimination, the white males on the bench embraced a new philosophy of judging—instead of a paternalistic model (most famously symbolized by Justice Potter Stewart's line "I know it when I see it"), judges would be merely referees in a neutral process. Instead of neutrality, however, they left a vacuum. At first gradually and now at a blinding pace, that vacuum has been filled with new theories and escalating claims by those who see justice as an entrepreneurial activity."[334]

333 Deborah Ng, (2007, October). "Top Ten Frivolous Lawsuits." Retrieved March 16, 2013, from http://www.legalzoom.com/lawsuits-settlements/personal-injury/top-ten-frivolous-lawsuits

The missing link in American justice is that judges have lost sight of the idea that lawsuits concern not only the particular parties to the dispute, but everyone in society.

> The mere possibility of a lawsuit changes people's behavior. That's why judges must act as gatekeepers, deciding who can sue for what. Law is supposed to uphold social norms of right conduct. Oliver Wendell Holmes Jr. said that this was "the first requirement of a sound body of law." By making people potentially liable for their negligence, law provides incentives for reasonable conduct. But the converse is also true. Allow lawsuits against reasonable behavior, and pretty soon people no longer feel free to act reasonably. . . . All life's activities involve risk, and therefore the inevitability of accident and disagreement. The role of law is not to provide a consolation forum for those who have felt the misfortune of risk, but to support the freedom of all citizens to make reasonable choices, including taking reasonable risks. That requires judges, wherever someone makes a claim, to balance the seriousness of the risk against the social utility of the claim. Those rulings are the building blocks of our common law system, which, the English Law Lords recently reminded us, "is just the formal statement of the results and conclusions of the common sense of mankind."[335]

Judges need to take seriously the social aspects to their adjudicated cases. This is even more relevant with the recent increases in cases involving doctors and class-action suits.

Malpractice Insurance and Class-Action Suits

In the US, virtually every doctor practicing in a high-risk specialty will face at least one malpractice claim during his/her career. In addition, physicians in low-risk areas have a 75% chance of facing a suit. In a study published in the *New England Journal of Medicine* based on data from more than 40,000 US physicians enrolled in a large nationwide professional liability insurance company from 1991 through 2005, it was noted that roughly 7% of doctors insured by the company were the subject of a malpractice claim each year. However, less than 2% had a claim leading to payment. By the age of 45, more than a third of doctors in low-risk

---

334   Op cit, Legalreform-now.
335   Ibid.

specialties had already faced their first malpractice claim. The rate was 88% in high-risk specialties. By age 65, the rates were 75% and 99%, respectively.[336]

> Amitabh Chandra of the Harvard Kennedy School in Cambridge, Mass., who headed the study, said the results show that doctors are correct when they say they face a constant threat of lawsuits, but the findings also show that the direct cost tends to be lower than most think. What the threat of a suit does do, he told Reuters Health in a telephone interview, is "generate emotional and hassle costs for doctors. Given that these suits take a long time—a typical suit takes five years to resolve—you spend your life in litigation."[337]

Psychiatrists and pediatricians faced the lowest risk of a malpractice claims with rates at 2.6% and 3.1% per year, respectively. Brain and thoracic surgeons faced the highest rates at 19.1% and 18.9%, respectively. But the specialties where the largest proportion of physicians faced a claim were not necessarily those with the highest average payment size. For example, physicians in obstetrics and general surgery, fields regarded as high-risk, were substantially more likely to face a claim than pediatricians and pathologists, but the average payments among pediatricians and pathologists were considerably greater.[338]

> Chandra and colleagues note that fear of malpractice claims may drive a large number of doctors to practice "defensive medicine," which can involve ordering lots of tests that a patient may not need and that can lead to harms and excess costs.[339]

As a result of the increase in suits, doctors are leaving the field of medicine or are limiting the scope of procedures they perform due to the increasing malpractice insurance costs, forcing, for example, one in 10 obstetrician/gynecologists to stop delivering babies.[340] The increase in malpractice insurance premiums is related to the increase in claims

---

336 Gene Emery, (2011, August 17). "Many doctors face malpractice claims, but few pay." Retrieved March 16, 2013, from
http://www.reuters.com/article/2011/08/17/us-doctors-idUSTRE77G5YS20110817
337 Ibid.
338 Ibid.
339 Ibid.
340 Op cit, Legalreform-now.

costs (i.e., amounts paid), poor pricing decisions or cost projections by insurance companies and decreased investment income by insurance companies due to the low returns on their investments in the recent downturns.[341]

> Unlike auto insurance, malpractice premiums are mainly determined by the class of physician (including type of work) and geography, rather than by an individual's practice experience. Auto insurance premiums are adjusted according to the insured's driving record. This is difficult to accomplish with malpractice insurance because claims experience is too variable over short periods of time. . . .

> In theory, a tort system to resolve malpractice claims is supposed to serve as a negative incentive to physicians to practice high-quality medicine. But the 1999 Institute of Medicine report on the occurrence and ramifications of medical errors, *To Err is Human,* provided evidence that the malpractice system has failed to accomplish this goal.[342]

Medical malpractice coverage costs are expected to experience modest increases over the short term starting in late 2012. However, as the Baby Boom generation begins to retire and more medical care is needed, increases in malpractice claims are expected. It is very likely that a large increase in malpractice suits will lead to increases in insurance rates due to a larger number of procedures being performed by a much smaller number of doctors and other healthcare providers.[343]

One of the major arguments for a healthcare system overhaul in the US is the rising costs of healthcare services. The cost increases are more related to the legal system, than the healthcare system and the systemic legal issues causing these cost increases have not been addressed by the PPACA.

Along with the increase in malpractice suits is a related increase in the number of class-action suits. Class-action lawsuits were created to

341 Eric Henley, (2006, August). "Malpractice crisis Causes of escalating insurance premiums, and implications for you." Retrieved March 17, 2013, from http://www.jfponline.com/pages.asp?aid=4325
342 Ibid.
343 Matt Dunning, (2012, October 11). "Medical malpractice rates expected to rise as healthcare providers keep consolidating." Retrieved March 17, 2013, from http://www.modernhealthcare.com/article/20121011/INFO/310119992

grant access to compensation for individuals whose individual claims would not be sufficiently profitable to persuade a lawyer to take their case. The small claims are combined into one case and litigated as a group. However, with the passing of time has come an increasing financial incentive to bring class-action suits to court, as amassing hundreds or thousands of claims into a single proceeding can generate substantial fees.[344]

Class actions do serve to reduce the number of overall court cases, but with that have come abuses. "The abuses that have arisen in the US with mass and class actions have been largely driven by the potential payoff offered by contingency fee financing of suits in which the winning plaintiffs' lawyers are entitled to roughly a third or more of the award or settlement. The more plaintiffs a lawyer can recruit, the greater the potential payoff. Thus, class actions in the US are largely lawyer-driven exercises in which the idea to bring a suit comes not from an injured consumer or investor, but rather from an entrepreneurial lawyer who sees an opportunity for profit."[345]

In an article in the *World Financial Review* discussing the class-action debate for Europe, Lisa Rickard reports:

> The explosion of US class actions over the past four decades has imposed a substantial cost on American business. Not only are US companies forced to allocate billions of dollars to legal fees and litigation costs every year, but the overall litigation climate in the United States deters significant foreign investment in US businesses and impedes research and development in important product areas, such as medical technology and pharmaceuticals.
>
> US-style litigation imposes crippling costs on the national economy. It is no secret that the US litigation system has had a tremendous economic impact. A study by the research firm Tillinghast Towers-Perrin estimates that the tort litigation system in the US costs $252 billion annually, or $835 per every American. These costs amount to 1.83% of US GDP compared with 0.5% to 0.7% in other OECD countries. . . .

344 Lisa Rickard, (2014, December 11.). "The Class Action Debate in Europe: Lessons from the U.S. experience." *World Financial Review.*
345 Ibid.

Litigation run amok dulls America's competitive edge. Notwithstanding recent improvements, there is growing concern that tort litigation costs undermine America's ability to compete in the global economy. A recent paper issued by the US Department of Commerce describes the chilling effect that the US litigation culture has on foreign direct investment. In an examination of the specific areas of concern cited by foreign investors, class action lawsuits are listed as one of four categories (in addition to punitive damages, forum shopping and litigation culture) meriting further examination for their impact on investment.

A number of other recent studies provide confirmation of the Commerce Department's findings. A survey of Chief Executive Officers of non-US-based companies conducted by the Organization for International Investment found class action lawsuits to be the top concern with the US legal system among foreign investors. In the same vein, the McKinsey and Company Global Capital Markets Survey found securities class actions to be a major concern affecting the health of the US capital markets.[346]

In many cases, companies are forced to pay for lawsuits that lack merit. The more class members in a lawsuit, the greater the likelihood that defendants will settle rather than risking a huge judgment against them, regardless of whether the facts are on their side. In fact, most class-action lawsuits rarely go to a trial at all in the US, with less than 2% of federal cases and only 5% of state cases going to trial.[347]

Securities class-action cases have been particularly problematic. "Regardless of the number of securities suits filed, the amount companies spend to settle securities litigation continues to grow ever larger. The average settlement size has increased dramatically in recent years. The average settlement for the period 1996 to 2001 was $16.3 million, [this] skyrocketed to $54.7 million for the 2002–2007 period, and, in 2008, for the first time ever, each of the top ten settlements totaled over $1 billion."[348] No other country in the world permits settlements that approach the size and scale of those that occur under US law.

346 Ibid.
347 Ibid.
348 Ibid.

The "King of Class"

One individual who was nearly elected President of the US made a living off malpractice and product liability lawsuits. From a partisan online article associated with *Newsweek* in 2004 before the presidential election: "Boyish Wonder" John Edwards' life story began when he was born in the mill town of Seneca, South Carolina in 1953. He eventually went on to obtain his law degree from the University of North Carolina in 1977 after receiving his undergraduate degree in textiles from North Carolina State University in 1974.[349]

In 1984, seven years after graduating with his law degree, Edwards tried his first big personal injury case. He had worked as a clerk for a federal judge, worked briefly for a firm in Nashville and then joined Tharrington, Smith & Hargrove, a small firm in Raleigh, North Carolina. With only limited litigation experience, Edwards won his first big jury verdict. The plaintiff in the case was disabled as a result of what Edwards said was an overdose of a drug used in alcohol aversion therapy, and the jury eventually awarded the plaintiff $3.7 million.[350]

In the following years, Edwards handled all sorts of cases. He sued the American Red Cross three times, alleging that AIDS was transmitted through tainted blood products, and obtained a confidential settlement in each case. Then, in 1985, he took on a case representing a five-year-old with cerebral palsy whose mother was not given a Caesarean section upon birth.[351]

Edwards initially won $6.5 million for his client in this case but this was reduced to $4.25 million upon appeal. After the trial, Edwards gained national attention as a plaintiff's lawyer. He filed at least twenty similar lawsuits in the years following against doctors and hospitals and achieved verdicts and settlements of more than $60 million for his clients, typically keeping about a third. The impact of his work has led to countless similar cases, returning large awards, and doctors have responded by changing the way they deliver babies, often seeing a relatively minor anomaly on a fetal heart monitor as justification for an immediate Caesarean section delivery. Subsequently, there has been a

---

349 Evan Thomas, Susannah Meadows and Arian Campo-Flores, (2004, July 19). "The Boyish Wonder: Happy warrior: He was no superstar. But John Edwards's determination and ability to read the defense took him to the top." *Newsweek*.

350 Adam Liptak and Michael Moss, (2004, January 31). "THE 2004 CAMPAIGN: THE NORTH CAROLINA SENATOR; In Trial Work, Edwards Left A Trademark." *New York Times*.

351 Ibid.

debate over whether the increase in Caesarean sections has done more harm than good. Studies have shown that the electronic fetal monitors now widely used during delivery often incorrectly signal distress. This then leads to needless Caesarean deliveries, which carry the risks of major surgery. The rise in such deliveries, from 6% in 1970 to about 26% in 2004, has failed to decrease the rate of cerebral palsy. Studies have indicated that in most cases, the disorder is caused by fetal brain injury long before labor begins.[352]

The biggest losers in the cases litigated over brain-damaged babies were the parents of children whose cases were rejected because personal injury lawyers deemed them unlikely of winning or producing large rewards.[353]

Edwards was on a winning streak, and after two profitable decades in law, he decided to try his skills in politics. He started "with a bang" in 1998, successfully winning the North Carolina Senate seat as a Democrat. Edwards spent $6 million of his own money in his campaign. While serving his first term as Senator, Edwards decided to run for the presidency in 2004. He lost in the primaries to John Kerry, the eventual Democratic candidate, who then selected Edwards as his vice-presidential running mate.[354]

Edwards' campaign was disproportionately financed by lawyers and people associated with them, according to the Center for Responsive Politics, which calculated that about half of the $15 million he raised in the 2004 election came from lawyers.[355]

Trial lawyers are known for supporting Democratic candidates like Edwards. As conservative writer Phyllis Schlafly notes, "The trial lawyers plow their lawsuit winnings back into politics to prevent anyone from interfering with their game. Nearly three out of every four dollars that attorneys contribute to political campaigns are to Democrats."[356]

In spite of Edwards' fellow trial lawyers' support, Kerry and Edwards lost the 2004 election to incumbents George W. Bush and Dick Cheney.

Edwards' next major move was when he announced his candidacy for the 2008 Presidential election. In 2007 at about the same time as his announcement, Edward's wife Elizabeth announced that she again had

352 Ibid.
353 Ibid.
354 Op cit, Campo-Flores et al.
355 Op cit, Moss et al.
356 Phyllis Schlafly, (2004, July 21). "Problems With John Edwards." Retrieved May 21, 2013, from http://www.eagleforum.org/column/2004/july04/04-07-21.html

been diagnosed with cancer.[357] This news and rumors about an affair did not help Edwards as he ended up third in the Democratic primaries behind Barack Obama and Hillary Clinton.

Edwards may not be the best example of a US malpractice, product liability or class-action suit lawyer in that he probably exhibits *more* integrity than the typical attorneys in these professions.

Clearly, something must be done about a legal system that encourages suits against companies and individuals for millions and even billions of dollars for accidental injuries, but adds no social value. A possible solution is a system that negates tort liabilities and punitive damages while focusing on the care and rehabilitation of those injured. Such a system is in place in the Asia Pacific country of New Zealand.

Origins of the Kiwi Disability System

New Zealand is not only known for its great national rugby team—the "All Blacks," but it is also known for its unique disability system, the Accident Compensation Corporation, the "ACC." New Zealand was one of the first countries to provide compensation for work injuries and was also one of the first to recognize the social and financial consequences of accidents involving uninsured motorists. "In 1900 New Zealand followed the example set by Bismarck in Germany 12 years earlier, and introduced a 'no fault' workers' compensation system. The Workers' Compensation Act lasted (with some changes) until 1974, and provided injured workers with weekly benefits and, in case of death, compensation for dependents."[358]

The New Zealand Workers' Compensation Act required that employers have insurance to cover themselves for injuries to employees. "Benefits provided by the Act were small and could only be paid for six years from the date of injury. Injured workers also had the right to sue an employer for negligence. The Act did not cover non-work injury, or motor vehicle injury."[359]

357 CQ Transcriptions, (2007, March 27). "Former Sen. Edwards Holds a News Conference on Wife's Health." Retrieved May 21, 2013, from
     http://www.washingtonpost.com/wp-dyn/content/article/2007/03/22/AR2007032201422.html
358 Accident Compensation Corporation, (n.d.). "History of ACC in New Zealand." Retrieved August 15, 2014, from
     http://www.acc.co.nz/about-acc/overview-of-acc/introduction-to-acc/ABA00004
359 Ibid.

In 1967, a Royal Commission was established to report on workers' compensation in New Zealand in response to complaints about the inadequacy of benefits. In a report from this commission, Sir Owen Woodhouse made the following statement: "Injury arising from accident demands an attack on three fronts. The most important is obviously prevention. Next in importance is the obligation to rehabilitate the injured. Thirdly, there is the duty to compensate them for their losses."[360]

The report, named after its chairman Mr. Justice Woodhouse (now the Right Honorable Sir Owen Woodhouse), recommended a completely new "no-fault" approach to compensation for personal injury. "It recommended the scheme to cover all motor vehicle injuries, funded by a levy on owners of motor vehicles and drivers, [as well as] all injuries to earners whether occurring at work or not, funded by a flat-rate levy on employers for the cost of all injuries to their employees. A levy on the self-employed to pay for injuries occurring at work or outside of work was also proposed. Employers would have to pay a compulsory levy for injuries to employees, but they would also be protected from being sued for damages. The right to sue for motor vehicle injuries and non-worker injuries to earners would also be removed."[361]

In 1972, the New Zealand Parliament voted unanimously to pass the Accident Compensation Act into law. The act covered injuries to income earners (both work and non-work injuries) and motor vehicle injuries. In 1973, an amendment providing cover for those not already covered by the 1972 act (including students, non-earners and visitors to New Zealand) was passed. Three schemes were established under the 1973 act. One, the earners' scheme, covered injuries to income earners and was funded from levies paid by employers on wages paid to employees, and paid by self-employed people. The second was the motor vehicle accident scheme, funded by levies paid by owners of motor vehicles, and the third, the supplementary scheme, covered those not in the other schemes. The government funded this third scheme.[362]

ACC benefits included:
- hospital and medical expenses;
- rehabilitation costs;
- associated transport costs;

360 Ibid.
361 Ibid.
362 Ibid.

- earnings-related compensation (payable from the seventh day after the accident at a rate of 80% of average weekly earnings before the accident);
- lump sum payments for permanent loss or impairment;
- lump sum payments (up to a maximum of $10,000 [US$8,000]) for pain and mental suffering; and
- funeral costs and lump sum payments to surviving spouses and children in cases of accidental death.[363]

The accident compensation scheme came into operation on April 1, 1974 under the administration of the (then) Accident Compensation Commission, (ACC) but by 1979, there was growing dissatisfaction with the overall cost of the scheme and employers had become increasingly vocal about paying non-work claims. The New Zealand government established a committee to review the ACC, and as a result, substantial changes were made to the Accident Compensation Act in 1982. The changes made included: reducing employers' obligations for providing weekly compensation from 100% to 80% for the first week following a work accident; joining the three schemes into a single one (which continued to be funded from the three levy sources); moving work-related motor vehicle accidents from the earners' account to the motor vehicle accident account and increasing the maximum amount payable for permanent loss or impairment from NZD$7,000 to $17,000 [US$5,600 to $13,600] (maximum payable for pain and suffering remained at NZD $10,000 [US$8,000]).[364]

In 1989 the ACC scheme was to be extended to cover those incapacitated by sickness or disease. With the 1992 Accident Rehabilitation and Compensation Insurance Act, the following major changes were implemented: employees paid for non-work injuries (instead of employers) through a premium collected by Inland Revenue; entitlements, eligibility and rates were specified in regulations; the calculation of weekly compensation was prescribed; lump sum entitlements were replaced by independence allowances and experience-rating discounts and loadings were introduced for employers. (As noted above, by experience-rating employers, the incentive to employers was to minimize the number of accidents and related claims reported by their entities.)[365]

363 Ibid.
364 Ibid.

In early 2000, the accredited employer scheme (ACC Partnership Program) was enacted. Employers who joined the program took responsibility for managing their employees' work-related injuries, and were given financial incentives to create safer work environments. Greater flexibility was also provided for determining self-employed premiums.[366]

The Kiwi ACC Scheme

Since 1974, New Zealand's ACC is the only scheme in the world that provides universal, 24-hour coverage for all accidental physical injuries. The ACC also covers mental injury under certain circumstances. The ACC was groundbreaking at its inception and is still today highly regarded by many experts in the field of accident compensation.[367]

In New Zealand, "ACC" is commonly used to refer both to the government organization (the Accident Compensation Corporation) which implements and delivers the scheme and the overall scheme itself, including the system of coverage, benefits and services available for all injured people in New Zealand. ACC can be characterized as a universal coverage, no-fault scheme, paying periodic income benefits for earners and some lump sum benefits for survivors. ACC has a comprehensive case management system for a range of benefits and treatments and rehabilitation services, currently underwritten and managed by a government monopoly corporation. According to "Big 4" accounting firm PricewaterhouseCoopers (PWC), "in a number of ways, ACC can be considered to be 'best practice' when compared to international schemes."[368]

The ACC currently is regulated by the Injury Prevention, Rehabilitation, and Compensation Act 2001. "The vast majority of ACC claims are for treatment only, but approximately 150,000 New Zealanders receive additional benefits for their injuries, typically including some level of weekly income benefits and often including rehabilitation services."[369]

---

365   Ibid.
366   Ibid.
367   Daniel Tess, (2008). *Accident Compensation Corporation New Zealand.* Sydney: PriceWaterhouseCoopers, p. i.
368   Ibid, p. ii.
369   Ibid, p. ii.

New Zealand has a population of 4.3 million, around 20% of whom currently suffer some level of disability, with approximately 20% of these incapacitated due to injury (4% of the total population). In fiscal year 2006/2007, 1.6 million injury claims were filed with the ACC, mostly for reimbursement of treatment costs. About 150,000 claimants received additional benefits for their injuries, typically including some level of weekly income benefits and often including rehabilitation services. New Zealand averaged around 500,000 hospital admissions due to injury per year over the period of 2000–2004. "Overall injury rates have been steadily declining in New Zealand as elsewhere in the OECD, although New Zealand reported injury levels remain comparatively high. Injuries are expensive to society, and it has been estimated that the social and economic cost of injuries in New Zealand is approximately NZD$6–$7 billion [US$4.8–5.6 billion] each year."[370]

Universal coverage on a no-fault basis is the most important feature of the ACC scheme, with the corresponding removal of tort law as a mechanism for compensating accidental injury.[371] From a review by PWC, international literature shows that no-fault systems are associated with the following outcomes:

- More injured people (70–95%) receive compensation.
- A higher portion of total costs (up to 90% in some schemes) goes directly to claimants' benefits, compared to perhaps only 50% in liability systems.
- Benefits are paid more quickly than in tort systems. The average settlement completion in the US tort system is 15 to 20 months, whereas benefits flow in three weeks on average in an uncontested workers' compensation claim and four months in contested claims.
- Claimant outcomes appear better than under periodic no-fault systems. A study by PWC for WorkCover NSW (a blended system in Australia) followed the outcomes for over 1,000 claimants receiving compensation under alternative compensation pathways. After standardization for known variables, Common Law and Commutations claimants were found to have poorer health outcomes and worse return-to-work rates than those receiving no-fault weekly benefits.[372]

370 Ibid, p. iii.
371 Ibid, p. vi.
372 Ibid, p. vi.

PWC also noted that no-fault systems are widely believed to facilitate more open communication and disclosure of treatment incidents, which can improve patient safety in the long run.[373]

Based on PWC's research, blended systems which allow access to tort law which are the norm in Australian workers' compensation schemes can be costly. "Evidence indicates that access to common law benefits, even where significantly limited in nature, has been one of the primary drivers of cost blow-outs in workers' compensation schemes in Australia."[374] If countries are to implement an ACC scheme similar to New Zealand's, it's cost effective not to include the access to tort laws which blended schemes offer.

ACC Compared with US, Canada and Australia

PWC compared the current ACC system in New Zealand with the typical situations in Canada, the US and Australia. Their study summarized the key economic and social benefits of the ACC scheme:

Economic values

- An increased pool of labor available, with the additional employment offering a boost to consumption spending as well as improved social outcomes.
- Potentially higher—although unquantifiable—levels of labor productivity due to improvements in the ability of injured persons to work, and higher workforce morale associated with a reduction of fear [of injuries due to accidents], improved care and higher perceptions of fairness.
- Reduced long-term spending on healthcare and other government services due to improved injury management.
- Legal cost savings, resulting in increased consumption spending and the generation of higher levels of economic activity in consumption-based activities. This includes the savings in legal fees in respect of unsuccessful claims and other claimant outlays.
- Increased participation in sport and other physical activities. (Due to the lack of fear of damaging disability claims.)

---

373 Ibid, p. vi.
374 Ibid, p. vi.

- Increased tourism activity related to New Zealand's ability to provide activities such as adventure sports, which are less developed in other countries due to the costs of liability insurance. At roughly 9% of total GDP, tourism accounts for NZD$19 billion [US$15 billion] in direct value and around NZD$6 billion [US$4.8 billion] in indirect value to the New Zealand economy.

Social values
- Lower rates of poverty by overcoming a key source of marginalization and enhancing the income earning potential of lower socio-economic groups who are least able to afford private insurance coverage or litigation.
- Improved quality of life for injured persons and their carers, families, and friends, as a result of improved injury management.[375]

PWC also noted that far more people are covered under the ACC scheme than would be the case with a disability program like that in the US, Australia or Canada. Over half (56%) of the current "other benefits" claimants in the ACC scheme would not receive any compensation or social security support, except for medical treatment, and would need to meet a significant portion of the cost of their injury through their own resources in these other scenarios.[376]

PWC also noted that interviewees expressed strong support for the ACC scheme and its major proposition: entitlement to 24-hour, comprehensive no-fault benefits in exchange for the loss of the right to sue for damages suffered from personal injury.[377]

ACC Compared with Other International Schemes

PWC compared the ACC with other international schemes. "Given the key identifying features of the ACC scheme—pure no-fault, universal 24-hour coverage of all accidental physical injuries, broad benefits, coordinated case management and a focus on claimant outcomes— there are only a limited number of similar schemes with which to

375   Ibid, p. ix–x.
376   Ibid, p. x.
377   Ibid, p. x.

compare. However, by any reasonable measure, ACC performs well when compared with these and other schemes."[378]

The ACC scheme offers broader coverage than every other scheme around the world due to coverage of all injuries and ACC's no-fault nature. "There are only a few countries in Scandinavia which provide no-fault coverage for treatment injury, a concept which was pioneered by Sweden. In relation to public and home environment injuries, no other comprehensive schemes exist, though a number of European countries provide stronger social welfare schemes to provide income and rehabilitation assistance. Perhaps the only system with conceptually wider coverage than ACC is the Netherlands workers' compensation scheme, which provides to workers (only) coverage for all incapacity including illness and sickness."[379]

The New Zealand ACC offers a more holistic approach to disability through a range of benefits covering income-replacement, impairment benefits, treatment costs, rehabilitation costs and death benefits. Case management is coordinated across all claimant benefits and services in pursuit of the best overall outcome for claimants in terms of participation and independence. Other systems around the world are typically more fragmented. These systems separate management and delivery of income benefits, treatment services and vocational and social rehabilitation where the New Zealand ACC does not.[380]

The ACC offers income-replacement benefits of pre-injury earnings of 80%, which is in line with or above many other schemes. Also, compared with other workers' compensation systems, ACC performs well in terms of return-to-work. "The clearest comparative evidence is for workers' compensation schemes across Australia, where the ACC (88% of claimants returned to work within six months) outperforms both the Australian average (85%) and all three comparable schemes (the state-monopoly schemes of NSW 86%, Victoria 85% and South Australia 77%) with similar results for durable (longer-term) return to work."[381]

The ACC is also less expensive than other schemes. "The ACC employer contribution rate as a proportion of wages is substantially lower (0.78% at June 2007) than in comparable Australian workers'

378 Ibid, p. x.
379 Ibid, p. xi.
380 Ibid, p. xi.
381 Ibid, p. xii.

compensation schemes (NSW 1.86%, Victoria 1.38%, Australian average 2%). The overall cost of ACC is quite low even after adjustment for coverage (e.g., common law access) and other known differences, and is also low relative to other international systems (Canadian average 2%)."[382]

The ACC has lower claims administration expenses (8% of total expenditure) than of all the Australian schemes measured (9% to 32%), and lower total administration expenses (24% of total expenditure) than of the schemes providing comparable benefits (NSW 28%, Victoria 31%).[383] "When one considers that, in addition to these administrative expenses, most Australian schemes also pay significant legal costs for common law claims, it is clear that ACC is paying a relatively high portion of total premiums directly to claimant benefits."[384]

Overall, the New Zealand ACC is one of the best, if not the best, government-run disability program in the world. The injured are taken better care of, a greater percent of costs is spent on the injured, and the overall costs of the program are less than those of other government-run disability programs. In addition, the legal cost savings with respect to unsuccessful claims and other claimant outlays due to the no-fault principle in the ACC result in increased consumption spending and the generation of higher levels of economic activity, which then ultimately benefit the New Zealand economy.

Disability Summary

Implementing a disability system in the US like that in New Zealand would result in many positive changes. Few patients in the US with injuries due to negligence file claims because of the difficulty in obtaining an attorney to represent them, and also the rigorousness of the litigation process.[385]

> Many meritorious cases do not result in compensation to the patient, while many non-meritorious cases do lead to settlements or jury

---

382 Ibid, p. xii.
383 Ibid, p. xiii.
384 Ibid, p. xiii.
385 Michelle M Mello, Allen Kachalia and David Studdert (2011, July). "Administrative Compensation for Medical Injuries: Lessons from Three Foreign Systems." Retrieved March 22, 2013, from http://www.commonwealthfund.org/~/media/Files/Publications/ /Issue%20Brief/2011/Jul/1517_Mello_admin_compensation_med_injuries.pdf

awards. The amounts awarded are highly variable across similar injuries, inadequate in some cases and excessive in others. The highly adversarial litigation process destroys physician-patient relationships and involves considerable emotional strain for both plaintiffs and defendants. Fear of litigation chills open discussion about medical errors, resulting in missed opportunities for learning and patient safety improvement, and leads physicians to order extra tests, referrals, and other services primarily for the purpose of reducing their liability exposure. Such defensive medicine, together with the high cost of malpractice insurance premiums that increases providers' overhead costs and the prices they charge, contributes to the upward growth of healthcare expenditures. It is estimated that defensive medicine alone accounts for more than $45 billion in healthcare spending in the United States annually.[386]

The ACC system in New Zealand is easy for patients to navigate. The focus is on the patients and the care they receive, not the attorneys and the income they can create. The ACC system, funded through general taxation and an employer levy, is remarkably affordable. The time to resolve claims takes weeks in New Zealand versus years in the US. The administration costs in New Zealand are low (under 10%) when compared to the US (just under 50%). Physician indemnity insurance costs in the US are astronomical and growing and very low in New Zealand.[387] The advantages to the ACC system over that of the US disability programs go on and on.

Any parents with children growing up in the 1980s in the US can tell you about going to McDonalds with their children for lunch or dinner and buying their little ones "Happy Meals" and going to the McDonald's playground. This was a safe and fun place to go for the whole family while enjoying an inexpensive dinner outside the home.

The McDonalds playgrounds are now gone. The threat of accidents have made it necessary for McDonalds to shut them down in order to protect itself from lawsuits. Instances like this can be found throughout the US. Granted some dangerous or unsafe behaviors or circumstances

---

386 Ibid.
387 Marie Bismark and Ron Paterson, (2006, February). "No-Fault Compensation in New Zealand: Harmonizing Injury Compensation, Provider Accountability, and Patient Safety," *Health Affairs,* January/February 2006 25(1):278?83

have been corrected in the US over time, but the pendulum has swung too far.

Behavior in the US has changed, and not for the better, as a result of the fear of being sued. Americans were once willing to help others when accidents occurred. In emergencies when someone was injured, strangers would immediately jump in and help. This is not the case now. People are afraid of helping the injured after hearing stories of "Good Samaritans" being sued as a result of their actions in emergencies.

In the US, there is now an attitude that having an accident is like winning the lottery. There were reports of individuals driving their cars in front of semi-trucks and hitting their brakes, knowing that if they survived, the trucking firm would pay millions to the "victim." The rewards negotiated through accident settlements have made individuals multi-millionaires.

In New Zealand, the ACC program is built around taking care of the injured. The awards for disabilities allow the disabled to maintain their lifestyle that existed before the disability, but do not make them millionaires. The focus of the ACC program is on recovery, assisting the disabled and getting them back to work, not on finding blame and seeking large settlements. The overall costs to society are much lower, and people and doctors are allowed to perform their professions while not worrying about being sued for performing their job or for helping others. The ACC program is one that answers the prayers of the disabled while eliminating the unethical actions of attorneys who prey on them.

CHAPTER 6

"Taxifornia" and the Hong Kong Tax Regimes

There are many reasons that Hong Kong was again named the world's top financial center, but one of the predominant reasons is its favorable tax regime. Policymakers in the US, and in particular California, have decided to raise taxes in an attempt to pay for their government spending. The result of high US taxation is sputtering US economic growth and stalling capital markets, while Hong Kong is thriving.

Tax Overview

Taxes have long been an issue for the people who pay them. American founding father Benjamin Franklin wrote: "In this world nothing can be said to be certain, except death and taxes."[388] About 200 years later in the 1900s, American humorist Will Rogers said, "The only difference between death and taxes is that death doesn't get worse every time Congress meets." The challenge for all governments is creating and maintaining a tax regime that produces enough revenues to cover government expenses while encouraging and not *inhibiting* economic growth.

Taxes are as old as are societies. Traditionally, taxes were collected to support defense and protect the community. Taxes were also required to build the infrastructure needed for economic progress and to pay the government workers who made this happen. In the last century, governments needed additional funding for social programs and public investments that provide for health, education and other amenities. All these programs require funding.[389]

Now more than ever, governments are challenged with determining the right mix of fiscal spending versus tax revenues. If revenues are less than expenses, deficit spending occurs. Deficits over a long period of

---

388 Benjamin Franklin (1789), Letter to Jean-Baptiste Leroy.
389 John Preston, Andrew Packman, Neville Howlett, Augusto Lopez Claros, Sylvia Solf and Tea Trumbic, (2012). *Paying Taxes 2012—The Global Picture*. London: PricewaterhouseCoopers, p. 5.

time can cripple a government, and we are seeing this today in both Europe and in the US.

A recent report by the World Bank and accounting firm PricewaterhouseCoopers (PWC) regarding corporate tax policies noted the current fiscal challenges to governments. "Over the past three years the world has experienced an extraordinary financial and economic upheaval. The financial turmoil continues to reshape the economic landscape and to present difficult choices for governments in terms of public spending and fiscal policy. Severe damage has been caused to the public finances in many economies and difficult measures are being taken to repair them. In an increasingly global economy, business investment, capital innovation and skilled people will quickly flow to countries where tax systems encourage and offer the prospect of economic growth."[390]

The rate of taxation and the complexity of administering the system are important. "All governments need revenue, but the challenge is to carefully choose not only the level of tax rates but also the tax base. Governments also need to design a tax compliance system that will not discourage taxpayers from participating."[391]

The total tax cost for a business will impact the decision to locate as it matters for a company's investment and growth. When taxes are high, individuals and businesses are more inclined to opt out of the formal sector. When looking at multinational firms' decisions on where to invest, research suggests that a 1% increase in the statutory corporate income tax rate would reduce the local profits from existing investment by 1.3% on average. Along with this, a 1% increase in the effective corporate income tax rate reduces the likelihood of a multinational firm establishing a subsidiary in an economy by 2.9%.[392]

Taxes on profits are only part of the total tax burden, less than 36% of a company's total tax on average. Businesses pay not only corporate taxes on profits, but also employment taxes, social contributions, indirect taxes, property taxes and a whole variety of smaller levies including environmental taxes.[393]

Both businesses and individuals care about what they receive for their taxes. Both are interested in a sound and extensive infrastructure. Good

390 Ibid, p. 1.
391 Ibid, p. 11.
392 Ibid, p. 12.
393 Ibid, p. 5&12.

healthcare is important because a healthy population supports a healthy workforce, which is vital to a country's competitiveness and productivity. Education increases the efficiency of the workforce, and ultimately, more educated workers produce more complex (and profitable) products and services.[394]

Taxpayers want their taxes to be used in the most efficient manner. Taxpayers want the entity that is taxing them to be around in the long term to protect their investment. They also want their tax payments to be fair, based on a set of common parameters, and not to pay more than others in similar economic situations. They want clear and transparent taxation systems that are not cumbersome or difficult to deal with.

> Efficient tax administration can help encourage businesses to become formally registered and the economy to grow—and thus expand the tax base and increase tax revenues. Administration that is unfair and capricious will bring the tax system into disrepute and weaken the legitimacy of government. In many transition economies in the 1990s, failure to improve tax administration when new tax systems were introduced resulted in very uneven imposition of taxes, widespread tax evasion and lower-than-expected revenue.[395]

Individuals as well as businesses want clear rules and regulations regarding tax payments. They want a payment scheme which is easy to comply with and which incurs little work on their part. They also want a tax regime that is transparent and fair.

> Compliance with tax laws is important to keep the system working for all and to support the programs and services that improve lives. One way to encourage compliance is to keep the rules as clear and simple as possible. Overly complicated tax systems are associated with high evasion. High tax compliance costs are associated with larger informal sectors, more corruption and less investment. Economies with simple, well-designed tax systems are able to help the growth of businesses and, ultimately, the growth of overall investment and employment.[396]

---

394 Ibid, p. 12.
395 Ibid, p. 13.
396 Ibid, p. 14.

It is important to keep the tax administration process simple. This is still true some 235 years after Adam Smith proclaimed simplicity to be one of the pillars of the effective tax system. The higher the number of tax payments for a company or individual, the greater the cost of doing business and the more inconvenience for both companies and individuals. The different forms that have to be filled out require different methods for calculating tax, a complex and frustrating process. This also increases the tax administration costs for authorities as well.[397]

Around the world, no matter where individuals live or where they do business, individuals and companies alike seek low tax rates. Tax administration is almost as important. Both individuals and companies want to deal with tax regimes that are low cost, simple and easy to comply with.

US Tax Oversight, Compliance and Abuse

The US tax regime is fraught with many challenges. For one, the system itself is massive. The US federal government was expected to bring in $2.6 trillion in revenues in fiscal year 2012. Revenues from income taxes were expected to bring in around $1.5 trillion, including more than $1.1 trillion from individual income taxes and more than $0.3 trillion from corporate income taxes. Social security taxes were expected to bring in $0.9 trillion in revenues. Excise taxes, transportation taxes and other taxes were expected to bring in $0.2 trillion in revenues.[398] (As noted already, these revenues are more than $1 trillion *less* than the amount of spending by the federal government for the same period, putting the US deeper in the hole.)

The agency that oversees the US federal tax system is the Internal Revenue Service (IRS). The roots of the IRS go back to the American Civil War in 1862 when an office of Commissioner of Internal Revenue was created to assist with costs incurred during the war. However, it was not until 1913 with the ratification of the sixteenth amendment to the US Constitution that Congress was given the power to enact an income tax. The agency set up under the Department of Treasury as the revenue service is the IRS.[399]

---

397 Ibid, p. 19.
398 Op cit, Chantrill.
399 IRS. (n.d.). "Brief History of IRS." Retrieved May 19, 2013, from
      http://www.irs.gov/uac/Brief-History-of-IRS

The IRS has grown since 1913. For the tax year ending in 2011, the IRS employed more than 94,000 people to conduct its business, ranking it as one of the largest employers in the US. The IRS operating budget was at its highest ever, at more than $12.3 billion, and it collected more than $2.4 trillion in revenues. It has offices located throughout the US and half of its personnel were involved in examinations and collections, with the remaining involved in filing, account services, information services, investigations and other activities.[400]

In addition to the already massive size of the IRS, with the advent of the PPACA, up to 16,500 new IRS agents are in the process of being hired. Some of the new positions will include criminal investigators to go after Obamacare tax evaders.[401]

The PPACA contains eighteen separate tax increases, which President Obama's administration has not been clear in communicating to the American public.[402]

The tax increases will add to the legendary annual headache Americans suffer when paying their taxes. The law will require more time to address more complicated tax returns and force individuals and entities to reveal additional tax information to the IRS, provide proof of government-approved healthcare and submit detailed sales information to comply with new excise taxes, thereby paving the way for future tax legislation and tax increases.[403]

> Characterizing Obamacare as a tax under the purview of the IRS is not a mistake. The near mythical authoritarian power of the IRS will be used to make sure Americans do not challenge Obamacare and unquestioningly submit to its unprecedented intrusion. . . . According to the noted polling service Rasmussen Reports, 43% of Americans fear the IRS more than the TSA. Only 20% feared the TSA more.[404] [The Transportation Security Administration (TSA) oversees security at airports.]

The reason for the fear of the IRS is because of its known or perceived abuses of taxpayers. In early 2013, for example, it was reported that the

400 Department of the Treasury, I. R. (2012). *Internal Revenue Service Data Book 2011 Publication 55B.* Washington, D.C.: Internal Revenue Service, pp. 66–67.
401 Op cit, Nimmo.
402 Op cit, Dubay.
403 Op cit, Nimmo.
404 Ibid.

IRS had targeted conservative nonprofit groups with a campaign of audits and harassment starting before the 2012 election. The IRS did not reveal that it had wrongly targeted conservative groups until after the 2012 presidential election.[405] These groups were critical of the Obama administration and subsequently were scrutinized in IRS audits and challenged when attempting to obtain certain required taxpayer status.

One news anchor in St Louis, Larry Conners, wrote on his Facebook page in May of 2013 that shortly after he interviewed President Obama and his wife in April of 2012, the IRS "started hammering" him. (In the interview, Conners asked more challenging questions of the president than he was used to.) "At the time, I dismissed the 'co-incidence', but now, I have concerns . . . after revelations about the IRS targeting various groups and their members," Conners wrote.[406]

Another example of recent IRS abuse relates to Republican presidential candidate Mitt Romney's former national campaign finance co-chair, Frank VanderSloot. This Wyoming businessman was tormented with two audits, one by the IRS and one by the Department of Labor. After being vilified as one of eight Romney backers described as "wealthy individuals with less-than-reputable records" in a post on the Obama campaign's website, he was notified of these audits.[407]

Sarah Hall Ingram was the IRS executive in charge of the tax-exempt division in 2010 when it began targeting conservative, evangelical and pro-Israel groups for harassment. It was reported that she got more than $100,000 in bonuses between 2009 and 2012. She has been recently promoted to a position that puts her in charge of the vast expansion of the IRS' regulatory power and staffing in connection with Obamacare.[408]

405 Daniel Halper, (2013, May 17). "Report: IRS Deliberately Chose Not to Fess Up to Scandal Before Election." Retrieved May 19, 2013, from http://www.weeklystandard.com/blogs/ /report-irs-deliberately-chose-not-fess-scandal-election_724711.html
406 KMOX. (2013, May 17). "KMOV's Conners Barred From Facebook, Interviews on IRS Controversy." Retrieved May 19, 2013, from http://stlouis.cbslocal.com/2013/05/17/ /kmovs-conners-barred-from-facebook-interviews-on-irs-controversy/
407 Jamie Weinstein, (2013, May 13). "FLASHBACK: Romney donor vilified by Obama campaign, then subjected to 2 audits." Retrieved May 19, 2013, from http://dailycaller.com/2013/05/13/ /flashback-romney-donor-vilified-by-obama-campaign-then-subjected-to-2-audits
408 Mark Tapscott, (2013, May 16). "IRS tax exemption/Obamacare exec got $103,390 in bonuses; Did Obama OK them?" Retrieved May 19, 2013, from Washington Examiner, http://washingtonexaminer.com/ /irs-tax-exemptionobamacare-exec-got-100390-in-bonuses/article/2529899

President Obama is not the first US President to be tied to abuses involving the IRS. In 1937, Democratic President Franklin Roosevelt launched a tax anti-avoidance campaign. Treasury Secretary Henry Morgenthau produced a memo which identified CEOs who were accused of tax avoidance through different schemes. The individuals identified included Amoco founder Louis Blaustein, Merrill Lynch patriarchs Charles E. Merrill and Edwin C. Lynch, electrical pioneer George Westinghouse Jr., General Motors President Alfred P. Sloan, as well as chemical titan Alfred I. du Pont, US Steel chief Myron C. Taylor, San Francisco banker William H. Crocker, and numerous others. Many of these individuals were also prominent Republicans. In reaction to the memo, Roosevelt encouraged Congress to investigate. The Democratic Congress at the time established a Special Joint Committee on Tax Evasion and Avoidance, and in a series of lurid hearings, the names came out.[409]

> Republican lawmaker Hamilton Fish, who represented Roosevelt's own district in Hyde Park, N.Y., asked to testify before the investigating committee. Fish, an ardent conservative and leading New Deal critic, accused Roosevelt of rank hypocrisy. The president was himself guilty of tax avoidance, Fish declared. And for that matter, so were his wife, sons, and Treasury secretary. The tax avoidance investigation, Fish argued, had deliberately targeted prominent Republicans.[410]

> . . . In his central charge that Roosevelt was guilty of hypocrisy, Fish was right. The president's tax returns did reveal a certain amount of tax avoidance. He had done nothing illegal, or even questionable. But using the president's own standard of tax justice—which demanded that taxpayers pay what they should owe, rather than what they did owe—the president was guilty as charged.[411]

Taxpayers are permitted to avoid taxes within the parameters of the law. However, the IRS has had constant challenges collecting revenues from individuals or companies who should have paid, but did not, or who underpaid. In fiscal year 2011 alone, the IRS assessed more than

409 Joseph J. Thorndike, (2009, April 30). "Tax History Project—Who You Callin' a Tax Cheat?" Retrieved December 30, 2012, from http://taxhistory.tax.org/thp/ /readings.nsf/ArtWeb/A03CE0C836330991852575B400689747?OpenDocument
410 Ibid.
411 Ibid.

$30 billion in civil penalties on more than 38 million cases. The penalties were related to such items as inaccuracy, bad checks and delinquencies, but more than half of the penalties were related to failure to pay.[412]

The IRS can pressure overdue taxpayers by placing a lien on an individual's property. A tax lien can stay on a taxpayer's record for seven years and negatively impact their credit rating and their ability to get back on their feet. The number of tax liens filed by the IRS increased from 168,000 in 1999 to 1.1 million in the 2010 tax year. The dilemma is that there is no evidence to suggest that these liens increase the likelihood of the IRS collecting revenues.[413]

Ironically, there are billions of dollars owed the US government from government employees themselves. According to an IRS study in 2009, federal employees and retirees owed the government more than $3.2 billion in back taxes. The agency with the largest number of individuals with tax debts was the US Postal Service, whose employees owed more than $283 million. The list of agencies included military personnel and numerous other agencies, including the Department of Veterans Affairs as well as even some who worked in the White House.[414]

There are others who make a living off of the federal government who do not pay their taxes. In a 2013 report by the IRS inspector general there were nearly 700 employees of Internal Revenue Service contractors who owed $5.4 million in back taxes. Many of these individuals (more than 50%) are ineligible for work with the IRS because they are not enrolled in installment plans to pay the back taxes they owe. "Unlike other federal agencies, the IRS requires employees and those who work on agency contracts to comply with federal tax laws. That means they have to file returns on time and either pay all the taxes they owe or enroll in a payment plan."[415]

In addition to people who are supposed to pay taxes who do not, there are a number of US taxpayers who are not required to pay federal income tax due to their not earning a high enough income. As already noted, roughly half the US population is related to individuals who do

412 Op cit, Department of the Treasury, p. 42.
413 Tom Murse, (2011, January 13). "How IRS Abuses Tax Liens." Retrieved December 29, 2012, from http://usgovinfo.about.com/od/incometaxandtheirs/a/How-IRS-Abuses-Tax-Liens.htm
414 Eaman Javers, (2010, November 16). "Government Employees Owe Billions in Delinquent Taxes." Retrieved December 29, 2012, from http://www.cnbc.com/id/40215318//Government_Employees_Owe_Billions_in_Delinquent_Taxes
415 Stephen Ohlemacher, (2013, October 23). "700 IRS Contract Workers Owe $5.4M in Back Taxes." Retrieved November 30, 2013, from http://www.breitbart.com/Big-Government//2013/10/23/700-IRS-contract-workers-owe—54M-in-back-taxes

not pay federal income taxes, and who are not claimed as dependents by someone who does pay them. This percentage has jumped from 14.8% in 1984 to 49.5% in 2009. "This means that in 1984, 34.8 million tax filers paid no taxes; in 2009, 151.7 million paid nothing."[416]

Tax Complexity

Tax has long been an issue of contention in the US. The rich are berated for making more and more money and not paying their fair share of taxes. Others feel that the rich pay more than enough and that raising rates will only slow the economy. But governments need revenue, and the challenge is to carefully choose not only the level of tax rates but also the tax base, and to design a tax compliance system that will encourage participation.[417]

Complexity is also an issue. "Congress frequently holds hearings on tax simplification so members can denounce the tax code's complexity. Each time, congressional experts and outside think tanks provide useful simplification ideas. Then when the TV cameras are turned off, Congress promptly ignores them and votes for more special interest breaks."[418]

Tax law complexity can be estimated by the number of pages in the tax code and regulations. According to tax service provider CCH, the tax code has increased from 400 pages in 1913 to 73,608 by 2012,[419] and 15,000 changes have been added to the tax code since 1986 alone.[420]

With the advent of Obamacare, the number of pages added to the tax code will increase dramatically.

Saving for education, retirement, and other items should be as simple as putting money in the bank. "Instead, Congress has manufactured hundreds of special savings rules, such as for 401(k)s, Keoghs, deductible IRAs, nondeductible IRAs, education IRAs, Roth IRAs, traditional pension plans, annuities, SIMPLEs, SEPs, MSAs, and others. The IRS guide to IRAs alone is 105 pages long!"[421]

416 Op cit, Tyrrell et al, p. 1.
417 Op cit, Trumbic et al, p. 11.
418 Chris Edwards, (2003, April 15). "10 Outrageous Facts about the Income Tax." Retrieved December 30, 2012, from
     http://www.cato.org/publications/commentary/10-outrageous-facts-about-income-tax
419 Politicalcalculations.com, (2012, April 17). "How Many Pages are there in the US Tax Code Today." Retrieved December 30, 2012, from http://politicalcalculations.blogspot.com/ /2012/04/2012-how-many-pages-are-there-in-us-tax.html
420 CCHGroup.com, (2012). Retrieved December 30, 2012, from http://www.cchgroup.com
421 Op cit, Edwards.

Income taxes are so complex that there are more than a million individuals involved in the US tax industry. In 2003 alone, there were up to 1.2 million paid tax preparers in the US, which was more than six times the number of troops in Iraq at the time. "The tax army includes legions of accountants, lawyers, and computer experts—some of the best minds in the country. Unfortunately, their brainpower is adding little to the nation's standard of living."[422]

As tax law grows more complex, the number of IRS tax forms has increased as well. "Congress hands the accountants business on a silver platter when they create special interest tax forms such as '8845-Indian Employment Credit' and '8834-Qualified Electric Vehicle Credit.' When Congress penalizes an activity, we get tax forms such as '6197-Gas Guzzler Tax.' It's time to end the micromanaging and adopt a simple flat-rate tax. Until then, Congress needs to supplement '6478-Credit for Alcohol Used as Fuel' with form 'XXX-Credit for Alcohol Used for Drinking.'"[423]

The US Tax Burden

US taxes are imposed on the net income of individuals and corporations by the federal, most state and some local governments. Citizens and residents are taxed on worldwide income and the US is the only country in the world that taxes its nonresident citizens on worldwide income, in the same manner and rates as residents, no matter where they live and regardless of how long they have been overseas.[424]

In 2010, the Foreign Account Tax Compliance Act (FATCA) was passed to root out Americans evading taxes by requiring foreign financial institutions to annually report to the IRS on US citizens who hold more than $50,000 at the end of the year. Paying taxes on worldwide income and forcing banks to report on US citizens bank balances has led some US citizens living abroad to renounce their citizenship; a number that has increased from 742 in 2009 to more than 1,850 in 2013. "FATCA is a textbook example of a bad law that doesn't achieve its stated

---

422 Ibid.
423 Ibid.
424 Randall Brody, (2012, August 30). "Why does the US tax its citizens on worldwide income regardless of where they live?" Retrieved May 19, 2013, from http://www.taxplannercpa.com/WP/foreign-earned-income-exclusion/why-does-the-us-tax-its-citizens-on-worldwide-income-regardless-of-where-they-live/

purpose but does manage to unleash a host of unanticipated destructive consequences," said Senator Rand Paul of Kentucky.[425]

United States taxable income is determined under tax accounting rules and includes almost all income from whatever source. Individuals are permitted to reduce taxable income for certain nonbusiness expenses, including home mortgage interest, state and local taxes, real estate taxes, charitable contributions and certain other expenses incurred above certain percentages of income.

The US utilizes a graduated tax rate scale system in which federal tax rates increase from 10% to 35% as the income per individual increases. Proponents of a flat tax state that the current system is unfair because it disproportionately discriminates against high-income earners. A flat tax program is one where the same rate (e.g., 23%) is charged to all participants.

Opponents of a flat tax regime state that the rich should pay more because they have more. But this policy discourages individuals from doing their best because "the more you make, the more they take." This is more relevant now than ever with only 50% of the US population paying federal income taxes.

Proponents of the graduated tax rate scale scheme believe that the current policy is fair and is a good way of distributing income from the rich to the poor and middle class. Besides, they argue that the top tax rate in the US is much less than the top rate of other industrialized countries. This is true when you compare the top tax rate in the US (at 35%) to the rates of other European countries such as Sweden (56.6%), Denmark (55.4%), the Netherlands (55%), Austria (50%), Belgium (50%) and the United Kingdom (50%).[426]

However, Big 4 accounting firm KPMG, which puts together an annual survey comparing top individual income tax rates across countries, notes that a country's highest personal income tax rate is only *one* indicator of what taxes individuals pay on their income. Just as influential are the other taxes that apply to individuals as well as the income thresholds those rates are charged at.[427]

---

425 William Douglas, (2013, November 13). "New tax law driving expats to renounce US citizenship." Retrieved December 27, 2013, from http://www.mcclatchydc.com/2013/11/27/209810/new-tax-law-driving-expats-to.html

426 KPMG. (2012). *KPMG's Individual Income Tax and Social Security Rate Survey 2012.* Zurich: KPMG, p. 5.

427 Ibid, p. 5.

For example, consider the actual taxes for an individual in the state of California. The individual made a little more than $48,000 annually in gross pay. After subtracting federal withholding tax (i.e., US income tax), Medicare, Social Security, state withholding tax and state disability tax, along with the tax paid by the individual's employer, the individual was left with annual take-home net pay of a little more than $30,000. However, the individual also paid state sales tax on roughly 60% of his/her purchased goods, property tax of 1% annually on the appraised value of his/her home, and telephone, road and gas taxes. When accounting for these, the individual paid taxes amounting to 52% of his/her gross income or a little over $25,000. (This calculation did not include alcohol or tobacco taxes.)[428] Ultimately, the taxpayers in California are paying real taxes of more than 50% of their income, and this increases as individuals move up the tax rate ladder.

As noted above, PWC puts together an annual survey of corporate tax rates by country, including not only corporate taxes on profits, but also employment taxes, social contributions, indirect taxes, property taxes and smaller levies, including environmental taxes. Out of more than 170 economies researched and included in the World Bank/PWC's 2012 study of corporate and business taxes, the average total tax rate was 44.8% of profits. Although the highest income tax rate on companies in the US is 35%, the US has a reported total tax rate of 131%, well above the world average.[429] This means that *in the US, corporations are taxed at a rate of 131% of their after-tax income.*

Many US tax deductions have been labeled as unfair. "The front of the Supreme Court building boldly declares "Equal justice under law," yet the income tax has hundreds of discriminatory provisions. For example, homeowners are treated more favorably than renters since they can deduct mortgage interest and other itemized deductions. Consider that a higher-income homeowner can effectively deduct car loan interest by shifting around his finances, but a lower-income apartment dweller cannot. Americans would not stand for such discrimination on other taxes—imagine if each shopper at Wal-Mart was assigned a different sales tax rate!"[430]

---

428 "Calculating Real Tax Rates." (n.d.). Retrieved from
       http://libertyforlife.com/tax/calculating_real_tax_rates.htm
429 Op cit, Trumbic et al, pp. 15, 69 & 115.
430 Ibid.

In addition, there is a unique calculation in the tax code, the "alternative minimum tax" (AMT). "The AMT is an unneeded parallel tax system alongside the ordinary income tax. It began life in 1969 after Congress was shocked (shocked!) to learn that 155 wealthy individuals were not paying tax because they used too many of the deductions that Congress had provided them. The AMT has been a complex nuisance ever since."[431] The AMT is a complex calculation with factors that discount deductions, so high-income earners ultimately pay more tax. Though this scheme was originally aimed at the rich, it now impacts millions of taxpayers.

Increasing US Tax Rates

In 2012 there was a push to tax the rich more. President Obama proposed increasing the tax rate of the top federal income tax bracket to 42% on anyone with more than $250,000 in income from salaries, small-business income and dividends. If passed, many Americans will face a total state and local income tax rate greater than 50% on their income. This action would cause much of those people's wealth, which might otherwise go toward creating jobs, to move to unproductive tax shelters, thereby reducing the revenue available to the government.[432]

There is a belief in the US that the rich are paying less tax than they have in the past. However, this is not true. "In 2007, the richest 3% of Americans contributed a larger share of tax revenues than they have in any year since 1960. For more than half its income, the federal government relies on what it takes from just that 3%. Every year, the Treasury Department examines the distribution of federal taxes by income group. The data for all recent years yield the same conclusion: people at the top not only make a disproportionate contribution to the nation's wealth; they also pay a higher proportion of their collective income than those at the bottom."[433] This is the opposite of what some politicians, the media and the general public would have you believe.

Low rates might be beneficial for the private sector, but the government needs funding. The challenge is to fund government without shrinking the private economy. The optimal tax rate is the lowest

---

431 Ibid.
432 Stephen Moore, (2012, August). "The US Tax System: Who really Pays?" Retrieved December 30, 2012, from http://www.manhattan-institute.org/html/ir_22.htm
433 Ibid.

possible rate that will produce sufficient revenues to pay for government's services.

The side effect of excessive tax rates is an economic downturn or, in the worst case, a recession, such as the US suffered repeatedly throughout the 1930s. "The near-doubling of tax rates on the rich in the 1930s under [Presidents] Herbert Hoover and Franklin Roosevelt played an important role in extending the length of, and the suffering from, the Great Depression. In recessions, the rich do a little less well, but the poor suffer terribly. Recoveries, like the 25-year boom launched by Ronald Reagan's tax cuts, lift all boats—especially those of the people most vulnerable to economic ups and downs."[434]

In the early 1960s, the highest income tax rate was 91%, which was cut to 70% during the Kennedy administration. The rate remained at 70% until 1981 when President Reagan slashed the top tax rate to 50%, then to 28% in 1986. "Even though the tax rate fell by more than half, total tax receipts in the 1980s increased; from $517 billion in 1981 to $1,030 billion in 1990, reflecting strong growth of the economy."[435] The increase in revenues during the Reagan years is used by economists to justify reducing taxes in order to increase government revenues.

Taxes also appear to have become fairer to some politicians since the late 1970s because even as tax rates fell by half, the amount of taxes paid by the wealthy, and their percentage of total income taxes paid, increased vastly. By 2007, the top 5% of taxpayers paid a larger share of individual federal taxes than the bottom 95%—for the first time since the Great Depression.[436]

> Along with fairness came opportunity, growth, and jobs because the money freed up for consumption and investment had a multiplier effect. Lower tax rates affect every economic decision. Just as consumers might forgo a vacation if they do not expect a tax refund, investors will take fewer risks if they expect their profits to be taxed away. Indeed, lower tax rates encourage investing in America (rather than China), where investors and entrepreneurs will start or expand businesses and create jobs. High taxes, by contrast, nudge people toward safe, sleepy investments or offshore tax shelters.

434 Ibid.
435 Ibid.
436 Op cit, Moore.

When President Kennedy was promoting tax rate reductions in 1963, he stated that the best way to promote economic growth "is to reduce the burden on private income and the deterrents to private initiative which are imposed by our present tax system—and this administration is pledged to an across-the-board reduction in personal and corporate income tax rates."[437]

Even though the top income tax bracket in the US is 10% to 20% lower than in most other industrialized nations, the US government is more dependent on rich people for taxes than are many of the more socialized economies of Europe. "According to the Tax Foundation, the US gets 45% of its total federal taxes from the top 10% of tax filers, whereas the average for industrialized nations is 32%. America's well-off bear a larger share of the tax burden than do the rich in Belgium (25%), Germany (31%), France (28%) and Sweden (27%)."[438]

In 2007, the richest 1% of Americans made 22% of all earned national personal income but contributed 40% of all personal income-tax revenue. The top 10% contributed 71% of all personal income-tax revenue. However, the bottom 50% of Americans earned 12% but contributed just 3% to the tax revenues.[439]

By 2010, households in the top 20% by income in the US paid 93% of net income tax revenues taken in by the federal government, according to a study by the Congressional Budget Office. The second quintile paid 13% of the net income revenues, leading to the top 40% of households in the US paying 106% of the country's net income taxes. The third quintile paid another 3%—bringing the total share of net federal income tax revenues paid by the top 60% to 109%. The extra 9% of tax revenues went to the lower 40% of the tax base. Households in the bottom 40% took in an average of $18,950 in what the CBO called "government transfers" in 2010, which were amounts collected from unemployment, Medicaid, food stamps, Medicare and other government programs.[440]

---

437 Ibid.
438 Ibid.
439 Ibid.
440 Terence P. Jeffrey, (2013, December 9). "CBO: Top 40% Paid 106.2% of Income Taxes; Bottom 40% Paid -9.1%, Got Average of $18,950 in 'Transfers'." Retrieved December 10, 2013, from http://cnsnews.com/news/article/terence-p-jeffrey/ /cbotop-40-paid-1062-income-taxes-bottom-40-paid-91-got-average-18950

Taxifornia

Revenue collections are a big deal, as exemplified in the state of California. Throughout 2012, the California Controller's office reported materially less revenues than the prior year. The reason for the decline in tax collections was due to businesses and successful people leaving California for the lower tax rates available in more pro-business states in the US.[441]

California has earned the sobriquet "Taxifornia" due to it having the highest personal income taxes in the nation and higher sales tax rates than all but four other states. But this was before the 2012 elections, where they passed legislation calling for an additional tax increase. "Spectrum Locations Consultants recorded 254 California companies moved some or all of their work and jobs out of state in 2011, 26% more than in 2010 and five times as many as in 2009. According to SLC President, Joe Vranich, the top ten reasons companies are leaving California are: poor rankings in surveys, more adversarial toward business, uncontrollable public spending, unfriendly business climate, provable savings elsewhere, most expensive business locations, unfriendly legal environment for business, worst regulatory burden, severe tax treatment and unprecedented energy costs."[442]

> Vranich considers California the worst state in the nation to locate a business and Los Angeles is considered the worst city to start a business. Leaving Los Angeles for another surrounding county can save businesses 20% of costs. Leaving the state for Texas can save up to 40% of costs. This probably explains why California lost 120,000 jobs last year and Texas gained 130,000 jobs.[443]

Democratic California Governor Jerry Brown's answer to his state's failing economy and crumbling tax revenue was to place an initiative on the November 2012 ballot to support K-12 public schools.[444] This initiative passed and is expected to bring in around $6 billion in additional revenues. However, California was expected to still have a $28 billion budget deficit for fiscal year 2012.[445]

---

441   Chriss W. Street, (2012, March 13). "Exodus—California Tax Revenue Plunges by 22%."
      Retrieved December 24, 2012, from http://www.breitbart.com/Big-Government/
      /2012/03/13/exodus-california-tax-revenue-plunges-by-22
442   Ibid.
443   Ibid.
444   Ibid.

California has about 15% of the US economy, but its expected budget deficit in 2012 represents about 30% of the deficits faced by all states in the US. California is legally required to balance its budget each year. However, according to one rating agency, Standard and Poor's (S&P), it is debatable whether California has had a balanced budget at any time over the past decade.[446]

The reason for the California state deficit appears to be due to overspending on social programs, large state employee pensions and retirement liabilities. However, S&P believes that as for the state's broader credit quality, the long-term source of credit pressure will be coming from retirement liabilities. "In our view, retirement liabilities have contributed little if anything to California's current budget problems." S&P believes the impact of these liabilities is yet to be incurred.[447]

California's solution has been to raise taxes on its wealthier residents. However, doing this has only encouraged them to move to another state. It is estimated that wealthy Californians over the past decade have put $5.67 billion into Nevada's economy, $4.96 billion into Arizona and $4.07 billion into Texas.[448]

One Californian who came under fire in early 2013 because of his complaints about paying a 60% tax rate as a resident of California was golfer Phil Mickelson. It was later reported by *Forbes* magazine that Phil had understated his tax rate. After winning the Scottish Open and the British Open golf tournaments in the summer of 2013 and garnering $2.16 million, it was reported that he would be on the hook for taxes of 61%. The UK would tax him 45%, for which he would receive a foreign tax credit so he would not have to pay this amount to the US federal government. But he would have to pay self-employment taxes, the new Medicare surtax and hand over 13.3% of his wages to the state of California, which does not have a foreign tax credit, *Forbes* reported.[449]

The challenges facing California are typical of those facing governments today. A government can raise taxes, reduce spending, print more

445 Joseph Weber, (2012, December 22). "New tax increases in California stir debate about adding to exodus." Retrieved December 24, 2012, from http://www.foxnews.com/politics/2012/12/22/ /new-tax-increase-in-california-stirs-debate-about-adding-to-exodus/

446 Gabriel Petek, (2012). "Anatomy Of A State Budget Deficit: California's $15.7 Billion Problem." Standard and Poor's. San Francisco: McGraw-Hill, p. 2.

447 Ibid, p. 2.

448 Op cit, Weber.

449 K. Sean Packard. (2013, July 22). "Phil Mickelson Wins Historic British Open And Incurs 61% Tax Rate." *Forbes*.

money or do nothing. When taxes are raised to solve fiscal deficits, and there are comparable alternatives, taxpayers will move to where taxes are lower. When government spending is reduced, the beneficiaries will be upset. When more money is printed, ultimately, inflation will occur. When nothing is done, massive deficits and eventual insolvency will occur. The solution is to have fiscal restraint on spending, a tax policy with rates that are not excessive and a tax program that is administratively efficient and fair. Hong Kong is one place that has achieved this.

Hong Kong Taxes

The beginning of an article posted by the *New York Times* in February 2012 states it best:

> The United States is shrinking its military and debating whether to cut social spending, raise taxes or both. European governments from Greece to Ireland are struggling to maintain payments to the unemployed and retirees. Japan is borrowing heavily to pay for earthquake reconstruction and care for a graying population.
>
> And then there is Hong Kong.
>
> Financial Secretary John Tsang announced a budget for the coming fiscal year that cuts income taxes, corporate taxes and real estate taxes. Household electricity bills will be subsidized, and people living in public housing will receive two months' free rent.
>
> Education spending will jump 7%. Senior citizens will receive an extra month's pension payment; government hospitals will expand; and 10 billion Hong Kong dollars, or $1.29 billion, will be put in a special fund to help the needy buy medicine.
>
> Perhaps most impressive, the budget is forecast to be roughly in balance—and Hong Kong's budget forecasters have a reputation for consistently underestimating surpluses. The city, an autonomous region of China ever since Britain handed it back in 1997, has accumulated a rainy-day fund equal to more than a year and a half of government spending.

Hong Kong is running another large budget surplus for the current year, which ends on March 31, despite giving 6,000 [HK] dollars to each adult permanent resident.

Economists attribute the bonanza to a series of factors: tight limits on senior citizen spending, no military spending and an economy that grew 5% last year, mostly because Hong Kong has cashed in on China's economic boom.[450]

Thanks to the strength of Hong Kong's business environment, infrastructure and favorable tax regime, Hong was named the world's top financial center for the second year running by the World Economic Forum.[451] Hong Kong has figured out the right balance between public spending and public revenues to support its spending. As important as keeping spending in check, Hong Kong has implemented and maintained a tax system that is regularly rated as one of the best in the world.

Hong Kong was also rated best in the 2014 Index of Economic Freedom put together by the *Wall Street Journal* and the Heritage Foundation. The index is a measurement of a nation's commitment to free enterprise, evaluating categories including fiscal soundness, government size and property rights. "Countries achieving higher levels of economic freedom consistently and measurably outperform others in economic growth, long-term prosperity and social progress."[452]

Hong Kong's Inland Revenue Department (IRD) administers tax collection under the leadership of the Commissioner of Inland Revenue. Hong Kong's income tax is broken up into three categories: salaries, sales and property tax. Income not falling within one of these three categories is exempt from income tax.[453]

[O]nly Hong Kong source income is subject to Hong Kong income tax. The nationality, domicile or residence of a person is not relevant in determining whether income is taxable in Hong Kong. It also makes no difference whether a business carried on in Hong Kong is in the

450 Keith Bradsher, (2012, February 1). "Bonanza in Hong Kong from Mainlands Boom." *New York Times.*
451 Reuters. (2012, October 31). "Hong Kong named top financial center for second year." Retrieved May 5, 2013, from http://www.reuters.com/article/ /2012/10/31/us-financialcentres-wef-report-idUSBRE89U0BD20121031
452 Terry Miller, "America's Dwindling Economic Freedom," *Wall Street Journal,* January 13, 2014.
453 P. K. Ho, (2007). *Hong Kong Taxation and Tax Planning.* Hong Kong: Elegance Printing & Book Binding Co. Ltd, pp. 2–9.

form of a sole-proprietorship, a partnership, a branch of an overseas company, a company incorporated either in Hong Kong or outside of Hong Kong, or a subsidiary, as long as the business is carried on in Hong Kong, and the profits from such business are derived in Hong Kong, those profits are subject to Hong Kong profits tax.[454]

How much more simple could it get?

There is no capital gains tax if an individual can show that he/she does not carry on a business and the gain made is capital in nature. There is no dividend tax on income payable to residents or non-residents. There is no profit remittance tax except in rare circumstances.[455] Also, Hong Kong has no estate, investment income, gift or wealth taxes.[456]

Hong Kong implements a direct assessment system for income tax rather than the "pay as you earn" method used in the US. A taxpayer prepares a tax form which is provided to the IRD. The IRD issues a tax assessment after receiving a completed tax form. Estimated tax assessments are prepared by the IRD if a return is not received, and a taxpayer has options to dispute his/her tax assessment.[457]

Hong Kong has a total corporate tax rate which is amongst the lowest in the world and is well known for its simplicity. Hong Kong's total tax rate on corporations is 23% with numerous incentives for corporations to reduce their tax rates further. One example is tax deductions for environmentally protective machinery and related installation costs.[458]

Out of more than 170 economies researched and included in the World Bank/PWC's 2012 study of corporate and business taxes, the average total tax rate was 44.8% of profits. Hong Kong at 23% is well below the global average. The US on the other hand, with a total tax rate of 131%, is well above the world average.[459]

In 2009, Hong Kong instituted a 100% tax deduction for capital expenditures on environment-friendly vehicles. In the 2010/2011 budget (Hong Kong has a fiscal year ending on March 31), the government proposed to introduce a tax deduction over a period of five years for capital expenditures on the purchase of registered trademarks, copyrights and registered designs. These incentives are in place to encourage

454 Ibid, p. 8.
455 Ibid, p. 8.
456 Op cit, KPMG, p. 61.
457 Op cit, Ho, p. 9.
458 Op cit, Trumbic et al, p. 69.
459 Ibid, pp. 15, 69 & 115.

environment-friendly activities as well as corporate research and development.[460]

Low tax compliance cost and efficient procedures can make a big difference for corporations when filing taxes. In Hong Kong, a typical firm is required to make only three payments a year, the lowest number of any economy in the World Bank/PWC's 2012 study of business taxes.[461]

> The Hong Kong SAR, China Inland Revenue Department is generally well regarded for its initiatives in employing the latest information technology, streamlining work procedures and maintaining communication with the tax-paying public. This has always been evident in the Paying Taxes study, with the 2012 report again revealing Hong Kong SAR, China as being among the easiest places in the world for business to comply with their tax compliance obligations. Hong Kong SAR, China's tax administration is highly transparent, with information on such matters as tax revenues, objection procedures and tax rules and guidance being published online and readily accessible to the public. . . . Much of the government's focus with regard to tax policy has been on maintaining the simple and easy-to-administer features of the existing system. As such, the ease of compliance is expected to be a continuing feature of the system. Moreover, the government's financial position is strong and therefore there is little reason to expect significant upward changes in the Total Tax Rate.[462]

Hong Kong's maximum individual income tax rate is 15%, and its top effective tax rate is the same. Effective tax rates consider deductions. The income tax in Hong Kong is charged on income less donations to charities and other very limited deductions.[463] An individual tax form can be completed manually in a matter of minutes.

The Hong Kong government collects a provisional tax in addition to the taxes due in the taxation year. The provisional tax is approximately 75% of the actual tax and is attributed to the next tax year's taxes. If an individual owes HK$10,000 in tax, he is charged HK$17,500 in his first

---

460 Ibid, p. 69.
461 Ibid, p. 14.
462 Ibid, p. 70.
463 Op cit, KPMG, p. 61.

tax assessment. The excess HK$7,500 is offset against the following year's tax.

Hong Kong's effective tax rate of 15% compares with a 35% maximum individual income tax rate for the US in 2012. A top effective tax rate for the US is difficult to locate and validate. However, as noted above, an individual in California can pay more than 50% in total taxes in a given year.

There are no social security taxes in Hong Kong, although there is a Mandatory Provident Fund (MPF) which employers and employees are required to contribute to.[464] The Hong Kong MPF is an example of the market providing subsistence for retirement for Hong Kong residents.[465]

The MPF program works in much the same manner as Australia's superannuation program. "The MPF requires workers and employers to each pay 5% of salary, up to a combined HK$2,500 a month, to MPF schemes run by banks, insurers and fund companies."[466]

The MPF was set up in 2000, and in the beginning only the employers were able to choose the providers. This changed in November 2012 when participants became able to choose. As a result, there was a mad dash by providers to attract new clients from other providers—some providing ice cream as an incentive to switch.[467]

One reason for Hong Kong's government surplus is the tax revenue on its retail sales. Nearly 100,000 mainland Chinese visitors a day come to Hong Kong and most head straight for the stores. They do not come because the Hong Kong stores are much nicer as practically every luxury retail chain now has shops in mainland China. Also, with sky-high rents in Hong Kong, the stores there charge more for a wide range of goods than in the United States and many other countries.[468] "Hong Kong's attraction instead has been as a tax haven to avoid the 17% value-added tax in mainland China, plus steep import and consumption taxes that can add another 10 to 50% to the price tag there. The tax savings on a single Louis Vuitton bag can cover round-trip airfare from practically any city in China."[469]

---

464 Ibid, p. 61.
465 Op cit, Jie, p. 21.
466 Enoch Yiu, (2012, November 1). "Battle to Lure Hong Kong MPF Switchers." *South China Morning Post.*
467 Ibid.
468 Op cit, Bradsher.
469 Ibid.

Despite low taxes, the government offers much more than basic benefits.

> Hong Kong provides free and universal primary education to all citizens; college students can receive substantial subsidies and loans from the government. Meanwhile, 92% of the hospitalization was provided by the public health system and over 90% of the cost was paid by the government in the 1990s. Moreover, more than half of the residents are either renting public flats or purchasing private ownership with subsidy from the government.[470]

Populists in Hong Kong have assailed the government for being less generous than the US and other Western countries to those who are poor, elderly or both. "Hong Kong is one of Asia's most expensive cities, but elderly residents typically receive [HK]$1,090 a month, or [US]$140, plus [HK]$2,820 dollars a month if they are needy."[471]

Cathy Chu, Financial Secretary John Tsang's deputy for Treasury, said, "the biggest reason for Hong Kong's fiscal strength [is] a combination of strong economic growth together with self-restraint in the share of economic output that is spent by the government, which is held to about 20%."[472]

Some individuals may say that you cannot compare the US to Hong Kong. The US is much bigger and larger in area and has a much larger population. This is all true. However, the principles used in Hong Kong—that is, low government spending combined with low tax rates and a simple tax system—demonstrably work and could be adopted in the US. Also, the increased costs in overseeing a tax system for 310 million people should not be that much more than Hong Kong's costs (if the programs were the same) due to the economies of scale. In theory, the costs per capita should be less in the larger economy.

The comparison between the US IRS and Hong Kong's IRD of costs for collecting tax revenues is staggering. As noted above, the US IRS employed 94,000 individuals and incurred US$12.3 billion in costs in 2011.[473] The Hong IRD employed 2,818 individuals in fiscal year 2011, which was the same number of employees as the prior four years in a

470 Op cit, Jie, pp. 21–22.
471 Op cit, Bradsher.
472 Ibid.
473 Op cit, Department of Treasury, pp. 66–67.

row, and incurred HK$1.2 billion (US$156 million) in costs in 2011.[474]
Based on these numbers, the cost per capita for collections of revenues
in the US is US$40, while Hong Kong's cost is half that, US$22. (Note
that this calculation doesn't include the additional costs of the new IRS
agents in the process of being hired for the implementation of the
PPACA.)

Hong Kong's government has one advantage over the US in that it
doesn't have to fund a military. However, even ignoring military and
defense spending, the US still spends in excess of its revenues by at least
$200 billion annually, not counting the massive amounts of non-funded
liabilities added annually in the trillions.

The answer in regards to taxation is for the US to cut government
spending to a reasonable level that can be sustained by a shrewd system
of government taxation. In addition, the US must simplify its tax code
and programs drastically while putting in place a tax model that does
not discriminate against the wealthy or the poor, yet still covers the costs
incurred needed to run the country now and into the future.

474 Hong Kong IRD, (2012). *Hong Kong Inland Revenue Department Annual Report: Human
     Resources.* Retrieved February 17, 2013, from
     http://www.ird.gov.hk/dar/2011-12/table/eng/hr.pdf

CHAPTER 7

Them Ponies Run and Pay

The Hong Kong Jockey Club is a non-profit organization that benefits from gambling in Hong Kong with the stakes provided to the Hong Kong government as well as Hong Kong charities.

Initiatives to Increase Government Coffers

Governments have always struggled to obtain revenues to keep them running. They have pillaged, plundered, stolen, begged and compromised to receive the funds necessary to maintain and stay in power. Governments throughout history have mismanaged their budgets and spent more than could possibly be supported by their revenues and then eventually suffered the consequences.

In the US, there are numerous taxes on various activities and products as already discussed in previous chapters. There are both federal withholding taxes (i.e., income taxes) and state withholding taxes, with some local communities having withholding taxes as well. Additionally, there are federal Medicare taxes, federal Social Security taxes and state disability taxes, which are paid by an individual and his employer. There are state sales taxes, personal property taxes on items such as cars and boats and real estate taxes. There are telephone taxes, gas taxes, road taxes, cigarette and tobacco taxes and alcohol taxes. The latter are sometimes referred to as "sin taxes." There are capital gains taxes and customs duties on imports as well as gift and estate taxes.

With all these taxes, Americans are giving more and more of their incomes to governments. But in spite of the growing tax burden, the government is still spending more than it brings in. The current army of tax inspectors and administrators is inefficient in collecting and using taxes and is missing many opportunities to tax revenues being produced.

US states are looking for ways to increase tax revenues. Washington and Colorado both passed laws in November 2011 making marijuana legal. One argument in favor of the law was that the government could tax sales of this product. The Washington initiative included a 25% tax rate imposed on the product at three points: "When the grower sells it to the processor, when the processor sells it to the retailer, and when the retailer sells it to the customer."[475]

However, the substance is still classified as an illegal drug by the federal government. The Controlled Substances Act classifies marijuana as a Schedule I controlled substance. This difference in interpretation of marijuana as being either illegal or legal between the federal government and the Colorado and Washington state governments is bound to be addressed through the US court system in the months ahead.[476]

Another potential source of revenue for state governments is in the gambling sector. Included in this category are casinos, gaming machines, lotteries, charitable betting (e.g., Bingo) and sports betting. Global gambling revenue in 2007 was estimated to be over $337 billion, with casinos and lotteries receiving roughly a third each.[477]

According to the estimates in 2007, the US was the largest gambling country in the world with estimated spending of $95 billion, nearly three times as much as the next largest gambling country, Japan, at $35 billion.[478] By the year 2013, gambling worldwide had increased to $450 billion, with the US still leading all countries with $119 billion gambled (and mostly lost) by Americans during the year. China had risen to second place world-wide in 2013 at $76 billion.[479]

In 2007 in the US, 48 states allowed charitable gaming, 44 states allowed lotteries, 40 states allowed paramutuel betting, 29 states allowed Indian casinos, 12 allowed commercial casinos and 12 allowed slot machines at racetracks. Las Vegas had the largest share of casino revenues in 2008 at $7.5 billion. This was considerably larger than the second largest US market, Atlantic City, which reported $4.5 billion in revenues that year. Las Vegas revenues during this time period were similar to that of Macau, the casino city near Hong Kong (although Macau's revenues have increased dramatically since 2007).[480]

---

475 Aaron Smith, (2012, November 8). "Marijuana legalization passes in Colorado, Washington." Retrieved March 29, 2013, from http://money.cnn.com/2012/11/07/news/economy/ /marijuana-legalization-washington-colorado/index.html
476 Ibid.
477 Elliott Morss, (2009, October 2). "The Global Economics of Gambling." Retrieved March 29, 2013, from: http://www.morssglobalfinance.com/the-global-economics-of-gambling/
478 Ibid.
479 John Aziz, (2014, February 5). "How did Americans manage to lose $119 billion gambling last year?" *The Week*.
480 Op cit, Morss.

In 2011, almost half the states in the US were adding tax revenues to their coffers through casinos. For example, Ohio added three casinos in 2011 and a fourth near Cincinnati was scheduled to open in 2012. Each Ohio casino pays a $50 million license fee to the state, and then gross revenue is taxed at 33%. With monthly gross revenues in casinos in Cleveland and Toledo at $40 million in August 2011, adding casinos in the cities of Columbus and Cincinnati will add significant amounts to Ohio's treasury.[481]

Around the world, governments use different means to tap gambling revenues. Hong Kong has a unique entity that produces revenues for the government by capitalizing on gambling: the Hong Kong Jockey Club..

History of the Hong Kong Jockey Club

1841 saw the arrival of the British in Hong Kong, bringing not only redcoats and drummer boys in gunboat diplomacy but also horseracing. The Brits immediately set about draining a malarial mosquito-infested swamp to form a racetrack at a location on the island named Happy Valley. This was literally the only flat land on the island of Hong Kong at the time. With the exception of a few years during World War II when the Japanese occupied Hong Kong, the track has seen non-stop action ever since.[482]

The Hong Kong Jockey Club (HKJC) was founded in 1884 and began organizing all racing activities in Hong Kong. The club also began taking a commission on bets, which at that time were still placed through private clubs. In 1907, the first company secretary was appointed and a club office was set up in the Central district of Hong Kong. By 1931, the first permanent stands at the Happy Valley racing facility were built. These two three-story stands were replaced in 1957 with two seven-story structures, which were further expanded in 1969 to form part of today's viewing stands, which can hold 55,000 racegoers.[483]

In 1971, the HKJC changed from being an amateur to a professional racing organization. Then, in 1973, due to the growth of horseracing's popularity and also to combat illegal bookmaking, the Hong Kong

---

481 Brian A. Shactman, (2012, October 8). "The Tax Gamble: States Double Down on Casinos." Retrieved March 29, 2013, from http://www.cnbc.com/id/49330592
482 HKJC. (n.d.). The Origin of Hong Kong Horse Racing." Retrieved March 24, 2013, from http://corporate.hkjc.com/corporate/history/english/index.aspx
483 Ibid.

government authorized the HKJC to operate off-course betting branches. Night racing began the same year. The HKJC opened six Off-Course Betting Branches and a telephone betting service in 1974.[484]

In 1975, the HKJC started the Mark Six Lottery. Initially, this was held weekly on Tuesdays, but today the Mark Six is held three times a week. In 1981, the computerization of "Telebet" was completed and in 1988, a hand-held Customer Input Terminal was introduced; there are now around 80,000 users. In 2003, the HKJC launched regulated football (i.e., soccer) betting services. Rather than dealing with illegal betting through confrontation, the problem was turned into a win-win scenario for the Hong Kong community.

In 1978, a second racecourse at Sha Tin opened, in the region between Hong Kong Island and mainland China. This racecourse has a capacity of over 80,000 and is generally considered to be among the finest in the world. By 1988, Hong Kong's first international race, the Hong Kong Invitation Cup, was held at Sha Tin, in which six local horses competed with six from Malaysia and Singapore. The international races have since grown and now include four international Group One races on the same day—the Hong Kong Cup, Hong Kong Mile, Hong Kong Sprint and Hong Kong Vase. These races are recognized around the world in horseracing and boast a total purse of HK$62 million [US$8 million] while attracting horses from some 10 overseas jurisdictions.[485]

During the 2008 Beijing Olympics, the HKJC assisted with the equestrian events. These events were successfully held at HKJC-provided venues, achieving high acclaim from international equestrian circles. In 2009, the HKJC was a principal contributor to the 5th East Asia Games, the first international multi-sports event hosted by Hong Kong.[486]

Hong Kong Jockey Club's Operations and Results

The HKJC is a company "limited by guarantee with no shareholders." (This type of legal makeup is similar to a non-profit organization in the US, which is provided tax advantages that for-profit entities do not enjoy.) The HKJC obtains its net earnings from racing and betting. "The money remaining after payment of dividends, prize money, taxes,

484 Ibid.
485 Ibid.
486 Ibid.

operating costs and investments to enhance Hong Kong's racing and betting facilities is donated to charitable and community projects."[487]

Racing, football betting and the Mark Six lottery are operated as separate entities by the HKJC. The club also provides a wide range of exclusive leisure facilities for its members, which fall under a separate company financed entirely by members' subscriptions and fees. "The club is directed by a 12-strong board of stewards, headed by a chairman, who provide their services gratis."[488]

The HKJC had a long tradition of donating to charitable causes, but it was in the 1950s as Hong Kong struggled to cope with post-war reconstruction and a massive influx of immigrants that the HKJC made this role integral to its operation. In 1955, the HKJC formally decided to devote its surplus each year to local charity and community projects. Donations from the HKJC became large enough to warrant the forma-tion of The Hong Kong Jockey Club (Charities) Limited in 1959. In 1993, this was replaced by The Hong Kong Jockey Club Charities Trust. Today, allocations to charities currently average HK$1 billion (US$128 million) a year.[489]

At the Annual General Meeting of the HKJC held on September 5, 2012, the chairman, Mr. T Brian Stevenson, told the HKJC's voting members that the HKJC's total direct return to the community had reached a record HK$19.06 billion (US$2.5 billion), adding together the HKJC's betting duty and tax payments, its charitable donations and its contributions to the Lotteries Fund, all of which also set new records. He noted the many other benefits the HKJC created for Hong Kong through employment, tourism and related spending.[490]

For the fiscal year ending in 2012, the HKJC's net margin on racing, football betting and the Mark Six lottery was HK$8.11 billion (US$1 billion), which was a 6.2% increase on the previous year. The net margin is the amount the HKJC has to cover operational costs and charitable donations after payment of dividends to customers and betting duties to the Hong Kong government.[491]

In the financial year ending in 2012, the HKJC made total tax payments, including betting duties and profits tax, of a record HK$16.17 billion (US$2 billion), growing 5.4% over the previous year. This

487 Ibid.
488 Ibid.
489 Ibid.
490 Ibid.
491 Ibid.

amount equaled 6.8% of all taxes collected by Hong Kong's Inland Revenue Department during the year, making the HKJC Hong Kong's largest single taxpayer. "In addition, the Mark Six operations generated a HK$1.15 billion contribution to the government's Lotteries Fund, which supports social welfare projects."[492]

The HKJC Charities Trust also set a new record in 2012 by providing HK$1.73 billion (US$220 million) to charities during the year. The HKJC Charities Trust supported 155 different charitable and community projects during the year which touched the lives of an estimated 5.4 million Hong Kong people. The HKJC Charities Trust charitable donations have increased by 70% over the past nine years.

Horseracing remained the key source of revenue for the HKJC during the fiscal year ending in 2012. Betting duty payments to the Hong Kong government increased by 6.3% and passed HK$10 billion (US$1.29 billion) for the first time since the fiscal year ending in 2002. Total racecourse attendance also increased to nearly two million for the year, the highest in eight years.

The HKJC's overseas race simulcasts continued to attract a growing following in line with the globalization of horseracing. Net margin on these simulcasts grew 20.4% to HK$59 million (US$8 million) while duty payments to the Hong Kong government grew 20.3% to HK$219 million (US$28 million).[493]

In a report in early 2013, it was predicted that revenues on overseas horseracing betting were expected to double in the upcoming year. A bill was passed that backed the two-way commingling of betting, allowing overseas betters access to the larger and more lucrative Hong Kong pools.[494] As a result, the HKJC was expected to add more than HK$200 million (US$26 million) to the government's coffers per year.[495]

The HKJC makes money on football betting and on the lottery as well. For football betting, the HKJC's net margin grew 10.7% to HK$3.94 billion (US$500 million) in 2012, generating betting duty payments to the government of the same amount. The Mark Six lottery saw growth of 12.0% in 2012 over the prior year with tax duty payments increasing to HK$1.92 billion (US$250 million).[496]

---

492 Ibid.
493 Ibid.
494 Alan Aitken, (2013, February 7). HK$200m windfall in betting change. *South China Morning Post*, p. A1.
495 Ibid.

One of the benefits to society of the lottery in the 2012 fiscal year was a HK$900 million (US$116 million) grant from the Lotteries Fund to refurbish Hong Kong's 250 public elderly centers. The Charities Trust complemented this grant with HK$110 million (US$14 million). Together, these were expected to provide upgraded facilities and special equipment at the refurbished premises to an eventual 200,000 senior citizens.[497]

A concern of the HKJC is the billions of dollars in local citizens' spending on gaming that could be benefiting Hong Kong which are now going instead to casino operations in Macau. Macau is *the* gaming center in the region because it is the only place with legal casinos in China. Macau reported annual revenues in excess of $35 billion in 2012, making it the world's largest casino market.[498] Other countries and territories in the Asia Pacific have legal casinos, such as Singapore, Malaysia, South Korea, Australia and New Zealand, but the biggest in total revenues by far is Macau.

Overall, however, the HKJC with its successful not-for-profit business model is something that many Hong Kong people cherish.[499] If you go to a horserace at Happy Valley in Hong Kong, it is an event you will not soon forget. The track is green and lovely with the amazing view of the massive skyscrapers in Hong Kong outside surrounding the stadium. Happy Valley now stands on a very expensive plot of real estate near the heart of Hong Kong. This land would have been swept up a long time ago by some sharp investor and sold for billions of dollars had the HKJC not been so successful and provided so much to Hong Kong. The Hong Kong government makes money, the horses race fast, and the people have fun, all the while helping society through tax revenues and gifts to charities.

Creative Revenue

There are opportunities for tax revenues that governments throughout the world are not taking advantage of. Revenues are being generated in gambling on racing, gaming and sporting events. Revenues are being

---

496 Op cit, HKJC.
497 Ibid.
498 Farah Master, (2013, January 2). "UPDATE 2-Macau gambling revenue hits record in December." Retrieved April 1, 2013, from
     http://www.reuters.com/article/2013/01/02/macau-revenues-idUSL4N0A710120130102
499 Op cit, HKJC.

generated online as well. Some of these revenue activities are and should stay illegal based on their negative impact on society. Other areas exist where governments could perhaps derive tax revenues in a logical manner.

The Hong Kong government has benefited for years from the tax revenues derived from horseracing, betting and the lottery. The unique aspect of this is that the government has done very little to administer the activities that generate the tax revenues.

The HKJC is an example of local people in a community putting together an organization with a vision to support the community while having fun. The key here is that the activities are run by an entity led by members in the community of good standing that do not work in the government.

There are costs to society from gambling. People can become addicted to gambling. This and related issues with gambling, alcohol, and marijuana cause concerns for many in that legalization may create an increase in addicts which is not in society's best interest. The social costs must be weighed with the tax revenues taken as a result of legalizing these products and activities. The argument from many proponents of legalizing these activities is that people will participate in them regardless, so you may as well legalize them, tax the revenues, and do all you can to assist those who are harmed by these substances or activities. These people would argue that the "punters" were going to be addicts whether these activities and substances were legal or not.

Singapore has a unique approach to the problem of gambling addiction. Singapore taxes locals entering casinos at a prohibitive rate while foreigners are allowed to enter free of charge.

The pros and cons to the legalization of activities that have inherent social costs should be thoroughly considered. There are many ways to tax revenues outside the normal channels. The best approach is to have them overseen by ethical members of society with no stake in the game.

The HKJC has withstood that test of time. It survived the World War II Japanese occupation of Hong Kong and the "handover" of Hong Kong from Great Britain to China in 1997. There was some concern as to whether the HKJC as well as other entities would remain in existence after the handover, but China's leader Deng Xiaoping reassuringly stated shortly before Hong Kong's reunification that, "The racing will continue, the dancing will stay." Deng was well informed and may have even been a racing fan. Obviously he knew a "gift horse" when he saw one.

CHAPTER 8

The Family and the State

A century ago in the US, the family unit bore the brunt of socio-economic challenges. Parents took care of their children and children took care of their elderly parents. It was shameful to ask for help. This mentality has slowly evolved over the past century into a "state-dependent mentality" as the responsibilities of the family have shifted to federal, state and local governments. The social and financial costs of this transfer of responsibility have been astronomical and are at least in part the cause of the US federal government's multi-trillion dollar debt burden. In China, the family still maintains the responsibility for each member of the family unit. China's policies have prevented the nation from incurring the annual deficits and related outstanding debt of the US.

The Family in the US

It was socially unacceptable to bear children out of wedlock in the US a half-century ago. If a single woman got pregnant, it was a shameful event that could only be rectified if the man responsible married her. The man was expected to provide for the family for life and begin the journey of raising a family together with the mother-to-be.

Even after such a marriage, the birthdates of firstborns might be postdated so the child would appear to have been conceived during the honeymoon.

The culture was one that respected the family and shamed those who did not. Promiscuity was not considered healthy or socially acceptable for men or women. It was shameful to go to the local government or church and ask for support. Families did all they could to make ends meet and were willing to go without rather than appear needy.

But people also helped each other. Community churches and other organizations were active in helping those truly in need. "Historically, individuals and local entities have privately provided more assistance to needy members of society than they do today. Particularly during the

20th century, government gradually offered more and more services that were previously provided by self-help and mutual-aid organizations."[500] In addition to the shift away from family and community assistance towards government assistance, the care that is provided has become more impersonal since the providers lack any relationship to the individuals in need.

Single-Parent Families

With the introduction of the social programs instituted under President Franklin Roosevelt and others from the 1930s onwards, the shame in having a child outside of marriage is gone. Today, single young mothers are more the norm than the abnormality. There are even TV shows about single mothers as it has become more socially acceptable.

Census statistics show that the number of children in single-parent families has increased dramatically over the past four decades.[501] According to the 2000 census, 28% of all families with children under the age of 18 are headed by single parents. Most (78%) of these families are headed by single females.[502]

The federal Centers for Disease Control and Prevention reported in early 2013 that of the 3,952,841 babies who were born in the United States in 2012, 1,609,619, or 40.7%, were born to unmarried mothers. 2012 was the fifth straight year that 40% or more of the babies born in the United States were born to unmarried women. In 1980, only 18.4% of births were to unmarried mothers.[503]

A study by Mark Mather revealed the impact of the single-parent family on the US populace. "The effects of growing up in single-parent households have been shown to go beyond economics, increasing the risk of children dropping out of school, disconnecting from the labor force, and becoming teen parents. Although many children growing up

500 Op cit, Tyrrell et al, p. 7.
501 Mark Mather, (2010, May). "Single-mother families." Retrieved October 27, 2012, from http://www.prb.org/pdf10/single-motherfamilies.pdf, p. 1.
502 Fran Hopkins, (2012, October). "Single-Parent-Family-Stats from the 2000 US Census-Single Parents-Families.com." Retrieved October 27, 2012, from http://single-parenting.families.com/blog/single-parent-family-stats-from-the-2000-us-census
503 Terence P. Jeffrey, (2014, January 8). "CDC: U.S. Fertility Rate Hits Record Low for 2nd Straight Year; 40.7% of Babies Born to Unmarried Women." Retrieved January 8, 2014, from http://www.cnsnews.com/news/article/terence-p-jeffrey/ /cdc-us-fertility-rate-hits-record-low-2nd-straight-year-407-babies

in single-parent families succeed, others will face significant challenges in making the transition to adulthood."[504]

Per the data Mather reviewed, the likelihood of having a single mother varies across different ethnic groups. Where about one-sixth (16%) of white children live in single-mother families, one-fourth (27%) of Latino children and one-half (52%) of African American children live in single-parent homes.[505]

Data also show that during the past 30 years, the proportion of single mothers who have never been married has increased while the number divorced or separated has decreased. In 2009, the number of single mothers who had once been married was still more than half of all single mothers (53%). This too varies by racial/ethnic group. While two-thirds (66%) of white single mothers were previously married, about half (48%) of Latino single mothers were once married, and a third (34%) of African American single mothers were once married.[506]

About 70% of children living in single-parent homes are in low-income families, compared to less than a third (32%) of children living in other types of families. Most single mothers have limited financial resources available to cover children's education, child care and health-care costs. Children of single mothers make up the majority (54%) of poor children in the United States and a large portion (42%) of children in low-income families. Ethnicity is also noticeable here. While a little over a third (35%) of low-income white children live in single-mother families, two-thirds (66%) of low-income African American children living in single-parent families. Only 21% of low-income Asian American children live in single-mother families, which is about half the national average.[507]

By ethnicity, white children account for the largest share of children living in single-mother families (38%), followed by African Americans (31%) and Latinos (25%). However, among low-income children in single-mother families, 34% are African American, 31% are white, and 28% are Latino.[508]

Social scientist Charles Murray stated, "Illegitimacy is the single most important social problem of our time—more important than crime,

---

504 Op cit, Mather, p. 1.
505 Ibid, p. 1.
506 Ibid, p. 1.
507 Ibid, p. 2.
508 Ibid, p. 2.

drugs, poverty, illiteracy, welfare or homelessness because it drives everything else."[509]

The number-one predictor of whether a person will end up in prison is whether he was raised by a single parent, when controlling for socioeconomic status, race and place of residence. The statistics are alarming. Seventy percent of inmates in state juvenile detention centers serving long-term sentences, 72% of juvenile murderers and 60% of rapists come from single-mother homes. "Seventy percent (70%) of teenage births, dropouts, suicides, runaways, juvenile delinquents, and child murderers involve children raised by single mothers."[510]

Other statistics on single-parent families are as grim. According to the Index of Leading Cultural Indicators, children from single-parent families account for 63% of all youth suicides, 70% of all teenage pregnancies, 71% of all adolescent chemical/substance abuse, 80% of all prison inmates, and 90% of all homeless and runaway children. A similar study by the *Village Voice* reported that "children brought up in single-mother homes 'are five times more likely to commit suicide, nine times more likely to drop out of high school, 10 times more likely to abuse chemical substances, 14 times more likely to commit rape (for the boys), 20 times more likely to end up in prison, and 32 times more likely to run away from home.' Single motherhood is like a farm team for future criminals and social outcasts."[511]

As Ann Coulter puts it, "however the numbers are run, single motherhood is a societal nuclear bomb."[512] This problem occurs not only in the US but also is prevalent in other countries with similar social programs.[513]

According to studies over the past 25 years on the relationship between family structure and adolescent sexual activity, there are characteristics of adolescents from intact families that further support that the family is the answer. Adolescents from non-intact family backgrounds tend to encounter their first sexual experience at a significantly younger age than their peers from intact family structures. Also, "adolescents from intact families are less likely to have ever had sexual intercourse, have had on average fewer sexual partners, are less likely to report a sexually transmitted disease, and are less likely to have ever experienced

509   Charles Murray, (1993, October 29). "The Coming White Underclass." *Wall Street Journal.*
510   Ann Coulter, (2008). *Guilty.* New York: Random House, p. 37.
511   Ibid, pp. 37–38.
512   Ibid, p. 38.
513   Ibid, p. 38.

a pregnancy or live birth when compared to their peers from non-intact families."[514]

Clearly, if children wait longer to have their first sexual experience and if they are less likely to become pregnant, then the children have less stressful lives and the social costs are greatly minimized.

In a recent article, Ann Coulter provided her take on the cause of the increasing single-parent family in the US. According to Coulter, Erol Ricketts, a black demographer and sociologist with the Rockefeller Foundation who researched the origin of black female-headed families in the 1980s, showed that the black family was thriving from the late 19th century through most of the 20th century.[515]

After examining US census reports between 1890 and 1950, Ricketts found that blacks had higher marriage rates than whites. Up through 1970, black women in the US were more likely to get married than white women. According to the reports, Ricketts determined that in three of four decennial years between 1890 and 1920, black men out-married white men. According to Coulter, these results show that the cause of illegitimacy and its associated problems is not poverty, discrimination, lack of education, unemployment or slavery. "Black Americans had all those handicaps—and yet they still had strong families and low crime rates from 1890 until the 1960s."[516]

According to Coulter, the increase in illegitimacy is due to granting benefits to unmarried women with illegitimate children. Coulter points out that even President Franklin D. Roosevelt's Secretary of Labor, Francis Perkins, knew that granting widows' benefits to unwed mothers would have disastrous consequences. An early-20th-century social welfare advocate, Homer Folks, warned back in 1914 that to grant pensions for desertion or illegitimacy would undoubtedly have the effect of a premium upon these crimes against society.[517]

But in the 1960s, under President Lyndon Johnson, the federal Bureau of Public Assistance eliminated the "suitable home" requirements for welfare—such as having a husband. The result has been calamitous. Illegitimacy has gone through the roof, particularly among

---

514 Samuel W. Sturgeon, (2011). "The Relationship Between Family Structure and Adolescent Sexual Activity." Retrieved August 17, 2014, from http://www.familyfacts.org/reports/1//the-relationship-between-family-structure-and-sexual-activity

515 Ann Coulter, (2013, August 7). "Bill O'Reilly is Smarter than Lawrence O'Donnell." Retrieved August 9, 2013, from http://www.humanevents.com/2013/08/07/bill-oreilly-is-smarter-than-lawrence-odonnell

516 Ibid.

517 Ibid.

blacks. "In 1970, for the first time, the marriage rate for black women fell below 70%. But even then, a majority of black children were still living with both parents. By 2010, only 30.1% of blacks above the age of 15 were married, compared to 52.7% of whites."[518]

As the government continues to subsidize unwed mothers, the illegitimacy rate continues to rise, which in turn leads to poverty, criminal behavior and more illegitimacy. However, though certain politicians claim that poverty causes illegitimacy and then demand more payments to unwed mothers, we now have empirical evidence that poverty does not cause illegitimacy. The data related to black American families from 1890 to 1960 proves it. As Coulter states, "If African-Americans started marrying again at their pre-Great Society rates, it would wipe out the entire black 'culture of poverty.' "[519]

Since the "suitable home" requirements for welfare were eliminated, America's welfare policy has been premised on the idea that being poor causes single motherhood and crime rather than single motherhood causing criminal behavior and poverty. "The result of treating a symptom rather than the cause was that all three—poverty, single motherhood, and crime—skyrocketed."[520]

Coulter, in her book *Guilty*, goes on to note case after case where the US society places single mothers in heroic victim roles rather than state the enormous burden single households put on society and, more importantly, on the children of single parent households.[521] Portraying the single mother as being admirable is not the answer.

The single-parent family is the catalyst that costs the US billions and billions every year. In a 2008 study, Georgia State University economist Benjamin Scafidi found that single mothers—unwed or divorced—cost the US taxpayer $112 billion every year.[522] Based on other changes noted throughout this book, this number has inevitably ballooned in recent years.

Finding a way to materially reduce the number of single mothers in the US is a key element to eliminating the annual US deficits and the many social ills associated with single-parent families.

The "one child" policy in China is not an answer that respects an individual's right to life. However, the family's accountability for its

518 Ibid.
519 Ibid.
520 Op cit, Coulter, *Guilty*, p. 40.
521 Ibid, p. 41.
522 Ibid, p. 51.

members, embedded in traditional Chinese culture, most definitely could be a solution.

China's "One Child" Policy

When Westerners think about the family in China, the first thing that comes to mind is probably the "one child" policy. This was initiated in 1979 by China's leader Deng Xiaoping.[523] This policy has been long identified as an infringement of the individual's (i.e., the baby's) right to life and a parent's right to bear children.

The "one child" policy in China has exceptions. It strictly applies to the urban population but not ethnic minorities. If the first child is a girl, then a rural family is permitted to have another baby after a few years have passed. The policy permits two adults who are the only children of their parents the right to have two children themselves. Parents are usually allowed to have another child if the first child is born with some type of defect or health issue.[524]

The Chinese government offers incentives for those who comply with the "one child" policy. There can be higher wages, better schooling and better governmental treatment in obtaining assistance with loans or other governmental applications. Those who do not comply with the policy can receive the opposite—fines, fees and poor service with governmental requests.[525]

The number of additional people that China says would be around today if not for the one-child-per-couple rule that took effect 40 years ago in China is *400 million*. The Chinese government reports that 336 million abortions and 196 million sterilizations have occurred since the policy was instituted, an average of 1,500 abortions every hour of every day for four decades.[526] The number of abortions alone is more people than the population of the entire US.

Numerous instances have been recorded of women forced to have an abortion in order to comply with the policy. Women are reported to have been literally dragged from their homes, screaming and crying for

523 Matt Rosenberg, (2012, 8 14). "China One Child Policy Facts." Retrieved 10 21, 2012, from http://geography.about.com/od/chinamaps/a/China-One-Child-Policy-Facts.htm
524 Ibid.
525 Ibid.
526 Daniel Greenfield, (2013, March 26). "China's One Child Policy Has Aborted 1,500 Babies Every Hour." Retrieved May 7, 2013, from http://frontpagemag.com/2013/dgreenfield/ /chinas-one-child-policy-has-aborted-1500-babies-every-hour/

help as they were being led to the local hospital to have a forced abortion performed on them as a result of getting pregnant with a second child.

One story reported in June 2012 was that a young married woman by the name of Feng Jianmei who was forcibly aborted at seven months term after failing to pay fines for violating the policy. Family planning officials waited until Feng's husband was at work, and then came and beat her and dragged her into a vehicle which took her to a hospital. When she refused to pay fines for her second pregnancy, she was forced to sign an abortion consent.[527] The officials then had the doctors inject a toxin into the unborn baby's brain. The mother recounted how she could feel the baby jumping around inside her until it went still. The family planning officials covered the mother's head with a pillowcase. "'She couldn't do anything because they were restraining her,' the husband stated."[528]

In another recent story, Pan Chunyan was grabbed from a grocery store when she was almost eight months pregnant with her third child. Men working for a local official locked her up for four days and then brought her to a hospital and forced her to put her thumbprint on a document saying she had agreed to an abortion. Shortly thereafter, a nurse injected the mother with a drug. "'After I got the shot, all the thugs disappeared,' Ms. Pan, 31, said in a telephone interview from her home in the southeastern province of Fujian. 'My family was with me again. I cried and hoped the baby would survive.' But after hours of labor, the baby was born dead on April 8, 'black and blue all over,' Ms. Pan said."[529]

Chinese demographers say the social and economic damage done by the one-child policy will be felt for many generations and may not reverse. The labor pool shrank by 3.5 million in 2012, the first decline in almost 50 years. The declining labor pool will cause the ratio of taxpayers to pensioners to decline from almost five to one to just over two to one by 2030, and there are fewer children to support their parents.

527 Lillian Kwon, (2012, June 12). "Chinese Officials Beat 7 month Pregnant Woman, Abort Baby." Retrieved October 27, 2012, from http://www.christianpost.com/news/ /chinese-officials-beat-7-month-pregnant-woman-abort-baby-76546
528 Lillian Kwon, (2012, June 14). "Chinese Woman Forcibly Aborted for Failure to Pay Fine (Graphic)." Retrieved October 27, 2012, from http://www.weirdasianews.com/2012/06/14/ /chinese-woman-forcibly-aborted-failure-pay-fine-graphic/
529 Katie J.M. Baker, (2012, July 23). "Forced Abortions Turn out to be Bad PR for China's One Child Policy." Retrieved October 27, 2012, from http://jezebel.com/5928193/forced-abortions-turn-out-to-be-bad-pr-for-chinas-one+child-policy

"Shanghai is an example of the demographic time-bomb facing China: its fertility rate, at 0.7, is among the world's lowest."[530]

In a reaction to the declining labor pool, in late 2013 the Chinese Communist Party announced that it will begin permitting parents to have two children if one spouse is an only child. This was the most significant adjustment in a policy that has defined Chinese family life for more than three decades and perhaps the most dramatic policy change out of the Chinese leaders' recent party conclave. It is not clear when the new policy will start.[531] Regardless, the new policy still limits the number of children parents may have and will still be the cause of millions of abortions annually.

Right to Life and Right to Choose

The most critical complaint outside of China of the one-child policy is the infringement on an individual's "right to life." How could a government force a mother to abort her baby?

The pro-life movement in the US interprets life as beginning at the moment of fertilization. This is the moment the sperm from the father unites with the egg of the mother.[532]

Some would argue that life begins when genetics are in place for the creation of the baby, or upon fertilization, as argued by the Roman Catholic Church. Others would say that life begins when the embryo begins gastrulation and twinning is no longer possible. Others argue that life begins at the 24-to-27-week period when brainwaves are noticeable. Finally, others believe that life really begins at or near birth, when the baby is able to survive outside of the mother's body.[533] Because of these differences in opinion, some "pro-choice" groups say that an abortion is acceptable because a baby is not a human being until some point close to birth.

The above may be an oversimplification of the abortion debate, but regardless of whether an individual believes that abortion is acceptable or not, the "one child" policy is an infringement upon an individual's

---

530 Op cit, Greenfield.

531 Laurie Burkitt, "China Eases One-Child Policy," *Wall Street Journal,* October 29, 2013.

532 Donna J. Harrison, MD (n.d.). "When Does Life Begin? Medical Experts Debate Abortion Issue." Retrieved 10 21, 2012, from http://familydoctormag.com/sexual-health/ /251-when-does-life-begin-medical-experts-debate-abortion-issue.html

533 Suzanne Holland, PhD. (n.d.). "When Does Life Begin? Medical Experts Debate Abortion Issue." Retrieved 10 21, 2012, from http://familydoctormag.com/sexual-health/ /251-when-does-life-begin-medical-experts-debate-abortion-issue.html

basic rights in either case. Abortion opponents argue that a baby's life and therefore "right to life" is terminated when an abortion occurs as a result of the one-child policy and pro-choice proponents would say that a parent's right to have any number of children and to the timing of their births is also infringed upon.

An overall observation is that if an individual believes that an unborn child's life begins at inception, then the number of people "murdered" as a result of the "one child" policy is somewhere between 200 and 400 million. These deaths would far surpass the 100 million deaths in China over the past 150 years at the hands of Chinese compatriots and leaders.[534] These deaths would be greater than the 30 million deaths in China attributed to Mao's Great Leap Forward, which in terms of lives lost as a result of the famines from this initiative, is the worst disaster of the 20th century.[535] Never in world history has a policy or war destroyed so many lives as the "one child" policy.

Single Parents in China

You will not easily find a single mother in China with a child born out of wedlock. The first reason is that it is expensive, and single girls are heavily dependent upon their parents for their own well-being. A child born out of wedlock will not be eligible to obtain a birth certificate and an ID. Without these important documents, the child would have a very difficult time getting into school, and the mother would have to pay large fines when the child is born or when she tries to register the child. The second and more pressing reason is that it is simply socially unacceptable for a young unwed girl to have and raise a baby. "An unmarried daughter with a child would be a constant source for rumors and gossip. Having sex before marriage is one thing, but having a baby before marriage would most definitely bring shame upon the girl's entire family."[536]

In addition, the social stigma of being a single mother may prevent a young man from marrying a young single mother. This encourages Chinese women to abort when pregnant outside of marriage.[537] Chinese mothers are known to discourage their girls from wearing makeup even

534 Op cit, Fenby, p. xxxii.
535 Ibid, p. 415.
536 Robert, (2009, 2 5). "Why Single Mothers in China Are So Rare." Retrieved 10 23, 2012, from
     http://teachabroadchina.com/abortion-china-single-mothers/
537 Ibid.

in their late teens in part due to cost but more so to encourage the girls not to focus on being with a boy. Good Chinese mothers constantly batter their young girls with the message of not having sex before marriage.

A large percentage of the population in China has *only* lived under the Chinese Communist Party regime which took power in 1949. From early on, the Party has built into the populace an attitude not to challenge it and not to even discuss displeasures with the government. When you travel in China you will not be able to find many, if any, who openly complain about the government. In addition, the Chinese people do not have a free press where they are able to obtain and share opposing views of their government. This is why any Chinese people who do not support the "one child" policy will not say much, if anything, in opposition to the policy.

The traditional family culture in China prevents children from being born outside of families. The resulting socioeconomic impact of this is that China saves billions in social programs and additional related savings to the Chinese government.

The Family in China

As abhorrent as the "one child" policy is to US citizens, the family philosophy in China is admirable. The family is an important aspect of the Chinese culture. China which has historically been very poor, has had to rely on the family to take care of its elderly. China does not have the subsidies and programs that are available in the US to help the poor, old or sick. Historically there have not been any support programs like those prevalent in the US. The irony here is that the socialist nation is the country without massive social programs.

In China there is no discussion in regards to what constitutes a family. Two individuals of the same sex are not permitted to marry. The Chinese Communist Party laid great significance to the term "familism" in order to legitimatize its welfare regime. In one of the articles of marriage law from 1950, it was stated that parents are obligated to ensure the upbringing and education of their children, and children are also under the obligation of supporting their parents.[538] This mandate is still present in

538 Op cit, Jie, p. 89.

the Chinese culture as self-reliance and family support receive primary importance in the welfare mix.

The Chinese government has limited welfare systems and therefore individuals rely on the family for subsistence.[539] Due to the fact that there are low levels of resources from the public and international sectors, the people rely heavily on the family or community for welfare support.[540]

Any casual observer of the "one child" policy would note that prospective parents in China want to have boys rather than girls, and that cases have been noted where girls in the womb were aborted because the parents wanted a boy. The attitude is that the daughter will marry and leave, but the son stays with the parents and takes care of them when they get old. The older generation relies on the younger generation for their care, not the government.

In fact, it is now a legal requirement for sons and daughters to see to their parents' physical needs. In addition, in December 2012, China's National People's Congress added to the law by requiring people to visit their elderly parents regularly or at least keep in touch with them in some way. "In an attempt to improve the well-being of the elderly, the amended Law of Protection of Rights and Interests of the Aged rules it is illegal for people to neglect the 'spiritual needs' of the elderly."[541]

The new clause says that family members who do not live with their parents should visit or "greet them" frequently. Parents can apply for mediation or take their children to court if the law is not complied with. There are questions in regards to, for example, what constitutes regular greetings with parents, but most Chinese (55%) in a recent poll supported the initiative as a means to urge people to take care of the elderly.[542]

Some scholars have stated that in China, due to Confucianism, the people will value family, corporations and the entire society more highly than individuals. This philosophy means that the people are more ready to fulfill their duties and obligations to others. "More importantly, individuals seldom have any expectation of what their governments should or should not do."[543]

539   Ibid, p. 21.
540   Ibid, p. 27.
541   Wang Yanlin, (2013, July 1). "Law demands visits to parents." *Shanghai Daily.*
542   Ibid.
543   Op cit, Jie, p. 23.

In 2000, Zhu Rongji reiterated that social security of peasants should be mainly supported by the family and supplemented by collectives.[544]

In addition to a culture that supports the family, companies offer products that reward families for sticking together. "Chinese insurance companies offer a baffling array of policies, from life policies with health insurance riders, to 'love' policies with accident riders, to endowment policies with annual wedding anniversary bonuses—with a big lump sum if the couple gets to golden."[545] These policies have made it financially prudent for families to stick together.

The result of a family taking responsibility for its own well-being is that in China, where there has been little or no public support, the government is not besieged with the annual deficits and related outstanding debt of the US. In every recent public election in the US, Americans are reminded that China "owns" the US. This is in large part due to the fact that China is not burdened by financing the massive debt resulting from social programs, as the US is.

The Family as a Solution

One family-related solution to the single-parent "societal nuclear bomb" in the US is to increase the number of adoptions. Ann Coulter notes that the number of adoptions in the US has decreased over the past few decades: "In 1979, only about 600,000 babies were born out of wedlock and one quarter of them were put up for adoption. By 1991, the number of illegitimate births had doubled to 1,225,000 annually, but only 4% were allowed to be adopted—and most of those babies were snapped up by either Angelina Jolie or Mia Farrow. By 2003, 1.5 million illegitimate babies were born every year, but only about 14,000 of them, less than 1%, were put for adoption."[546]

Clearly, changing the US culture to make adoption easier is an important step. However, this is only a part of the family solution. The US should address the single-mother issue immediately in order to solve problems with poverty, crime and other social ills. Implementing broader policies and initiatives that promote the family is the answer.

The ultimate solution lies in an all-out culture shift. The family should be idolized in the US culture. Marriage should be promoted and

---

544 Ibid, p. 128.
545 Patti Waldmeir, (2013, August 28). "When Insurance is a Girl's Best Friend." *Financial Times*.
546 Op cit, Coulter, Guilty, p. 43.

the family encouraged to stay as a unit. Politicians from both parties would have to be on board as this would not work if one party says they are for the single motherhood and the other against.

The movies, TV shows and general media should show the family in a positive light. This is currently the case in Chinese TV shows, "soaps" and movies. There are few, if any, divorcees in Chinese daytime soaps. Encouraging children to refrain from sex until married would not only agree with most Americans' religious beliefs but would also encourage a family culture. Rather than making sex easier through government programs, government policy should be to promote the family. If the US wants to continue with social programs to assist those in need, the number of individuals in need must be reduced in order to maintain these social programs.

China has shown that a country can survive and even thrive without massive spending on social programs from the government through reliance on the family. Ultimately, the family is the major social vehicle and the primary source of welfare. The reliance on the family appears to be in inverse proportion to the amount of government support provided to a country's citizens. When no material government support is provided to individuals, they rely on their family for support. This was as true a century ago in America as it is in China today. This also implies that the poorer the country, the more the family is the primary support for the welfare of its citizens.

Under current policies in the US, each child represents additional benefits from the government. This policy has enticed single women to have more and more children who then are more likely to go on to live lives in poverty and crime. These policies must change.

In the summer of 2013, a big story in the US news was about a young African American by the name of Trayvon Martin who was shot and killed in Florida by George Zimmerman, a neighborhood watchman. Cable news anchor Bill O'Reilly added his thoughts in his nightly show:

> The reason there is so much violence and chaos in the black precincts is the disintegration of the African-American family. Right now, about 73% of all black babies are born out of wedlock. That drives poverty. And the lack of involved fathers leads to young boys growing up resentful and unsupervised. . . . So raised without much structure, young black men often reject education and gravitate towards the street culture, drugs, hustling, [and] gangs. Nobody forces them to do that; again, it

is a personal decision. But the entertainment industry encourages the irresponsibility by marketing a gangster culture, hip hop, movies, trashy TV shows to impressionable children. . . . The solution to the epidemic of violent crime in poor black neighborhoods is to actively discourage pregnancies out of marriage, to impose strict discipline in the public schools, including mandatory student uniforms, and to create a zero tolerance policy for gun and drug crimes imposing harsh mandatory prison time on the offenders. And finally, challenging the entertainment industry to stop peddling garbage.[547]

O'Reilly's comments could as well be applied to a growing portion of the US population that is finding themselves dependent on the government. No matter what race, color or creed, the family is the answer. Pope John XXIII knew that "the family . . . must be regarded as the natural, primary cell of human society."[548] Many of society's problems could be addressed through a renewed focus on the family and a move away from government dependency.

Government incentives and a change in the culture promoting family living and unity as well as incentives for getting married and staying married would have long-term beneficial effects on both US society and government coffers. A culture like that in China of taking care of both your own children and elderly parents would generate equally long-term massive savings. This has to occur because the growing costs of social programs and demands placed on the fragile society in the US are fast approaching unsustainable levels.

A final argument in promoting the family as the main catalyst in addressing society's ills is that the family knows you better than anyone. Your family is there for you when you need help the most. Your family may not always be able to provide you with a monetary fix to your problems, but more importantly, your family will have the knowledge of your situation and the wisdom to suggest proper fixes, the courage to call out your denials and the love you need the most. A social worker does not have the historical information necessary to make the right decision that family members may have, and certainly the government will never care for you like your family does.

547 Bill O'Reilly, (2013, July 22). "President Obama and the Race Problem." Retrieved July 26, 2013, from http://www.foxnews.com/on-air/oreilly/2013/07/23/ /bill-oreilly-president-obama-and-race-problem#ixzz2Zsr7j2Pm
548 Pope John XXIII, (1963, April 11). *Encyclical on Establishing Universal Peace in Truth, Justice, Charity, and Liberty.*

CHAPTER 9

It's not all Cherry Blossoms

It's not all cherry blossoms in the Asia Pacific Region as each country faces its own unique challenges. However, when compared to the US, the Asia Pacific countries as a whole are in a much better place.

Asia Pacific Challenges

Although there has been rapid expansion in the Asian economies, there have also been increasing gaps in income along gender and ethnic lines with the rich getting richer and at a faster rate. These rising disparities will challenge social stability despite substantial declines in poverty levels. There is also growing urbanization, and Asia Pacific countries will have more demand for capital, energy, minerals, water and food.[549] These challenges are clear, and the countries of Asia will have to address them to continue their upward rise in the world's economic rankings while maintaining social cohesion.

Not all things are "cherry" in the Asia Pacific Region.

Japan

Every spring in Japan, the cherry blossoms bloom. This magical event has been celebrated for millennia. The trees' pink and white blossoms are not just beautiful; they have been a symbol of the nation for hundreds of years. "Most Japanese visit their country's trees in groups for special cherry blossom viewings known as *hanami*. Students visit the trees taking a half or full day off from lessons. Neighborhoods organize their own viewings. Companies send their newest employees to stake out areas for corporate picnicking under the trees. When the flowers burst out of their buds, the Japanese people celebrate their New Year with food, dance and music."[550]

---

549 Op cit, Australian Government, pp. 49–50,59,68–70.
550 Ellen Rolfes, (2013, April 12). "For Hundreds of Years, Cherry Blossoms Are Matter of Life and Death." Retrieved May 11, 2013, http://www.pbs.org/newshour/rundown/

Held above all other flowers by the rulers, the "trees have been used as symbols for everything from predicting successful harvests of rice to giving the World War II kamikaze pilots courage for their one-way missions."[551]

The cherry blossom's symbolism today is more apposite than ever because Japan is in a situation similar to the US: its magnificence and beauty, like that of the cherry blossom, may be short-lived. Anyone who travels Japan can only be amazed at its beauty, the attention to detail, the kind spirit of the people and the massive economic machine the country has created. However, its social ills have put Japan in a precarious position.

Japan's modern economic success can be traced predominantly to two significant periods in its history—the pre-war Meiji era and the post-war economic miracle. During the Meiji restoration period in the mid-19th century, the Japanese government actively pursued Western-style reforms and development. Over 3,000 Westerners were hired to teach mathematics, science and technology to Japan. The Meiji government also created a business environment favorable for private businesses to thrive.[552] This was the period that ended the feudal system of the samurai, as Japan transitioned into a modern, more Western, society.

Although World War II devastated Japan, the social foundations set up by the Meiji era contributed to the post-war economic miracle from the 1960s through the 1980s. One of the greatest contributing factors of the Japanese transformation was the establishment of the Ministry of International Trade and Industry in 1949, which implemented numerous policies that led to heavy industrial growth in Japan. The post-war economic transition was so successful that Japan experienced economic growth at an average of 10% annually in the 1960s, 5% in the 1970s, and 4% in the 1980s.[553]

Growth slowed in the 1990s in Japan, causing this period to be known as the "Lost Decade." But by the time the 2008 global financial crisis had come and gone, the Japanese economy had a strong period of economic recovery. In 2010, Japan's economy was the fastest growing among the G-7 nations for the year. Then the 2011 Tohoku earthquake and tsunami came and derailed Japan's economic growth again.[554]

/2013/04/for-more-than-1000-years-cherry-blossoms-move-world-to-emotion.html
551   Ibid.
552   EconomyWatch World Economy Team, (2010, March 15)."Japan Economy." Retrieved April 4, 2013, from http://www.economywatch.com/world_economy/japan
553   Ibid.

Japan has a population of 127 million with a labor force of 66 million and in 2010, its unemployment rate was the lowest among the G7 nations at 5.1%. One of Japan's biggest challenges is its aging population and negative population growth rate with 22.9% of the Japanese population above the age of 65 and Japan's total fertility the 5th lowest in the world. Most (70%) of Japanese land is forested and unsuitable for agricultural, industrial or residential uses, and as a result, much of Japan's economic activity is concentrated in major cities such as Tokyo, Yokohama and Osaka.[554]

Tokyo is the world's largest metropolitan area by far with more than 34 million people in its vicinity. The next closest cities in size are Guangzhou, Jakarta, Shanghai and Seoul, reportedly with a little more than 25 million inhabitants each.[555] For a city as large as Tokyo, it is clean, well-kept and safe, and its transportation systems are remarkably punctual.

Japan imports about 60% of grain and fodder crops from other countries because only about 15% of its land is arable, and it also relies on imports for most of its meat products. Japan is the largest agricultural market for the EU and the third-largest market for the US. However, Japan does boast the largest fishing fleet in the world, accounting for almost 15% of the global catch. Because of its lack of natural resources, Japan also relies on the import of commodities (such as fuels, foodstuffs, chemical, textiles and raw materials) from various countries for its industrial sectors. As noted previously, Japan is the world's third largest oil importer.[557]

Despite having an overall stagnant economy for the past few decades, Japan's industries are still among the most highly advanced and innovative in the world. Japan is the world leader in the manufacturing of many products, but especially in electronics and automobiles, where Japan tops the world in both production and technological advancements.[558]

Industry is accountable for 23% of Japan's GDP. Major industries include motor vehicles, electronic equipment, machine tools, steel and nonferrous metals, ships, chemicals, textiles, and processed foods. Japan's automobile industry produces the second-largest amount of

554   Ibid.
555   Ibid.
556   Citypopulation. (2013, January 1). "Agglomerations." Retrieved April 5, 2013, from
       http://www.citypopulation.de/world/Agglomerations.html
557   Op cit, EconomyWatch.
558   Ibid.

vehicles in the world behind China, and Japanese automobile companies remain among the most valuable and technologically advanced
in the world. Japan is home to six of the top twenty largest vehicle
manufacturers in the world—Toyota (1st), Renault-Nissan (4th), Honda
(8th), Suzuki (10th), Mazda (14th) and Mitsubishi (16th).[559]

Japan is the world's largest electronics manufacturer with companies
such as Sony, Casio, Mitsubishi Electric, Panasonic, Canon, Fujitsu,
Nikon, Yamaha and others, whose products are renowned for their
innovation and quality. Major services in Japan which account for
75.9% of Japan's GDP include banking, insurance, retailing, transportation and telecommunications.[560]

The Tokyo Stock Exchange is the third largest stock exchange in the
world with a total market capitalization of $3.8 trillion (at year-end
2010). "Japan is also home to 326 companies from the Forbes Global
2000. The once government-owned Japan Post is also the world's largest
postal savings system, and quite possibly the world's largest holder of
personal savings—presently it holds about $2.1 trillion of household
assets in its savings accounts and $1.2 trillion of household assets in its
life insurance services."[561]

Japan is the 5th largest importer and exporter in the world with China
being Japan's largest export and import partner.[562] In 2011, Japan had
the world's third largest economy in terms of GDP at $4.5 trillion
behind the US at $15.3 trillion and China at $11.5 trillion. In 2012, Japan's
GDP gained little, remaining nearly the same at $4.5 trillion, but its
world ranking fell to fourth as India surpassed Japan as the world's third
largest economy. The US ($15.7 trillion), China ($12.4 trillion) and
India ($4.8 trillion) compromised the world's top three economies in
terms of GDP in 2012.[563] Japan has done well on the world economic
stage for decades but its stagnant GDP growth may be a sign of things
to come.

The foremost economic problem Japan faces is its crushing burden
of government debt. "Japan's ratio of government debt to GDP, currently
about 2.28, is by far the highest in the industrial world, almost double
that of even Greece and Italy, and steadily growing. Already, the

559   Ibid.
560   Ibid.
561   Ibid.
562   Ibid.
563   Op cit, CIA.

combined costs of interest on that debt and social security are approximately equal to total government tax revenue."[564]

Japan has now reached the point that they call the *waniguchi* (crocodile's mouth) effect. After two decades of economic stagnation, together with an ageing population, total public expenditure have soared whereas tax revenues have dropped. Like the US, the fastest-rising expenditures in the Japanese budget are related to social security pensions, medical insurance, welfare and employment programs. These costs have risen from ¥11.5 trillion (US\$121 billion) in 1990 to a forecast ¥27.2 trillion (US\$287 billion) in 2010 with some 70% of all social-security payments now going to those over 65.[565]

Japan's social-security benefits are still less than that of many European countries, but because of the national debt, Japan has limited ability to increase them. Like the US, this is not good with a growing elderly population. Pension payments are absorbing a growing share of the total social-security bill. "In 2006 they accounted for 13% of national income, almost double the level of 1990, and their share is due to rise further."[566]

One compensating factor for the Japanese is that their private pensions complement the public ones, covering 45% of their workforce. However, after years of meager investment returns, especially after the 2008 financial crisis, several of their big life insurers have gone bust. Their real dilemma is that the mandatory retirement age and the age from which employees can start drawing corporate pensions will rise to 65 in 2013, just when lots of people born in the middle of the Baby Boom start to retire. Due to this glut in pension payments, the cost of pensions may begin to look unsustainable.[567] As noted earlier, this statistic is not unique to Japan but is a major issue in the US as well.

Even worse, the longer the people of Japan live, the fewer workers are left to support them. "When public pensions were introduced in the 1960s there were 11 workers for every pensioner. Now there are 2.6, compared with an OECD average of four. In a sign of growing disillusion with the pension system, almost 40% of the self-employed fail to pay contributions."[568]

564 Jared Diamond, (2012, April 26). "Three Reasons Japan's Economic Pain is Getting Worse." Retrieved April 4, 2013, from http://www.bloomberg.com/news/ /2012-04-25/three-reasons-japan-s-economic-pain-is-getting-worse.html
565 The Economist, (2010, November 18). "Social insecurity." *The Economist*.
566 Ibid.
567 Ibid.

Along with the pension problem, healthcare costs are rising inexorably as well. Estimates are that total healthcare expenses will almost double between 2005 and 2020, making them increasingly unaffordable. In addition, the quality of care has decreased with emergency wards already turning away patients because they are understaffed.[569]

To date the Japanese government has been able to fund its growing fiscal gap by raising debt in its domestic market. Due to banks and pension schemes primarily, the Japanese hold 95% of the country's huge public-sector debt. Also, household and corporate savings still comfortably exceed the level of debt. However, as people age these piggy banks will quickly decrease.[570]

One worry of the government is that the more companies and ordinary savers believe that their investments in Japan are not profitable or safe, the more likely they are to invest their money overseas. Companies could do this by setting up factories overseas and not repatriating the profits. Personal savers are already seeking higher returns in markets overseas, such as Brazil's.[571]

If the "perfect storm" occurs where investments are sent overseas and Japan has to borrow abroad, its current-account surplus would vanish and it might suffer in the same manner as Greece did in 2010. More than likely, to prevent this, Japan will progressively push up the consumption tax, cut back on social services and possibly even inflate away its debts. "The most serious inconvenient truth in Japan is that the government will—reluctantly—have to cut social spending," said Masaaki Kanno, chief economist of JPMorgan in Japan.[572]

Japan is a beautiful country and its people are smart, generous and kind. But its history is scarred. Japanese soldiers killed millions of Asians during World War II—17 million Chinese alone. Perhaps this is the cause of its current fiscal quandary? In recompense for its despicable past abuses of the peoples of Asia, the country and its leaders have overcompensated its poor and elderly in the form of social programs. Just as a wayward father provides excess gifts to his children to compensate them for his being absent or abusive, or the way the US has perhaps overcompensated its poor and elderly in restitution for slavery, Japan

568   Ibid.
569   Ibid.
570   Ibid.
571   Ibid.
572   Ibid.

has created a social system that overcompensated its people to the point of bankrupting the entire country.

If there is any cause for optimism, it lies with the Japanese themselves. Many times throughout their recent history they have faced challenges, and have not just survived, but thrived. They have a mountain of debt as high as Mount Fuji, but with their national resolve and character and after making good and difficult choices and with lots of work, they may again have many more enjoyable spring days picnicking under the cherry blossoms of the sakura trees.

China

Confucius once said: "Understanding what the future holds requires grasping the lessons of the past."[573] When Mao's Communist regime took over China in the late 1940s it had two tasks: to socialize industry and to eliminate private ownership and handicrafts in favor of a collective ownership.[574] The tragic end result was the Great Leap Forward and 30 million deaths.

Clearly, China and the Asia Pacific region have changed since the years of Mao. Much has improved for the better as already discussed; however, China still has its fair share of challenges. For all its economic expansion and enormous size, China is still a poor country overall. "Output per person in China is currently only 20% of that in the United States, while India and Indonesia have barely reached 10%."[575]

Healthcare and other concerns are evident. A recent survey of wealthy individuals in China noted that more than half of the wealthy interviewed said that they intended to leave the country. This is due to concerns that China's growth may be slowing and other private concerns about social issues such as the one-child policy, food safety, pollution, corruption, poor schooling and a weak legal system.[576]

As previously discussed, never before has this world seen a program instituted by a government like China's one-child policy, which has accounted for hundreds of millions of abortions since its inception in 1979. This may be about to change. For years, the individuals who administered the policy were government workers, who became

---

573　Op cit, Fenby, p. xlviii.
574　Op cit, Jie, pp. 61–62.
575　Op cit, Australian Government, p. 54.
576　Jeremy Page, "Many Rich Chinese Consider Leaving," *Wall Street Journal*, November 2, 2011.

despised by the Chinese citizens. In March of 2013, the family planning bureaucracy was combined with the health ministry to create a Health and Family Planning Commission. Outsiders believe that this may be a sign that China is possibly ready to get rid of its one-child policy.[577]

The social and economic damage created by the one-child policy may last for generations. In 2012, the labor pool shrank by 3.45 million, which was the first decline in China in almost 50 years, and as already noted, the ratio of taxpayers to pensioners will decline from almost five to one to just over two to one by 2030. There are fewer children to support their parents, and as a result, there is a demographic time bomb facing China. Massive cities like Shanghai, for example, have a fertility rate which is among the world's lowest. Parents who have lost their children will have no one to take care of them in their old age.[578] The shrinking labor pool, the unwanted abortions and perhaps recognition of its citizen's rights are all reasons for ending the one-child policy.

Corruption is another major issue facing China today. When China set out to build a socialist market economy, the government's heavy hand created many opportunities for corruption. "Meanwhile, political reforms have dragged on, and there is little oversight of office-holders. Inevitably corruption has grown rife, exacerbated by globalization."[579]

Repeated instances of corruption of Chinese officials, citizens and companies continue to be reported. One instance described in April 2013 was of Huang Sheng, a former deputy provincial governor of Shandong, who was being tried in the city of Nanjing for accepting bribes. He was accused of accumulating 12.23 million RMB or almost US$2 million in bribes. What was more astonishing than the bribe amount was the news that the former official had 46 mistresses. The fact that Huang had mistresses is not shocking to the Chinese as a recent study showed that of all officials revealed to be corrupt in 2012, 95% were proven to have mistresses.[580]

Another story reported in early April 2013 related to Liu Zhijun the former Railways Minister, who was once one of the country's most

---

577   The Economist, (2013, March 16). "Monks without a temple: China may have begun a long end-game for its one-child policy-Experts say it cannot end soon enough." *The Economist.*
578   Ibid.
579   Caixin Online, (2012, December 19). "How to Fight China's Corruption Cancer." Retrieved April 14, 2013, from http://english.caixin.com/2012-12-19/100474378.html
580   Liz Carter, (2013, April 9). "China's Latest Corruption Target Allegedly Embezzled Millions and Kept 46 Mistresses: Where's the Shock?" Retrieved April 15, 2013, from http://www.tealeafnation.com/2013/04/ /chinas-latest-corruption-target-embezzled-millions-and-kept-46-mistresses-wheres-the-shock/

important men. He was in charge of China's vast railway system and oversaw a huge infrastructure investment, notably including High Speed Rail. Liu's alleged crimes were that from 2003–2011, he pocketed 60 million RMB in bribes (almost $10 million) for giving out contracts. He was also accused of taking sexual bribes. "One businesswoman allegedly arranged for Liu to have sex with TV starlets, including actresses from popular TV series *The Dream of Red Mansions* (there have been some reports in Chinese media that he used his power to have sex with every female member on staff on the show)."[581]

Liu is concerned about the allegations against him and with good reason. One recent report suggests China may secretly execute thousands of people each year, sometimes for relatively minor infractions. Additionally, Liu is credited with creating a railway system seen by many as overpriced, inefficient and unsafe, and his mismanagement has been linked to the tragic Wenzhou train crash in 2011 that killed 40 people. He was ousted from the Communist Party in 2012 and will reportedly face trial in Beijing for taking bribes and abusing power.[582]

The challenge to rein in corruption is formidable. Firstly, China must eradicate the conditions that breed corruption by reforming its market and legal systems through comprehensive reform and instituting a system that effectively targets corruption. This includes the features of a sunshine law (i.e., requiring government workers to report their incomes and assets), robust public and media scrutiny and an independent judiciary.[583]

Secondly, over the long term, China must work towards having an independent judiciary. This is a crucial task. China's current legal system is based on the Soviet model. In a more mature system, the state's power would be separate from the power of the judiciary.[584]

A third area requiring reform in China is related to its political arena. According to Human Rights Watch, China is an authoritarian one-party state that imposes sharp curbs on individual freedoms of speech and religion. China also rejects freedom of the press and often restricts and suppresses human rights defenders and organizations, often through extra-judicial measures.[585]

581 Adam Taylor, (2013, April 13). "China's Ex-Railway Boss Could Face Execution For Corruption Charges." Retrieved April 15, 2013, from http://finance.yahoo.com/news/man-allegedly-ruined-chinas-railway-213248459.html
582 Ibid.
583 Op cit, Caixin Online.
584 Ibid.

China also censors the Internet and maintains highly authoritarian policies throughout the country but especially in ethnic minority areas such as Tibet, Xinjiang and Inner Mongolia. The government abuses its power in dealing with these minorities and then says that its actions were done in the name of "social stability." China dismisses international comments about its human rights record as attempts to destabilize the country. While having a large defense budget, the government spends more on "social stability maintenance" expenses.[586]

Although rights-consciousness among citizens continues to grow, the government's lack of effort to allow genuine judicial independence encourages the status quo where the Chinese Communist Party has authority over all judicial institutions and mechanisms. The police control the criminal justice system, which relies disproportionately on defendants' confessions, many of which are extracted by torture. In addition, China continued in 2011 to lead the world in executions with the exact number being a state secret but which are estimated to be within the range of 5,000 to 8,000 per year.[587]

China's form of government is still a long way from the democracies in the West. A move towards an independent judicial system with rights of speech, religion and the press for its citizens as well as honoring the rights of the family and unborn would be miraculous.

However, fiscally, China is in a much better position than the US. As noted earlier in this book, China's total revenues from its social programs in 2011 amounted to $382 billion, which exceeded its cash outflows of $287 billion for the same programs by nearly $100 billion.[588] The US, on the other hand, has amassed more than $1 trillion in deficit spending in each of the four years since 2008, and this does not count the increasing unreported liabilities and continued massive deficits.[589]

China has many challenges ahead. "But the speed and scope of its transformation since the country's dynamic forces were unleashed at the end of the 1970s have been blinding and unprecedented, with world-wide impact because it has taken place in the context of globalization."[590] Overall, the fiscal picture that lies ahead for China is promising. Mixed

585   Human Rights Watch, (2012). *World Report 2012: China*. Retrieved April 17, 2013, from
         http://www.hrw.org/world-report-2012/world-report-2012-china
586   Ibid.
587   Ibid.
588   Op cit, Ministry of Human Resources and Social Security of the People's Republic of China.
589   Op cit, Chantrill.
590   Op cit, Fenby, pp. xxxi–xxxii.

with desperately needed social, judicial and political reforms, the Chinese have much to look forward to as they work their way through the possibilities and challenges of the 21st century.

India

India with its massive population is becoming economically more prominent. While, as noted above, in 2012, Japan's GDP gained little and remained at $4.5 trillion, India's grew to $4.8 trillion. As a result, India surpassed Japan as the world's third largest economy behind the US and China in that year.[591] According to a 2012 US National Intelligence Council (NIC) report, by 2030 India could be the rising economic powerhouse of the world that China is seen as today.[592]

According to the NIC report which is aimed at providing a framework for thinking about the future, by 2030, India's rate of economic growth is likely to rise while China's slows. The total Chinese working-age population is expected to peak in 2016 and decline from 994 million to about 961 million in 2030. In contrast, India's working-age population is unlikely to peak until about 2050 or almost 20 years later. By 2030, Asia will have surpassed North America and Europe combined in terms of GDP, population size, military spending and technological investment.[593]

India, however, faces many of the same problems and traps accompanying rapid growth that China does. For one, India has large inequities between rural and urban sectors within its borders. Also, India will have increasing constraints on resources such as food and water and will need greater investment in science and technology in order to continue to move its economy in the upwards direction.[594] Anyone who has visited India will attest to the depths of poverty and crime faced by a majority of the population. You either swim (work) or sink (die on the streets).

A major advantage India has over China is that India's democracy provides it with a safety valve for discontent in a way that China's one-party rule does not. In addition, the NIC report said that long-term

---

591 Op cit, CIA.
592 NDTV. (2012, December 11). "US Intelligence Sees India as Rising Economic Powerhouse in 2030." Retrieved April 20, 2013, from http://www.ndtv.com/article/india/ /us-intelligence-sees-india-as-rising-economic-powerhouse-in-2030-303799
593 Ibid.
594 Ibid.

forecasts show Indian economic power growing steadily throughout the 21st century and overtaking China at the end of the century because of China's maturing age structure.[595]

In order for India to maximize its advantage from its youthful population, it will need to boost its educational system in both attainment and quality at the lower levels. India will also have to make substantial governance improvements in countering corruption. India also must undertake large-scale infrastructure programs to keep pace with its rapid urbanization and the needs of a more advanced economy in the future.[596]

India is the current "sleeper" in the world economic scene. In recent years, it has become known for its highly educated IT workforce. This niche created a shift of IT work from the US and other countries to India due to the low labor costs for well-educated Indian IT personnel. This trend was only the beginning as India is in a position to become the major economic power in the world by the end of this century.

Australia

In the past half-century, Australia has benefited from its proximity to Asia by being an important and reliable supplier of mineral and energy resources fueling economic growth. Australia currently provides Japan with over three-quarters of its domestic consumption of coking coal (for steel production) and half of its consumption of thermal coal (for power generation). Australia also supplies one-sixth of Japan's natural gas imports and is Japan's largest supplier of important minerals such as zinc and bauxite. The minerals boom in Australia began in the 1960s and 1970s, caused by Japan's economic rise, and led to the creation or revival of towns in Australia's outback mining regions.[597]

Since 2003, the demand for Australian commodities has reached an elevated level, with the economic emergence of China and India. China now accounts for two-thirds of Australia's total iron ore production and has a relatively small but growing market for Australian coal and natural gas. India, on the other hand, is the second-biggest importer of Australian coking coal (behind Japan).[598]

---

595 Ibid.
596 Ibid.
597 Op cit, Australian Government, pp. 91–92.
598 Ibid, p. 92.

In addition to the economic benefits, Australia's ethnic diversity has also been impacted by Asia. Tourism from Asia has increased and many Asians come to Australia to obtain their educations.

> More people from Asian countries live, study and work in Australia than ever before. Of the 5 million overseas-born people living in Australia, almost 2 million were born in Asia—an increase from 276,000 in 1981. Close to 1 in 10 of Australia's population identifies with Asian ancestry. Today, there are more speakers of Chinese languages in Australia than speakers of Italian or Greek. In 2010–11, for the first time in Australian history, Britain was not the main source of permanent residents—more people moved here from China than from any other country, and in 2011–12, India was the number one source of permanent migrants.[599]

Just as the future was looking bright for the "Aussies," their government passed a carbon tax law in its legislature. This is something that some are beginning to regret. Australia has been taxing carbon emissions since July 1 of 2012 at a rate of $AUD23 per ton.[600] (Note that the Australian dollar is very close to the US dollar in value at the time of this writing.) "A carbon tax is an environmental tax applied to the burning of fossil fuels in order to discourage the production of greenhouse gas emissions such as carbon dioxide. Normally, this is conceived as a levy on the production of fuels such as natural gas, coal and petroleum, thus encouraging non-carbon fuels and technologies to emerge in the market and better compete against large carbon emitting corporations."[601]

Australian businesses are now feeling the effects of the carbon tax. Data from the Australian Securities and Investments Commission showed that a record 10,632 businesses faced insolvency in 2012. The largest manufacturing firms in Australia are asking the government to scrap the nation's carbon tax as it disadvantages the local businesses that compete on a global market. Critics argue that the carbon tax ultimately

599 Ibid, pp. 97–98.
600 Michael Bastasch, (2013, March 19). "Report: Australian Carbon Tax contributes to record number of Businesses Insolvencies." Retrieved April 21, 2013, from http://dailycaller.com/2013/03/19//report-australian-carbon-tax-contributes-to-record-number-of-businesses-insolvencies/
601 Ecolife. (n.d.). "Dictionary: Carbon Tax." Retrieved April 21, 2013, from http://www.ecolife.com/define/carbon-tax.html

leads to job losses. When other trading partners are not held to similar tax schemes in their countries, it puts tremendous pressure on Australian companies and inevitably leads to Australian job losses and business closures.[602]

Some estimates are that the carbon taxes and other green programs make up as much as 30% of the Australian small- and medium-sized businesses' electric bills. Australia's tourism business has also been impacted by carbon pricing. One study by Tourism Accommodation Australia reports that the carbon tax will add $115 million in costs to Australian hotels and motels, and these costs are coming straight off the bottom line.[603]

Overall, however, the prospect for Australia is bright. The country in mid-2013 voted in a new government led by Tony Abbott, who stated: "The carbon tax was basically socialism masquerading as environmentalism, and that's why it's going to get abolished."[604]

According to the white paper published by the Australia government in 2012, "Australia has an enviable combination of solid growth, contained inflation, low unemployment and strong public finances. This stands in stark contrast to the weak and challenging economic conditions faced in many parts of the developed world."[605] Australia has a democratic government, a growing population and abundant land and resources. With the exception of its recent carbon tax legislation, which may soon be abolished, Australia's future is perhaps best expressed with the Aussie slang phrase: "She'll be right, mate."

Southeast Asian "Tigers"

The ten countries that make up Southeast Asia seem to make no sense together. They include the small, hugely rich oil kingdom of Brunei; the post-conflict poor society of Cambodia and the wealthy but small and regulated economy of Singapore. In addition, there is Myanmar, a country that has been under military rule since 1962; Laos, a poor, landlocked economy blessed with hydropower and minerals; and Vietnam, a populous nation whose growth rates rival China's. In addition, there are four diverse middle-income economies that aspire to join the

---

602 Op cit, Bastasch.
603 Ibid.
604 Michael Bastasch, (2013, October 25). "Aussie PM: Carbon Tax is 'Socialism'." Retrieved December 1, 2013, from http://dailycaller.com/2013/10/25/aussie-pm-carbon-tax-is-socialism/
605 Op cit, Australian Government, p. 106.

ranks of advanced countries in the region: Indonesia, Malaysia, the Philippines and Thailand.[606]

These countries share a strategic location and access to abundant natural resources. They are diverse and yet increasingly integrated. They manifest the amazing economic growth coming from this region. Politically, most have stability, and with the region's continued development—which depends on investments in infrastructure and education as well as improvements in business climate—they are becoming more and more important for the rest of the world.[607]

In 2011, these ten countries had a combined GDP of $1.9 trillion, bigger than India's GDP. They have a diverse population of almost 600 million, nearly twice that of the US, and have an average per-capita income near that of China. Over the last decade, these countries have averaged a growth rate of more than 5% per year. If Southeast Asia were one country, it would be the world's ninth-largest economy.[608]

In the 1970s, several of Southeast Asia's countries were noticed for having economic promise. "Singapore was deemed an 'Asian tiger' (along with Korea, Hong Kong, and Taiwan), while Indonesia, Malaysia, the Philippines, and Thailand were dubbed 'tiger cubs.'"[609] All five countries in the region (Singapore, Indonesia, Malaysia, the Philippines and Thailand) have since lived up to this prediction, with Singapore now a high-income economy and the four "cubs" all middle-income economies. The latest member of Southeast Asia's middle-income group, Vietnam, adopted China's economic reform model and has enjoyed similarly explosive growth and poverty reduction.[610]

The countries of Southeast Asia made it through the 2008 financial crisis with few scars. The export-dependent countries of Malaysia, Singapore and Thailand benefited considerably from China's early rebound because of their close trade linkages. Indonesia, the Philippines and Vietnam, with relatively large domestic markets, also proved resilient and avoided material economic downturns.[611]

606 Vikram Nehru, (2011, July 7). *Southeast Asia: Crouching Tiger or Hidden Dragon.* Retrieved April 21, 2013, from Carnegieendowment.org: http://carnegieendowment.org/ieb/2011/07/07/southeast-asia-crouching-tiger-or-hidden-dragon
607 Ibid.
608 Ibid.
609 Ibid.
610 Ibid.
611 OECD. (2010). *Southeast Asian Economic Outlook.* New Bedford, Ct: Development Centre of the Organisation for Economic Co-Operation and Development, p. 9.

Southeast Asia owes its success in part to geography. "The countries sit astride the Malacca Straits, the world's second busiest shipping channel (after the English Channel) and second most popular oil tanker route (after the Straits of Hormuz). Well over half of the world's merchant fleet capacity uses the channel each year, and closing the Straits would be highly disruptive and possibly even catastrophic for world trade."[612]

The region also has a wealth of natural resources with oil, hydro- and geothermal power, various minerals, timber, rice, palm oil, cocoa and coffee in abundance. For centuries, the region has attracted traders and colonists, with foreign investors a more recent phenomenon.[613]

According to the Australian government's 2012 white paper, Southeast Asia's cumulative economic, political and demographic importance is growing. "With a combined population of 600 million, these countries have embarked on a drive, through the Association of Southeast Asian Nations (ASEAN), towards regional integration and connectivity by 2015."[614]

In 1980, income per person in developing countries in Asia was about one-thirtieth of that in the United States. By 2025, this gap is expected to close, and income per person in the United States will be only four times that of Asia's developing countries. Higher living standards and access to goods and services will transform the lives of millions in the region. The people of Southeast Asia will have access to a broader education through the global reach of communications and digital technology. Indonesia alone is expected to have the world's 10th largest economy by the year 2025.[615]

For Southeast Asia, the biggest challenge may be its biggest opportunity—China. As China emerges over the next two decades and becomes the world's largest economy, it will bring risk. As noted above, China has its own set of economic, social, environmental and international challenges that it must face. Southeast Asia will undoubtedly be impacted by any instability in China and may always view China's regional dominance as a possible security risk.[616]

The "tiger cubs" should have concerns about their economic development due to precedents set during the last half-century. Few countries

612 Op cit, Nehru.
613 Ibid.
614 Op cit, Australian Government, p. 52.
615 Ibid, pp. 52–53.
616 Op cit, Nehru.

have moved from medium to high incomes per capita on the strength of their manufacturing and services alone. In order for countries to move up the value chain and compete with advanced economies, it is necessary to have a highly educated and innovative workforce. In addition, advanced economies have a culture of excellence, entrepreneurial skills, access to finance, a solid infrastructure and a competitive business environment. "Southeast Asia's middle income economies are gradually putting these in place, but their efforts will need to be more vigorous and coordinated if genuine progress is to be achieved."[617]

If the countries of Southeast Asia move up the value chain and further their economic prosperity by putting in place the programs needed to enable their workforce to compete with the rest of the world, they could well become full-fledged tigers in the future world's socio-economic jungle.

The Current State of the US

Although the US was doing well in many respects, the perception amongst Americans in 2008 was that the country was declining. For example, many Americans and others around the globe perceived China to be the country with the world's largest economy. A Gallup poll taken in 2008 in the US reported that 40% of Americans considered China to be the world's leading economic power while only 33% of Americans chose the US.[618] However, as of 2010, the US not only had the world's largest economy, it also was the world's top manufacturing producer.[619] The US has had the world's largest economy by some measures for more than 100 years, since the end of the 19th century.

Clearly, the US is not as strong as it was before the 2008 financial meltdown. In fact, in 2013, the US was suffering from the worst economy in 83 years with GDP growth in the midst of its longest sub-3% annual growth rate since 1929, the beginning of the Great Depression. The economy had not topped 3% GDP annual growth since 2005, and unemployment numbers that count the discouraged and under-employed as well as the jobless (often called the "real" unemployment

617 Ibid.
618 Op cit, Fenby p. xxxvi.
619 Economics in Pictures, (2013, January 28). "Changing Top Manufacturing Countries (1980–2010)." Retrieved May 11, 2013, from
      http://www.economicsinpictures.com/2013/01/changing-top-manufacturing-countries.html

rate) remained stubbornly high as of early May 2013 at 13.8% of the workforce.[620]

Although world economic freedom has reached record levels, according to the 2014 Index of Economic Freedom released by the Heritage Foundation and the *Wall Street Journal,* in 2014, after seven straight years of decline, the US dropped out of the top 10 most economically free countries. (Hong Kong was number one.)[621]

According to the 2014 Index of Economic Freedom, countries achieving higher levels of economic freedom consistently and measurably outperform others in economic growth, long-term prosperity and social progress.

> It's not hard to see why the US is losing ground. Even marginal tax rates exceeding 43% cannot finance runaway government spending, which has caused the national debt to skyrocket. The Obama administration continues to shackle entire sectors of the economy with regulation, including healthcare, finance and energy. The intervention impedes both personal freedom and national prosperity.[622]

The US may still be the world's number one economic power, but it is not accurate to say that the fiscal status of the US federal government is good or even fair. However, most Americans do not know this because the media simply will not report that the dysfunctional social programs in the US are destroying the US at an ever increasing rate. Instead, the media berates Americans as being selfish or racist if they speak out about the dysfunctional social programs. The American people may be the world's largest donors and philanthropists and have contributed more than $15 trillion to the welfare of the poor, elderly and sick in America through governmental social programs alone since 1964 when Medicare came into existence. Still, the American people are shamed by the media as being selfish, racist and uncaring.

The cost of its social programs is staggering. If the US government confiscated the entire adjusted gross income of all American taxpayers making more than $66,000 a year ($5.1 trillion), and then confiscated all corporate taxable income in the year before the 2008 recession ($1.6

620 Cox, J. (2013, May 1). "'Real' Jobless Rate Still Above 10% In Most States." Retrieved May 1, 2013, from http://www.cnbc.com/id/100691168
621 Op cit, Miller.
622 Ibid.

trillion), it still wouldn't be nearly enough to fund the over $8 trillion per year in growth of US liabilities related to its social programs. "Some public officials and pundits claim we can dig our way out through tax increases on upper-income earners, or even all taxpayers. In reality, that would amount to bailing out the Pacific Ocean with a teaspoon. Only by addressing these unsustainable spending commitments can the nation's debt and deficit problems be solved."[623] The massive and increasing US federal deficit and the even greater and increasing un-funded liabilities growing as a result of the country's dysfunctional social programs are a fiscal time bomb.

In 2008, the whole world was impacted by the financial meltdown that began in the US. The Federal Housing Administration, which guaranteed banks' mortgage risks, and the Federal National Mortgage Association (FNMA—also known as Fannie Mae), which effectively insured mortgages by purchasing mortgages from lenders (both created in the 1930s), shifted risks from the lenders to the US taxpayers. These government social programs, along with the Federal Home Loan Mort-gage Corporation (FHLMC—also known as Freddie Mac), another government housing program similar to FNMA, were at the center of the 2008 financial meltdown. These programs, along with laws that made credit-worthiness no longer relevant in an effort to provide minorities house loans, created the glut of subprime loans that led to the 2008 financial disaster.

When the financial markets were in their most dire state in the fall of 2008, the federal government stepped in and created the Troubled Asset Relief Program (TARP). The TARP, along with a separate bailout programs for Fannie Mae and Freddie Mac, loaned money to troubled institutions to help them stay afloat. Altogether, accounting for both the TARP and the Fannie and Freddie bailouts, $606 billion was invested, loaned or paid out by the federal government to assist troubled companies as well as Fannie Mae and Freddie Mac ($421 billion to various entities and $187 billion to Fannie Mae and Freddie Mac).[624]

As of November 2013, the US government had provided $421 billion of TARP money to 934 recipients other than Fannie Mae and Freddie Mac. Those recipients had returned $380 billion and the US Treasury had earned a return on the TARP money of another $52 billion. About

623 Op cit, Archer.
624 Paul Kiel and Dan Nguyen, (2013, December 2). "The Bailout Scoreboard." Retrieved December 2, 2013, from http://projects.propublica.org/bailout/

$9 billion of the TARP money was in the form of subsidies that will not be coming back.[625] The government loaned auto-maker General Motors $50 billion and then transferred this loan into ownership in the company. Even though the market has gone up considerably since 2008, after selling its stake in General Motors, the US government will incur a loss of $10 billion.[626] Banks and insurance companies who were loaned TARP money in 2008 have been income producers for the federal government while General Motors has been the opposite. The decision to loan to General Motors over the long run and to meddle in the auto maker's business proved to be yet another example of how socialism does not work.

When the TARP was created in 2008, the media criticized the G. W. Bush administration for catering to the Wall Street elites, while conservatives criticized the administration for transferring the risk of failing companies to the taxpayer through large bailouts. One company, AIG, was singled out and demonized for being given a large bailout. As much as $182 billion of aid was committed at the peak of the bailout to AIG, and the US Treasury at one point owned more than 90% of the company. However, by the end of 2012, it was announced that the government had been repaid all that it loaned to AIG, and in addition, the government made a profit of $22 billion.[627] The AIG loans were a big part of the TARP payout.

The meddling with Fannie Mae and Freddie Mac is another story. The federal government placed these two entities under conservatorship in 2008, which was intended to be a temporary measure to keep the entities solvent. These entities combined hold $5 trillion in US residential mortgages, or almost half of the nation's outstanding loan volume. In 2008, it was imperative for the government that these entities stay afloat in order to prevent further catastrophes in the financial markets. In the few years following 2008, the federal government provided more than $187 billion to these two mortgage institutions. It was doubtful whether they would ever pay a single penny of the money provided to them until 2012, when the markets suddenly made a minor comeback. Since 2012 the Treasury has recovered more than $213 billion in

625 Ibid.
626 Peter Flaherty, (2013, November 14). "The Government's Bailout Of General Motors Is Strangling GM," *Forbes*.
627 Jeffrey Sparshott and Erik Holm, (2012, December 11). "End of a Bailout: U.S. Sells Last AIG Shares." *Wall Street Journal*.

dividends from Fannie Mae and Freddie Mac. However, there was a catch.[628]

When the market changed in 2012, the Treasury Department, seeing an opportunity to speed up debt collection, issued a "sweep" rule that effectively barred Fannie Mae and Freddie Mac shareholders from realizing any profits on current or future earnings. Private investors were angry and have filed suit with the US government to claim what is rightfully theirs.[629]

Fannie Mae and Freddie Mac escaped much criticism by the press in relation to the 2008 financial meltdown and resulting government bailouts, though the policies that these organizations put in place were directly responsible for the collapse. Their underwriting guidelines for loans were altered to encourage loans to individuals who were not creditworthy. These "subprime," or less than creditworthy, loans were purchased and packaged with other Fannie Mae and Freddie Mac good loans and sold to the public. When the subprime loans began to fail in record numbers, the entire world's economy was shaken. Companies and individuals began hoarding cash, and liquidity in the markets dissipated until the governments around the world stepped in to prevent further company bankruptcies and eventually calmed the markets.

In early 2013, the Obama administration was pushing the same policies that created the 2008 financial meltdown. In early 2013, administration officials said they were working to get banks to lend to a wider range of borrowers by taking advantage of taxpayer-backed programs—including those offered by the Federal Housing Administration—that insure home loans against default. It was reported that housing officials were requesting the Justice Department provide assurances to banks that they would not face legal or financial recriminations if they made loans to riskier borrowers who meet government standards but later default. "Officials are also encouraging lenders to use more subjective judgment in determining whether to offer a loan and are seeking to make it easier for people who owe more than their properties are worth to refinance at today's low interest rates, among other steps."[630] Critics charged that

628 Carl Horowitz, (2014, July 28). "Court Forces Government to Release Documents in Fannie/Freddie Suit." Retrieved August 8, 2014, from http://www.progressivestoday.com/ /court-forces-government-to-release-documents-in-fanniefreddie-suit/
629 Ibid
630 Zachary A. Goldfarb, (2013, April 3). "Obama Administration Pushes Banks to make Home Loans to People with Weaker Credit." *Washington Post.*

these efforts will ultimately result in another crisis exactly like the one that the US has been desperately trying to get out of since 2008.

Another shocking report from early 2013 stated that the US Federal Reserve was supporting subprime lending on automobiles. Loans to subprime borrowers surged in 2012, up 18% from a year earlier, to 6.6 million borrowers. With low interest rates pinching yields on their traditional investments, insurance companies, hedge funds and other institutional investors hunger for riskier, higher-yielding securities— like bonds backed by subprime auto loans, and lenders have rushed to meet that demand. Wall Street banks and big private-equity firms have provided the capital lenders need to sell ever-greater amounts of subprime auto loans in the form of relatively high-yield securities, with the proceeds going to fund even more lending to more subprime borrowers.[631] Can this really be happening?

Not only has the US not learned from the 2008 financial meltdown, it is in the process of creating another financial explosion as a result of its overspending on social programs. Just like the 2008 financial meltdown, which was ultimately created by social programs Fannie Mae and FHA which originated in the 1930s, the impending financial meltdown has been created by overspending and overpromising by social programs like Social Security which were also created in that decade. Unless the US federal government changes the policies recently redeployed that led to the 2008 financial meltdown and stops the spending that will lead to the next worldwide financial crisis, another financial bomb is going to blow.

What is the US government's answer for addressing the massively excessive annual deficits and unfunded liabilities occurring as a result of its dysfunctional fiscal policies? Well, to print more money, of course. This plan is setting up future generations for more massive misery because once the US currency is debased, the lifelong financial savings of Americans will be worthless. The government has instituted "quantitative easing" programs by which they have pumped $2 trillion into the economy since 2008 by buying government bonds and other securities.[632]

631   Carrick Mollenkamp, (2013, April 3). "Special Report: How the Fed Fueled an Explosion in Subprime Auto Loans." Retrieved April 28, 2013, from http://finance.yahoo.com/news//special-report-fed-fueled-explosion-subprime-auto-loans-110501752.html
632   Neil Irwin, (2013, March 13). "No, printing money won't solve the United States's debt problem." Retrieved April 28, 2013, from http://www.washingtonpost.com/blogs/wonkblog//wp/2013/03/13/no-printing-money-wont-solve-the-united-statess-debt-problem/

Another option to address the massive debt burden and unfunded social liabilities is to confiscate the savings from hard-working Americans. This was recently done in Cyprus by its government. One provision in Obama's 2013 budget proposal concerning retirement accounts triggered alarm bells. The provision called for tax laws to prohibit individuals from accumulating over $3 million in tax-preferred retirement accounts. The provision was expected to raise $9 billion over the next 10 years. "Immediately, many analysts jumped to the conclusion that the provision might involve actually taking away money from retirement accounts."[633]

Neither printing nor confiscating money are reasonable, viable long-term alternatives for addressing the US government's financial woes as a result of its dysfunctional social programs. There are only two alternatives that will solve the financial mess the US is in—one, replace the dysfunctional social programs with programs similar to ones working in the countries in Asia Pacific, and two, spread the message to Americans that the government is not the answer.

Rick Newman in *US News and World Report* noted: "If you think politicians will help you get ahead then you'll be less likely to take action on your own to make yourself better off. What politicians and policymakers really ought to be telling struggling Americans is this: You're on your own. The government is running out of money and is borderline dysfunctional besides. Instead of new policies that will make the economy fairer, we need more self-sufficient workers who aren't looking to government for answers."[634] Newman is correct in that the US needs more self-sufficient workers, but it needs to revamp its current policies to enable this to happen.

How Did the US Arrive at its Current State?

How did the US get into such a fiscal mess? There are many reasons and root causes. The first is that the politicians who put together the US social programs really believed that the programs were good and would help the old, sick and poor in their times of need. These may have been

633   Dan Caplinger, (2013, April 21). "Will Obama Really Confiscate Your Retirement Savings?" Retrieved May 1, 2013, from http://www.fool.com/retirement/general/ /2013/04/21/will-obama-really-confiscate-your-retirement-savin.aspx
634   Rick Newman, (2012, July 24). "What no one's telling US workers." Retrieved December 29, 2012, from http://money.msn.com/personal-finance/what-no-ones-telling-us-workers-usnews.aspx

admirable aims, but they had two major flaws. One flaw was simply that they did not work. The programs and promises put in place were impossible to maintain and keep financially afloat, and the bureaucracies they created have become archaic and impossible to manage.

Another flaw with America's social programs is that the programs take from working Americans and give to non-working Americans. The working Americans perhaps even initially happily agreed to give because many Americans are good and generous people who feel obliged and are happy to help a person in need. The problem is that these Americans could not give enough to support the dysfunctional social programs, and so now their children and even their children's children are on the hook for the current costs and obligations of these programs.

Another root cause for the fiscal mess the US is related to the guilt Americans feel as a result of slavery and racial and gender abuses. One explanation for the US disability fiasco is that the judiciary abdicated its role as gatekeeper in the 1960s and started letting anyone sue for almost anything as a result of being embarrassed by their complacency on racial and gender discrimination.[635]

The judiciary is merely a microcosm of US society as a whole. Americans too often forget the good things they have done for the world and instead focus on their regret for the sins of their forefathers. Similar to the study of micro- and macroeconomics, societies often reflect the nature and behaviors of individuals. It is time for Americans to see the good that they have done and forgive themselves for the past. Did not American forefathers also stand up against tyranny from the British, and was not America a key ingredient in stopping Hitler and communism while saving the lives of millions as a result?

Too often today in the US, politicians abuse the good nature of Americans by reminding them of the past abuses. This guilt is used as a tactic to ask for more. It is also used in other countries as well. The time has come for good Americans to say enough is enough. Yes, America has been involved in past transgressions and abuses that have scarred its history, but in order to defuse the fiscal time bomb of dysfunctional social programs, America must move on past these demons of the past.

Another reason for the horrible fiscal state of the US is related to the media. It could be argued that the media has a responsibility to find and

635 Op cit, Legalreform-now.

tell the truth. When the US has a debt of over $17 trillion and unfunded liabilities for Medicare and Social Security alone at over $60 trillion,[636] Americans should be debating, or even out protesting, the state of the Union. Clearly, there is a communication problem: the media is failing to present an accurate picture of America's fiscal status.

The denials of politicians are very much to blame for the current state of fiscal calamity as well. Politicians deny the magnitude of the financial situation or outright mislead the public in order to win votes. This was the case with the recent debate about the "sequester" held in early 2013. The sequester put in place cuts of $1.2 trillion to various parts of the federal budget over the next ten years, including $85 billion by October 2013. The sequester was in the cards since August 2011, and neither side expected it would ever be invoked. Neither side tried to stop the legislation when it was proposed, and President Obama did not even summon the leaders of Congress to discuss the issue until the day the sequester took effect, and the meeting lasted less than an hour.[637]

The sequester was set for failure for many reasons, but the two most obvious were that the Democrats did not like cuts to government-funded healthcare and pensions, and Republicans did not like higher taxes. Failing any compromise, the sequester set automatic across-the-board cuts, with few exceptions.[638]

As a result of the sequester, lines of travelers grew at airports because air traffic controllers were being furloughed and the White House announced no more tours as they were too costly, with many similar painful examples being reported. Both parties were blaming the other for the discomfort being dealt to Americans. Politicians arguing over $85 billion in cuts from the sequester is like a family arguing over the cost of toilet paper in a $300,000 home under foreclosure. This is nothing—stop your bickering—much more needs to be done!

A final reason for the fiscal cancer in America is ultimately related to American nature. Fear of change may the culprit. Maybe some are afraid of losing their jobs if the government bureaucracy is streamlined, though clearly, new jobs would be created. Lack of information may be their excuse. Without good information, how can any issue be truly solved? But there are many sources of information available to get at the truth.

636 Op cit, Archer.
637 The Economist, (2013, March 1). "The sequester: No Reprieve." Retrieved May 1, 2013, from http://www.economist.com/blogs/democracyinamerica/2013/03/sequester
638 Ibid.

Maybe Americans are lazy and selfish and not willing to give up what they have already been given. Maybe Chinese leaders were right when they professed that it is difficult to take back governmental programs or benefits that have already been promised. Whatever the reason and whatever the excuse, Americans must take a deep look at the freedoms they cherish and stand up and change the programs killing the country before it is too late.

The bald eagle has long been known as the symbol for America and became the national emblem in 1782 when the great seal of the United States was adopted. It is a beautiful and majestic bird. It can fly as high as 10,000 feet, shares the same mate and nest for life, can swim and hunt and sits on top of the food chain. It lives up to 30 years and molts in patches, taking almost half a year to replace its 7,000 feathers, starting with the head and working downward.[639]

The US, like the bald eagle, has great strength and has lived a long life. The time has now come for the US to make a choice to continue to fly like an eagle or to perish.

639 Baldeagleinfo.com. (n.d.). "General Facts about Bald Eagles." Retrieved May 3, 2013, from
      http://www.baldeagleinfo.com/eagle/eagle-facts.html

CHAPTER 10

Conclusion

It is clear that changes have to be made to address the social policies driving up America's debt burden. Hopefully, these changes will address the socioeconomic problems as well. There are viable alternatives currently in place today in Asia Pacific countries that address both.

When man goes against the laws of nature, nature wins. One principle is very simple and clear—if you spend more than you take in, you will eventually run out of money. This applies to individuals, companies, corporations and governments. If you spend more than you take in, then in order to comply with the laws of nature, you must either cut spending, increase revenues or some combination of both in order to stay alive. The alternative is to ultimately perish. You can print money or take money from your people, but these alternatives are short-lived and will not work.

Another law of nature is that in order to give money to one individual or group, a government must take money from another individual or group. The social policies in America were touted as programs to eliminate poverty, poor health and to ease the suffering of the elderly. They never would have come to pass had they been proposed as programs that would eventually bankrupt the country while taking hard-earned money and savings from working Americans, their children and their children's children.

Solutions

This book has detailed programs and attitudes working in Asia Pacific countries that hold the keys to America's long-term success. These programs consist of solutions to simplify government administration, reduce both costs and free handouts, and, where possible, privatize government programs. They have worked well in Asia Pacific countries and there is no reason they can't work equally well in the United States.

Reduce Social Program Costs

The first step in its road to success is for the US to recognize that it is giving way too much to the American people. By conservative estimates, "capitalist America" is giving more than 30 times the amount of subsidies to its people than is the socialist country of China. In so doing, the US is spending more than $1 trillion more than the revenues that it brings in annually. The US debt load is setting world records at over $17 trillion at the time of this writing, and estimates of the US's total debt and unfunded promises related to its social programs and pensions are nearly $100 trillion.

The first step in addressing the fiscal challenges is to agree that the US gives way more to its citizens than is financially reasonable, prudent and practical, and this policy must stop. Decreasing the federal government's costs does not mean eliminating social programs or not providing for the country's sick, elderly and poor. Services and social programs can be even better with smart changes in social programs in the US mirroring effective programs in countries in the Asia Pacific region.

Replace Social Security

Throughout this book, information was provided showing the US Social Security program is busted. This program, created in the 1930s, promised a government pension for a small number of Americans once they reached a retirement age. Both the number of participants and the age when benefits start have gradually increased over the years. The revenues provided by American workers were promised to be there, safe and secure, once they retired. Unfortunately, this is not the case, as the revenues paid into the program by workers have been used to pay for current beneficiaries, and now, since 2010, Social Security revenues are less than the amounts paid to retirees. Also unfortunate is the fact that this social program, the world's largest, is projected under its current makeup to never have revenues that exceed benefits. Added to this, due to the Baby Boom generation reaching retirement age over the next 20 years, 10,000 Americans are expected to retire every day. The US Social Security program, considered by some the world's largest Ponzi scheme, cannot survive.

At the other end of the world, the "superannuation" social program in the land down under, Australia, was created for the same purpose as the US Social Security program: to provide benefits for individuals in their old age. This program is functioning quite nicely as it provides guaranteed benefits for retirement with workers' savings being credited to their own accounts. Upon retirement, the amount paid into an individual's account is available for that individual. Because of this program, Australians are market savvy, and the Australia pension fund assets are the fourth largest of any country in the world.

The Australia superannuation schemes are flourishing while the US Social Security program is bankrupt. Implementing a program similar to superannuation in the US and replacing the current Social Security program would increase the well-being of current and future generations. This program would solve Social Security's long-term financial problems without the necessity for either huge tax increases or draconian benefit cuts, while providing enormous capital for the US economy. Not only this, but it would provide a real increase in income for every American.

Start Over with Healthcare

When the PPACA was hastily pushed into law in President Obama's first two years in office, the opinions of the Republican lawmakers were not considered or invited. Insurance companies were condemned by Democratic Party members as being unethical entities which deny people coverage while their CEOs enjoy lavish salaries and perks. Individuals who spoke out against Obamacare were condemned as simply being partisan, and the opinions of the majority of individuals who provide healthcare, the doctors, were for the most part ignored.

The PPACA has numerous faults. It was developed and passed in haste, and, as a result numerous legal challenges have ensued. The costs were understated and misleading, and the complexity was not necessary. Many optimistic statements that were made about the new healthcare law have been proven false and misleading. This new law, along with the current federal health programs of Medicaid and Medicare, will lead the federal government further and further into insolvency while providing less healthcare for the citizens, all at a considerable expense to the taxpayer.

The Hong Kong Health Protection Scheme is a model for healthcare reform around the world. Obamacare is not. The US spends more than 2.5 times on public healthcare per capita than does Hong Kong, and this measurement materially understates the US costs because it only includes Medicare and Medicaid and not other federal, state and local government healthcare program costs. The HPS is voluntary for insurance companies and individuals alike, no mandates are necessary and fines are not assessed on individuals who decide they don't want to pay for health insurance at the current time.

The Hong Kong Healthcare regime is one that works, and the US would be prudent to study the Hong Kong HPS as a solution for both future solvency and quality of care. In addition, the US could save billions in healthcare costs by creating public hospitals and clinics rather than public healthcare regimes, bureaucracies and policies.

Recreate the Disability Framework

In the US, the number of individuals receiving benefits from the government's disability programs has never been higher, with each month the number of individuals receiving benefits setting a new record. The increase has led to skyrocketing cost increases. While government payouts are increasing, so are the settlements and payments to attorneys as a result of malpractice, product liability and class-action suits. The costs for the disabled and the settlement amounts cannot continue to increase.

Implementing a disability system in the US like that in New Zealand would result in many positive changes. The New Zealand Accident Compensation Commission system is easy for patients to navigate, and claims are processed much faster than in the US. The focus of the ACC is on the patients and the care they receive, not the malpractice, product liability and class-action attorneys and the fees they make. The ACC system, funded through general taxation and an employer levy, is remarkably affordable. The time to resolve claims takes weeks in New Zealand versus years in the US. The administration costs in New Zealand are low (under 10%) when compared to the US (just under 50%). Even physician indemnity insurance costs in the US are astronomical (and growing) compared to very low premiums in New Zealand. The advantages to the ACC system over current US disability programs go on and on.

Americans need a disability program that will allow children to be children and people to enjoy life without fear of being wrongfully sued due an accident. The fear of lawsuits has changed the behavior of

Americans, and not always for the better. In the US, there is now an attitude that having an accident is like winning the lottery.

The ACC program is built around taking care of the injured, and the awards for disabilities in New Zealand enable a disabled person to maintain their lifestyle that existed before the disability. The focus is on recovery, assisting the disabled and getting them back to work, not on finding blame and seeking large settlements like in the US. The overall costs to society are therefore much less in New Zealand than the US, and people and doctors are allowed to perform their professions while not worrying about being sued for performing their job or for helping others.

Overhaul the US Tax Regime

The US tax regime is administratively costly and cumbersome with over 73,000 pages to its tax code, and this is before additional tax code will be added related to the PPACA. The tax rates in the US are high compared to the rest of the free world, and yet do not produce enough revenues to offset the massive amounts of spending by the federal government. The answer to raising revenues for some public entities in the US, like the state of California, is to tax individuals more rather than less. This ludicrous policy is causing Californians to leave the state by the thousands. Not only is the tax pool being drained, it is dwindling in numbers.

In the Asia Pacific region, Hong Kong is financially solvent in spite of having low income taxes and a simple tax system. Hong Kong's approximate 15% corporate and individual tax rate is amongst the lowest in the world, and Hong Kong is famous for its simple tax system, leading it to be one of the most favorable places on the planet to do business. In addition to this, the cost of collecting tax revenue in Hong Kong is half that of the US on a per capita basis. Hong Kong's efficient and simple tax system is a model the US should mirror.

The first step of tax reform for the US is to cut government spending to a reasonable level that can be sustained by a reasonable level of taxation. Then the US must simplify its tax code and reduce tax rates to increase revenues while putting in place a tax model that does not discriminate against the wealthy or the poor, yet still covers the costs incurred in running the country now and into the future.

Make Good out of Vices

There are ample opportunities for tax revenues that governments throughout the world are not taking advantage of. Revenues are being generated in gambling on racing, gaming, sporting events and through sales on the Internet. Areas therefore exist where governments could perhaps tap these revenues in a logical manner.

The Hong Kong government has benefited for years from the revenues derived from horseracing, betting and the lottery. The unique aspect of these tax revenues is that the government does very little to administer the activities that generate the tax revenues. The not-for-profit Hong Kong Jockey Club is a unique institution that provides entertainment for the community and generates billions in tax revenues and charitable bequests.

Save the Family

The family always has been the center of society. When you get hurt or need help, it is your family who is there for you to pick you up and help you get back on your feet.

When social programs were conceived, the intent and selling point was to help people in need. Gradually, these programs have created a population of dependency in the US while the family has been slowly destroyed. Americans need to get back to taking care of themselves and their families. The social programs that are currently in place need to change to encourage the building of the family, not its destruction. Supporting family initiatives is one major way that the US can reduce its social program costs while benefiting society and individuals in the long run.

In the poor or developing countries of Asia Pacific, the family *is* the social system with individuals receiving little or no support from the governments that run them. These countries are more like the way the US used to be. It's time for the US to get back to its roots and encourage family attitudes.

Falling Eagle—Rising Tigers

The US has many challenges, but with these come opportunities. There are working, efficient and fiscally responsible solutions to the current significant problems faced by the US. But before these solutions can be applied, there has to be recognition of the materiality of the problems in the US today.

In the 1970s, several Asia Pacific countries were singled out for their economic promise and labeled "Asian Tigers," namely, Singapore, Korea, Hong Kong and Taiwan, while the countries of Indonesia, Malaysia, the Philippines and Thailand were dubbed "tiger cubs." All of these countries are rising in the economic jungle of the world like tigers climbing a rainforest summit. All have flourished over the past few decades and show signs of even more future promise.

The Asian Tigers, along with the rest of the countries in Asia Pacific, are flourishing. The historical rise in their economies is unprecedented and despite each of these countries having their individual challenges (most, if not all of which, are their own making), the countries of Asia will be major players on the world stage.

The US is in a different position. It has been at the top of the world economically for more than a century. Like an eagle flying high in the sky all alone, the US had no economic predators to fear nor challengers for leadership of the clear blue skies. Over the past century, the US triumphed or survived challenges from the likes of Hitler, communism and the more recent threats from Islamist extremists. At the same time a more sinister threat was silently undermining the US. The social programs in the US are creating a financial burden that is great and deadly like a cancer destroying the county from within.

Only time will tell if the US, like the eagle, is at the end of its life cycle or is just in a molting stage. If the US reforms its dysfunctional social programs and makes every effort to support the family, and therefore society, it will survive. If it does not, then perhaps President Lincoln will be proved correct in his declaration:[640] "As a nation of freemen, we must live through all time, or die by suicide."

---

640 Abraham Lincoln, (1838, January 27). Address Before the Young Men's Lyceum of Springfield, Illinois.

Acknowledgments

Many people have contributed to the creation of this book. Special thanks to all friends and family who have supported me in this endeavor.

Thanks to Mason Choy who introduced me to his ideas in healthcare in Hong Kong and who offered additional thoughts on the differences between Obamacare and Hong Kong's healthcare system.

Thanks to Warren Britton, my good Kiwi All Blacks friend, who introduced me to the unique New Zealand disability program called the ACC. Another good Kiwi friend, Tina Paap, provided invaluable information on this subject and I am very grateful for her support as well.

Thanks to Michael Cox, sportswriter and good friend. He introduced me to horse racing in Hong Kong. Although, I haven't won much betting on the races at Happy Valley, his insights opened me up to a marvelous review of the Hong Kong racing culture.

Many thanks to Roger Robertshaw, author and retired Harrier pilot in the Royal Air Force, who read and provided expert comments on the initial transcripts of this book. He delivered gentle and honest feedback and his encouragement kept me going.

Thanks to sisters Lynne and Becky. Lynne for her expert review and comments, and Becky, the best artist I know, for her work on the cover.

Special thanks to Jack Cashill. After reading one of his books it was apparent that he knew what he was talking about in regards to reading, writing and editing books. From my earliest requests he was generous in leading me in the right direction and offered support and direction which I desperately needed.

Special thanks to David Limbaugh who took an interest in this project and encouraged my continued efforts to complete it. He was a great inspiration and his interest helped me move forward with this endeavor. As successful as he is as an agent and writer, he was courteous, kind and more than willing to help me. This book would not have been published without his efforts, so I thank him immensely.

Special thanks to Alan Sargent who edited and compiled the final version of this book. His comments were spot on and straight forward. Also, special thanks to Peter Gordon from Inkstone Publishing who responded to my queries which eventually led to this book being published. These two Hong Kong residents were instrumental in this book seeing the light of day.

Special thanks to my twin brother Jim, the "Gateway Pundit." His efforts and energy stirred me to make an effort to help the US through the creation of this book. He has been a great example and wonderful friend. I am so lucky to know and share my many years with him.

Finally, special thanks to my lovely wife Catherine who introduced me to China and the Chinese way of life. Our experiences that we have shared in China led me to the realization of the good things working in China and the wonderful people who live there and throughout Asia. No matter what you think about the politics of China, Catherine showed me that the people there are as wonderful, generous and as loving a culture as any on earth.

About the Author

Joe Hoft is an Executive Director of a Fortune 300 company based in the dynamic mega region of Hong Kong. He has spent the majority of his professional career in the financial industry and much of this time involved in the Asia Pacific region. As a result of his travels and experiences he has accumulated a unique perspective of the activities and policies of Asia Pacific countries that could be used to help stop the economic calamity looming in the US.

Joe has written articles and reports that have been published and presented in academic journals and corporate board meetings. His career positions have involved attending and presenting at corporate and non-for-profit board meetings and dealing with executives and board members stationed in companies and entities in the US, Asia Pacific and throughout the world. Joe's expertise in financial reporting, accounting, auditing and insurance, in the US and in Asia Pacific, enable him to see things as no one else can. He has held controller roles overseeing the financial reporting activities for more than $1 billion in revenues and is an expert in process reviews and problem identification and resolution in the finance and insurance industries. Joe has drawn from this skillset in crafting this book.

Joe has obtained three degrees including an MBA with an emphasis in finance from Iowa State University. He also has obtained seven designations including receiving his Certified Public Accountant (CPA) designation and his Certified Information Systems Auditor (CISA) designation. He is also a Fellow of the Life Managers Institute (FLMI).

Joe is the identical twin brother of provocative and acclaimed US political blogger Jim Hoft. Jim is the author's best friend and closest confidant and the sole proprietor of the *thegatewaypundit.com*, consistently ranked one of the top political Internet sites in the US and recently ranked as the 10th most popular political blog in the US.

Jim and Joe are brothers and best friends who enjoy discussing what can be done to make the US a better place. This book is in part, a product of these discussions.

For more information on related topics and to contact the author, see *joehoft.com*.

Select Bibliography

Books

Bush, G.W., (2010). *Decision Points*. New York: Crown Publishers.

Coulter, A., (2008). *Guilty*. New York: Random House.

Department of the Treasury, I.R.,(2012). *Internal Revenue Service Data Book 2011 Publication 55B*. Washington, DC: Internal Revenue Service.

Fenby, J., (2009). *The Penguin History of Modern China – The Fall and Rise of the Great Power 1850–2009*. London: Penguin Books.

Ho, P.K., (2007). *Hong Kong Taxation and Tax Planning*. Hong Kong: Elegance Printing & Book Binding Co. Ltd.

Lewis, M., (2010). *The Big Short*. London: Penguin Books.

Smith, C.K., (2009). *Economic Contractions in the United States: A Failure of Government*. Fairfax: The Locke Institute.

White Papers, Articles and Presentations

Australian Government, (2012). *Australia in the Asian Century*, Canberra: http://pandora.nla.gov.au/tep/133850

Freeman, Andrew, J.Y.G., (2010, December 21). *The Impact of Health Care Reform on the Financial Services Industry*. Deloitte Dbriefs Financial Services. Deloitte Development LLC.

KPMG, (2012). *KPMG's Individual Income Tax and Social Security Rate Survey 2012*. Zurich: KPMG.

Ministry of Human Resources and Social Security of the People's Republic of China, (2012). *2011 Social Services Review*. Beijing: Ministry of Human Resources and Social Security.

OECD, (2010). *Southeast Asian Economic Outlook*. New Bedford, Ct: Development Centre of the Organisation for Economic Co-Operation and Development.

Pang-Hsiang, C., (2010). *Milliman Limited:Feasibility Study on the Key Features of the Health Protection Scheme*. Hong Kong: Milliman Ltd.

Petek, G., (2012). *Anatomy Of A State Budget Deficit: California's $15.7 Billion Problem*. Standard and Poor's. San Francisco: McGraw-Hill.

Preston, J.; Packman, A.; Howlett, N.; Claros, A.L.; Solf, S.; Trumbic, T.; (2012). *Paying Taxes 2012—The Global Picture*. London: PricewaterhouseCoopers.

Tess, D., (2008). *Accident Compensation Corporation New Zealand*. Sydney: PriceWaterhouseCoopers.

Tyrrell, W.W., (2012). *The 2012 Index of Dependence on Government*. Washington, DC: The Heritage Foundation.

Government Websites

Accident Compensation Corporation (ACC), New Zealand:
  http://www.acc.co.nz
Australian Prudential Regulation Authority, Australia: http://www.apra.gov.au
Australian Taxation Office, Australia: http://www.ato.gov.au
Department of Health, Hong Kong: http://www.dh.gov.hk
Food and Health Bureau, Hong Kong:
  http://www.myhealthmychoice.gov.hk
GovHK, Hong Kong: http://www.gov.hk
Hospital Authority, Hong Kong: http://www.ha.org.hk
Inland Revenue Department, Hong Kong: http://www.ird.gov.hk
Internal Revenue Service, USA: http://www.irs.gov
TreasuryDirect, USA: http://www.treasurydirect.gov
United States Census Bureau, USA http://www.census.gov
United States Social Security Administration, USA: http://www.ssa.gov
US Energy Information Administration, USA: http://www.eia.gov

News, Current Events and Reference Media Websites

ABC News, New York: http://abcnews.go.com
Alliance Defending Freedom: http://www.alliancedefendingfreedom.org
Bloomberg, New York: http://www.bloomberg.com
Breitbart News Network, Los Angeles: http://www.breitbart.com
Caixin, Beijing: http://english.caixin.com
Cato Institute, Washington, DC: http://www.cato.org
CBS Local Media, New York: http://cbslocal.com
Center for American Progress: http://www.americanprogress.org
Christian Post Reporter: http://www.christianpost.com
CNBC, New York: http://www.cnbc.com
CNN Money, Atlanta: http://money.cnn.com
CNSNews.com, Reston: http://cnsnews.com
Conservative Crusader: http://www.conservativecrusader.com
Council for Disability Awareness: http://www.disabilitycanhappen.org
Crawford Broadcasting, Denver: http://www.crawfordbroadcasting.com
The Daily Caller: http://dailycaller.com
Detroit Free Press, Detroit: http://www.freep.com
Disabled World: http://www.disabled-world.com
Ecolife Dictionary: http://www.ecolife.com/define
Economics In Pictures: http://www.economicsinpictures.com
The Economist, London: http://www.economist.com
Economy Watch: http://www.economywatch.com
Financial Times, London: http://www.ft.com
Forbes, New York: http://www.forbes.com

Fox News, New York: http://www.foxnews.com
Gateway Pundit: http://www.thegatewaypundit.com
Global Finance Magazine, New York: http://www.gfmag.com
Heritage Foundation: http://www.heritage.org
Human Rights Watch: http://www.hrw.org
The Independent, London: http://www.independent.co.uk
Infowars.com: http://www.infowars.com
InvestorDaily, Sydney: http://www.investordaily.com.au
Journal of Family Practice: http://www.jfponline.com
McClatchy DC, Washington, DC: http://www.mcclatchydc.com
Modernhealthcare.com: http://www.modernhealthcare.com
The Motley Fool, Alexandria: http://www.fool.com
MSN money: http://money.msn.com
My Family Doctor: http://familydoctormag.com
National Review, New York: http://www.nationalreview.com
New Delhi Television, New Delhi: http://www.ndtv.com
New York Post, New York: http://nypost.com
New York Times, New York: http://www.nytimes.com
Political Calculations: http://politicalcalculations.blogspot.com
Population Reference Bureau: http://www.prb.org
ProPublica, New York: http://propublica.org
Public Broadcasting Service, Arlington: http://www.pbs.org
Reuters, London: http://www.reuters.com
South China Morning Post, Hong Kong: http://www.scmp.com
TeaLeafNation: http://www.tealeafnation.com
Time, New York: http://www.time.com
USAToday: http://www.usatoday.com
USfederalbudget.us: http://www.usfederalbudget.us
Wall Street Journal, New York: http://online.wsj.com
The Washington Examiner, Washington, DC: http://washingtonexaminer.com
Washington Free Beacon, Washington, DC: http://freebeacon.com
The Washington Post, Washington, DC: http://www.washingtonpost.com
The Washington Times, Washington, DC: http://www.washingtontimes.com
WebMD: http://www.webmd.com
The Week, New York: http://theweek.com
The Weekly Standard, Washington, DC: http://www.weeklystandard.com
World Atlas: http://www.worldatlas.com
The World Fact Book:
    https://www.cia.gov/library/publications/the-world-factbook
World Financial Review: http://www.worldfinancialreview.com
World Trade Organization: http://www.wto.org
Yahoo Finance, Sunnyvale: http://finance.yahoo.com
Zerohedge.com: http://www.zerohedge.com

Index